FRUITS OF EMPIRE

*Among James Walvin's previous books are:*

BLACK IVORY: A History of British Slavery
ENGLAND, SLAVES AND FREEDOM, 1776–1838
FOOTBALL AND THE DECLINE OF BRITAIN
THE LIFE AND TIMES OF HENRY CLARKE OF JAMAICA
MANLINESS AND MORALITY (*editor with J.A. Mangan*)
THE PEOPLE'S GAME: The History of Football Revisited
QUESTIONING SLAVERY
SLAVES AND SLAVERY: The British Colonial Experience
VICTORIAN VALUES

# Fruits of Empire

## Exotic Produce and British Taste, 1660–1800

James Walvin
*Professor of History*
*University of York*

First published 1997 by
MACMILLAN PRESS LTD
Houndmills, Basingstoke, Hampshire RG21 6XS
and London
Companies and representatives
throughout the world

ISBN 0–333–67062–0 hardcover
ISBN 0–333–67063–9 paperback

A catalogue record for this book is available from the British Library.

This book is printed on paper suitable for recycling and made from fully managed and sustained forest sources.

10 9 8 7 6 5 4 3 2 1
06 05 04 03 02 01 00 99 98 97

Typeset by EXPO Holdings, Malaysia

Printed and bounded in Great Britain by
Antony Rowe Ltd, Chippenham, Wiltshire

# Contents

# Acknowledgements

In the course of writing this book I have acquired a host of debts which I am happy to acknowledge. I was prompted, initially, to consider the idea at the heart of this study by reading a number of key books by other scholars, notably Alfred Crosby, Henry Hobhouse and Sidney Mintz.[1] My gratitude to them is reflected in the fact that I could not have begun this venture without their work. Sections of the book were first presented at various academic seminars; at the University of York, at Flinders University, at the Australian National University in Canberra, and at the Colonial Williamsburg Foundation. Comments by colleagues at the Annual Conference of Caribbean Historians in Jamaica in 1993 were also useful.

I am especially grateful to the two anonymous reviewers whose reports on the original draft were remarkably detailed and constructive. I hope those reviewers will see that I have tried to put their suggestions to good effect.

I am most grateful to the libraries and staff of the Wellcome Institute in London and the National Library of Jamaica (Kingston). The bulk of the book was written in York (courtesy of the J.B. Morrell library) but I revised the manuscript in the civilized environment of The Library Company of Philadelphia. Once again, I was helped by an expert, congenial and willing staff. I would however like to single out Phil Lapsansky whose advice and witty companionship made my visits so fruitful and enjoyable. I could not have worked in Philadelphia without the warm hospitality of Rod McDonald. I hope he accepts this note as part repayment of a major debt of gratitude. I am, like so many scholars, indebted to James Axtell for his elegant scholarship; but I also owe Susan Axtell thanks for her hospitality. Rosie and Tolly Taylor were my other generous hosts in Williamsburg. Alan Forrest was always available to help my efforts with timely backing.

Finally, this book is dedicated to my mother-in-law, Elizabeth Tate, born and bred in India and long-time resident of York. I had looked forward to giving her a copy of this book. Instead, I have to dedicate it, lovingly, to her memory.

James Walvin
York
May 1995

# Introduction

## THE TOPIC

What could be more British than a cup of sweet tea? Is there anything more typical of British cuisine than the over-emphasis on the potato? Has there been a greater plague on recent British life than the inescapable presence of tobacco smoke? Each – and more – is as British as rainy summers. But, of course, they are British only by adoption. Each of these social habits emerged around items which, initially, were imported great distances and which, at first, were objects of great social and intellectual curiosity. They took root in Britain roughly between the years 1660–1800, i.e. in the period between the development of a powerful British imperial and global trading presence and the early days of modern industrialization and urban growth. When, in the nineteenth century, Britain became a highly-urbanized and industrial giant, its people (of all sorts and conditions) took for granted the exotic commodities and associated habits which had been intruded into British life in the years between 1660–1800.

It was in these years that certain commodities from the far reaches of empire and the most distant points of trade entered everyday British life and changed forever the domestic face of Britain itself. Of course a very similar story could be told of other western nations. I could just as easily have begun with a similar question – what is more American than apple pie? – and pointed out that there were no apples in America before the arrival of the Europeans. In the British case tropical staples which began life as the expensive luxury of the wealthy eventually became the cheap, commonplace pleasure and necessity of the masses. This process was part of a much broader domestic revolution which has attracted a great deal of historical attention in recent years, namely the rise of modern material consumption. This book is designed partly as a contribution to that debate. But it is primarily about the way in which British material well-being developed as a function of global trade and imperial settlement.

The purpose is not however to tell a comprehensive story (of all imported exotica and their impact on Britain), nor to write the history of British overseas trade and settlement. The concentration here is on certain tropical staples; on some of those ingestible items, cultivated huge distances from Britain which quickly established themselves as prominent features of British social life.

What follows is a book which seeks to show the link between the emergence of key areas of British social experience and the development of British imperial and commercial history. Its purpose is to tell the historical origins of key British social habits and to reflect on the way they were brought into being and shaped by British involvement with the regions, peoples and products of the wider world. It was a process which did much more however than change the habits of the British people. In order to sustain this expansive British addiction to key tropical staples, wide regions of the globe were utterly transformed. This, in its turn, was but one aspect of a much broader story: of the impact of a curious, later an aggressive and acquisitive European onslaught on the wider world post-1492.

As Europeans made maritime contact with distant regions and peoples, they set in train a fundamental recasting of the world itself. They remade key regions of the globe not so much in their own image, but in order to serve their broader self-interests. So fundamental, so seismic were the global changes inaugurated by European overseas expansion and settlement, that even the appearance of the world began to change.

## POINT OF DEPARTURE

It is virtually impossible now to imagine what much of the inhabited globe looked like five centuries ago. The migrations of peoples, animals, flora and fauna, from one region to another so transformed the human and natural habitat that what is local and indigenous, what is alien and exotic, is now barely discernible. Areas of human settlement provide perhaps the most obvious but dramatic examples. Vast sprawling cities now dominate regions where once there was nothing but wilderness. Similarly, modern landholding and agricultural systems have served to reconstitute indigenous nature and to impose shapes, settlements and produce which owe little or nothing to the original habitat. Wherever we look, the consequences of human settlement and development – in urban and rural areas – are so obvious that it is easy to forget how *new* much of it really is. Put crudely, much of the world *looked* very different five centuries ago.

Even when we turn to 'nature', closer scrutiny often reveals a physical world utterly transformed from its original state. Of course this begs the fundamental question – what is native and natural? – in a world characterized by a slow, evolutionary process of human and natural change. Yet even if we accept this basic point, it is impossible to deny the explosive rate of change in the transformation of the world over the past five centuries.

A few simple examples will help to make the point. When Columbus first sighted the islands of the Caribbean, that lush 'Garden of the Indies' presented a very different face to European invaders from its modern form. The tropical beauty – so beloved of modern travel and tourist literature – is, by and large, alien and relatively new. Much of the flora and fauna, the trees, bushes, grasses and flowers which today help to define what we mean by the West Indies, were imported often from the far side of the globe. From trees to bananas, from the sugar cane to the breadfruit trees, from the dazzling flame trees to majestic royal palms; all were conspicuous by their absence when Columbus first made landfall in the fifteenth century. The greenery of the Caribbean was then transformed by flora and fauna which were alien. But so too was human society in the islands. The people we now know as West Indians are themselves arrivals of relatively recent vintage: the descendants of Africans, Europeans, Indians, Chinese and others who went to the islands (mainly against their will) as part of a much broader story of human migration in the years after Columbus. Indigenous peoples survived in small, generally isolated and inaccessible regions. Similar stories could be told of course of other regions of the world – of North America, Australasia, South and East Africa. Indeed, in time, few regions of the habitable globe remained untouched by the process.

Put this way, however, it is tempting to view the development of the post-Columbian world as merely a continuation, at a quickening pace, of a slow, long-standing human and natural evolutionary process. Here then is an aspect of world history which, not surprisingly, has begun to attract serious intellectual scrutiny. Pioneering studies over the past generation have exposed the massive phenomenon of global change since 1492 largely through examination of relatively small, detailed examples. By looking at the changes wrought by the migration of specific plants, foods, crops and diseases, a small band of imaginative historians have given us some fascinating histories and, more important still perhaps, have provided the intellectual stimulus to reassess the wider phenomenon itself. This study seeks to push the argument in a different direction. And while acknowledging my debt of those earlier scholars, notably Alfred Crosby and Henry Hobhouse, I begin from a very different perspective – and come to a very different conclusion. But without their stimulating work I would not even have been able to begin.

Like those earlier scholars, I seek to advance my argument through a study of particular crops – tropical staples – but this study seeks to locate those crops in a very different and defining context. Stated crudely, context is all. The central, unavoidable and seminal force in the story of tropical staples is that of aggressive European colonial expansion. Though the book which follows is not a history of European expansion, the story of that expansion, post-1492, is the context which shapes, directs and determines the history of those commodities. In the post-1492 global movement of peoples, plants and diseases, some commodities became remarkably important, others much less so. What determined their respective importance was the course and direction of empire itself. There were of course elements of the accidental – the serendipity – at work here, as in other historical arenas. But the demands of empire, the imperative of using empire for the broadly defined advantages of imperial peoples, was the fulcrum on which all else hinged.

Plants and commodities which had previously been of minor or local significance were transformed by the integrated forces of colonial and commercial expansion. It was the astonishing ability to conquer, control or overawe huge regions of the globe (and its peoples) that enabled European powers to transmute some crops into major instruments of profit, public taste and global exploitation. In their turn, such staples themselves became agents of imperial and commercial advancement. European rivalries were nurtured and exacerbated by the urge to gain access to the land, peoples and routes to the profitable cultivation of certain tropical staples.

Though the broad outline of this story is a western European phenomenon, this study concerns itself with Britain. Indeed in the rise of British power in the seventeenth and eighteenth centuries – the development of that remarkable fiscal-military state described by John Brewer – the role of empire was crucial.[1] Central to the course and success of that empire were commerce and colonial production. By the late eighteenth century it seemed, as Adam Smith recognized, that the British empire had come into being to satisfy a nation of customers.[2] It was, of course – and Smith pointed it out – much more complicated than that. Yet it was an indisputable fact that the British people's material comforts, their luxuriant pleasures (and even life's basic neccessities) had been conjured forth and were guaranteed by the instruments of empire and by the aggressive conduct of global trade and commerce.

From the mid-seventeenth century onwards, Britain was able to integrate itself into a much broader global role and setting. In a word, Britain became a global power. And it was this global power which shaped the particular relationship between the British people and those tropical staples discussed here – what I have termed the 'fruits of empire'. Before we can concentrate on this aspect of British history however, we need to focus our attention to other peoples and other regions; to see what happened when Europeans began to make encroachments to their east.

# 1 Attractions of the East

In a series of daring maritime explorations from the fifteenth century onwards, Europeans made direct contact with distant parts of the world which were previously unknown, or known largely through legend or complex, indirect and often mysterious trading links. Then, and since, Europeans looked with pride on those feats of imaginative daring which, 'discovered' Africa, the Americas and Asia. Henceforth Europe was in direct maritime contact – initially tentative and insecure – with the wider world. Those voyages were seen to represent Europe's rising strength and power, displaying to the wider world that here was a powerful new commercial and military axis, generally unknown to other civilizations. The power of individual European states waxed and waned, the dominance of one being surpassed by its next European rival. The wider world dazzled Europeans with the apparently limitless prospects of trade, wealth and global power. They began to compete and to fight each other, not simply in Europe but right round the world, grappling for those military and strategic toe-holds which would surely confirm prosperity and power at home. But in the broad rise of European power (which lasted effectively until the emergence of the modern USA in the nineteenth century), few stopped to consider the remarkable cultures and civilizations that Europeans encountered (and in many cases destroyed).

One by-product of this global dominance was that Europeans came to view themselves as the world's superior people, able to dominate great swathes of the globe by a varying mix of military and commercial power. European influence around the world became a presence more potent even than the power of familiar, ancient empires. Time and again, the ascendant European nation-state – by turns the Portuguese, the Spanish, the Dutch, the French and then the British – looked at their achievements and compared themselves favourably with the greatest of imperial and trading peoples of the past. Yet each in their turn waned as surely as they had waxed.

What lured Europeans to embark on their 'discoveries' of the wider world was above all else, those costly and much-prized products and commodities which they had previously acquired indirectly. Most dazzling of all, of course, were the precious metals and jewels that bedecked the homes, the persons and regalia of governing and clerical elites. No less important, though infinitely more mundane and prosaic, were the spices and natural produce of distant regions, so vital to the culinary life of those same elites. Yet long before men stepped ashore from the first Portuguese and Spanish vessels to sail to Asia, these items had been well known and widely used throughout western Europe. Spices and material valuables from Asia and the Levant had for centuries found their way to Europe by other routes. Henceforth, trade was about to be redirected. The world's commodities began to arrive in Europe in the holds of European ships sailing directly back from the most distant of foreign trading posts and entrepots. The world's centre of trading gravity began to shift from Asia to Europe.

This age of European trading ascendancy was indeed remarkable. It was an ascendancy however which was forged by an aggressive and rapacious determination to render the peoples, the regions – the very fruits of the wider world – malleable and biddable to the interests of dominant Europeans. But its success, so often interpreted from a European viewpoint, has often overshadowed what went before. No less remarkable were the trading systems which were already in existence in the Indian Ocean and Asia long before Europeans' vessels tentatively rounded South Africa and South America.

For almost a millennium before Europeans made direct maritime contact with the civilizations of Asia, complex trading networks had drawn widely scattered societies into economic contact with each other. While Europeans came to feel proud about the global trading systems they set in train – especially in the Atlantic – they had lagged long behind the pioneering efforts of traders in Asia and the Indian Ocean. There was a fine web of trade linking greatly different societies (from Japan to the Levant) in a massive trading system. The communities of the Red Sea and the Persian Gulf, united by the ties of Islam, had their own clearly defined trading systems. And they had links, by long distance trade, which pushed out to India, South-East Asia and on to China.[1] Long before Columbus set foot in the Americas, there was a trading system which stretched from the Pacific to the Mediterranean. It was on the whole a maritime trade dominated by professional merchants, with little state involvement. But this pattern later changed with the rise, in the Mediterranean, of powerful European city-states which were prepared and willing to use military power to get their economic way. Here was a physically aggressive way of conducting business – of grabbing markets, produce and land – at the end of a gun – which was at variance with the older trading systems that had characterized the East for a thousand years.

The Indian Ocean trade forged connections between a number of very different civilizations: 'the Irano-Arabic, the Hindu, the Indonesian and the Chinese.'[2] All were linked by seaborne trade and supplemented by overland trade routes (for example the caravan routes of Central Asia). Along these trade routes, on land and water, goods and produce from all parts of the world found their way to distant regions. Thus did various societies come to value commodities found or manufactured in the far ends of the earth. A simple example will suffice. The cowrie shells of the Maldive Islands became valuable first in India, before being translated to East Africa and on to the Middle East. Later still they took hold in West Africa as objects of trade and value. By the eighteenth century, Europeans would barter for African slaves using cowries as a means of exchange. Yet here was a simple sea-shell – beautiful and decorative – which had become a major item of global barter and trade and was exchanged by Europeans and Africans many thousands of miles away from its isolated place of origin.

Europeans had quickly learned to prize exotic Eastern commodities which found their way to Europe: the spices, silks, cotton textiles, porcelain and glass, jewellery and finely cut precious stones. There was also a host of other items which seem less obviously appealing but which were no less important to contemporary style and taste. Uses for the spices from Asia (pepper, cloves, nutmeg, mace, cinnamon and others) were various in a western world which lacked the means of preserving many of its foodstuffs, or of heightening their taste. European domestic styles – of food, clothing and habitat – absorbed the commodities produced by cultures and civilizations on the far side of the world, long before Europeans traded directly to Asia. Of course this was only an extension of a pattern already long in evidence in Asia itself. Luxuries from China, for instance, spilled out to please the wealthy in a string of distant societies. Satins and silks, strictly controlled by the Chinese government, were traded through merchants in Central Asia and Arabia. Jade too passed from China to far-flung regions. Fruits from Central Asia were the costly pleasures of the rich in India and Persia. Indian textiles, from the cheapest to the finest, were traded throughout Asia. Indeed, a series of foodstuffs, notably tea, were consumed by a string of societies from the Himalayas to the islands of South-East Asia.

This movement of goods, criss-crossing great stretches of the globe, was a response to a host of factors; to changes in prices, to simple utility and to the appealing cachet of novelty. The exotic caught the eye, tickled the fancy, flattered the rich; it helped to reinforce their status and wealth, confirming them as people cut off from lesser beings. It was no accident that, throughout the trading world of the Indian Ocean, it was the rich who first acquired the taste for exotic goods. The wealthy and the governing elites first encountered, sampled, and then acquired a taste for clothing, foodstuffs and luxuries brought to their door from the far reaches of the known world. This was a well-established pattern which was to be repeated, in Europe, Africa and later North America,[3] when the western world became the most powerful nexus of military and commercial interests, able to tap the wealth and luxuries of the whole world, using by turns the fearsome firepower of their advanced technology and the seductions of their commercial offerings.

Long before European ships rounded the Cape and intruded into the existing trading systems of the Indian Ocean, many of the exotic goods of the East were well established in Europe. The much-prized spices of Asia, for example, had found their way to Europe via complex, time-consuming trade routes, partly overland, partly by sea. Spices were important (at least to the rich): they flavoured bland food, rendered edible the unpalatable, preserved food for future consumption and adornment of the tables and the homes of the rich. But their supply routes were easily threatened by political convulsions. The rise of Islam for example effectively threw up a trading barrier between east and west – a barrier which had to be circumvented. The Mediterranean had long been the link between the systems of Asia and mainland Europe, but an ascendent Islam threatened to isolate the Mediterranean; to reduce it from the crossroads of international trade to an unimportant lake. It was, in part, to bypass these obstacles of the Islamic nations, and to gain direct access to the important markets of the East, that the Portuguese launched their maritime explorations in the fifteenth century. Significantly, when the first two men from Vasco da Gama's crew reached Calicut, they declared: 'We have come to seek Christians and spices.' Returning to the Tagus in 1499 they presented King Manuel with cloves, cinnamon and other spices and 'rubies and all kinds of precious stones'.[4] The spectacular but accidental landings in the Americas have often deflected attention from the no less important meetings between European commercial activities and the trading systems of the East.

Though the agents of Spanish interests laid initial claim to much of the New World, perhaps the most spectacular achievements were those of the Portuguese on the other side of the globe. The sixteenth century was the beginning of a remarkable period in Portuguese history, for they came to dominate, in a very short period, key maritime trading routes and posts in the Indian Ocean and beyond, with bases as far east as Malacca (with onward links to even more distant Asian markets). The exotic riches of Asia tumbled forth, like an annual cornucopia, from Portuguese vessels returning from Asia. Some 400–500 ships unloaded their wares in Lisbon each year as Portugal became in effect the 'wharf between two seas'.[5] Lisbon soon established itself as the centre of European international trade, and major trading houses and companies from Italy, Spain and France hurried to set themselves up in Lisbon.

The Portuguese quickly developed a remarkable global trading empire, with lucrative and fiercely defended bases and links in the Americas, Africa, India and Asia. Within this global system, goods shifted back and forth. Produce from China and Japan, precious metals from the Americas, the fabrics and spices of India, the raw muscle power of Africa – all and more were ferried to and fro. One consignment covered payment for the next in a complex worldwide transaction – all hinging on the thriving financial and service centre of Lisbon. In the East, their first task was to establish a string of bases – in Hormuz, Goa and Malacca – achieved by dint of careful planning, ruthless military action and shrewd commercial strategy. In this way they secured control over the crucial spice-trade routes across the Indian Ocean. The end result was that the exotic produce of the East entered Europe via Lisbon. From there it was distributed throughout Europe, to satisfy the demand of the expanding and ever more prosperous elites. They bought the peppers of Malabar and Indonesia, the nutmeg and mace of Banda, cinnamon from Ceylon, cloves from Ternate, Tidore and Amboina; silks and porcelain from China, silver from Japan, cotton goods from Gujarat and Coromandel.[6] Perhaps the most remarkable fact was that all this flowed through a Portuguese nation of only one and a quarter million people; a nation, moreover, chronically short of shipping.

Above all else Europeans wanted spices from the East. In the second half of the sixteenth century imports of spices into Europe doubled, prices perhaps tripled. The bulkiest of all Portuguese cargoes was pepper (though much of it was transhipped to the Turkish empire).[7] To buy the pepper, the Portuguese needed specie, mainly gold, from other parts of its vast and growing empire. Thus there came into being that complex global system of trade and transactions which linked the European heartland with distant colonial peripheries and with even remoter trading outposts. Europeans were able to command produce from one region of the world to promote their interests in another. Coercion, domination – crude power exercised in a number of forms – was exerted to advance the Europeans' broader interests. It was power first displayed by the Portuguese. Their presence and power in the Indian Ocean was remarkable. From Mozambique they defended the coast of East Africa, from Goa they controlled links to the rest of Asia. There were Portuguese forts or trading posts to assert their power along the western coast of India, to Ceylon, the Straits of Malacca and on to the South China Sea (all in addition to similar posts in Africa and Brazil). But this grand edifice of empire and trade was not to last. The centres of European control began to shift with the rise and collapse of different European trading dynasties and empires. First the Dutch, then the British and the French slipped into regions initially opened to European influence by the Portuguese. The faces and languages were different, but the aims were very similar; to secure for themselves as much of the valuable trade in Asian products as military power and commercial cunning would allow.

The Portuguese were a natural target for those emergent European powers, drawn by the wealth and potential of the Portuguese sphere of influence. In the early seventeenth century the Dutch systematically picked off the Portuguese trading and military posts one by one. A declining Portuguese trading empire slowly gave way to an ever more powerful Dutch ascendancy. By the mid-seventeenth century the Dutch had ursurped the pioneers and now effectively controlled the flow of goods from Asia to Europe. Henceforth the European centre of that trade shifted from Lisbon to Amsterdam. The northern Europeans had been able to push aside the Portuguese pioneers in the Asian trades (and elsewhere) by dint of their ascendent military and political power. But they also brought to the task new commercial systems – notably the joint stock company – which tapped the riches of empire as never before. The United Dutch East India Company and the English East India Company 'embodied the spirit of mercantilism in its manipulation of political power and privileges for commercial goals'.[8] Here was a political and commercial tool which was to bring even greater power and prosperity to its European proponents.

By the end of the seventeenth century the Dutch had secured firm control of the trade from Asia, ousting their various competitors. Together, the power of the Dutch and then the English trading companies were able to alter permanently the trading patterns of Asia itself, bending them to the interests and requirements of the Europeans. Previously the Portuguese had, by and large, simply redirected local trade. Henceforth the northern Europeans were determined (and able) to dictate much of the internal pace and direction of Asian trade. Ever greater sectors of Asian economic life began to dance to a European tune; orchestrated by alien trading companies, managed by powerful agents with fleets and armies at their disposal. In the process there developed a major European presence throughout Asia, communities of exiled Europeans which became a permanent feature of life in the region from that time forward. But just as the Europeans changed the face of Asia, so too had Asian products begun to change the tastes of Europe.

Europeans were often confused by their discoveries in the wider world; often too they were amused by the peculiar customs they encountered in their dealings with the peoples of Asia. It was to be one of history's quirky ironies that, in time, Europeans often came to realize that they quite liked what they found. What sometimes seemed odd at first, in time became enjoyable and, later still, essential. This was to prove spectacularly true of that most distinctive of Asian pleasures – tea.

# 2 Tea

Long before Europeans acquired the taste for tea, the drink was firmly established as a popular beverage, with a string of associated social customs, throughout large areas of Asia. Tea-drinking began in and spread from China. By the third century AD a number of societies had their own tea-drinking ceremonies; there was also tea as medicine, as a source of taxation, as a religious ceremony – and as a simple popular beverage. All these and more could be found among the Chinese – and later the Japanese. Tea was a simple crop which yielded a great variety of types, all prepared, processed and consumed in a multitude of fashions: dried, ground, pounded, mixed with water and other items. It was a drink which warmed and revived, which calmed the agitated, succoured the sick. Eventually it was available to everyone. Although the more elaborate drinking ceremonies were, understandably, to be found among society's ruling elites, tea quickly became the basic drink of the humble labouring poor. When the British came to know tea, it was widely accepted that the drink was universal in China. 'Tea is the common beverage of all labouring people in China ... [and] the Tea pot and Tea cup' appeared in most pictures of Chinese life.[1]

It was the ideal beverage, easily grown and gathered and, perhaps most important for poor people, easily and quickly prepared. These qualities ensured the drink's popularity throughout Asia. In Japan, as in China, tea began life as the drink of Emperors, but soon became the drink of the common people. In time the expansion of trade and empire ensured that tea-drinking found its way into the remotest corners of Asia. The spread of Chinese influence and trading contacts took Chinese commodities and produce into the most inaccessible corners of the continent. When in 1784, a Captain Turner of the Bengal Army explored the recesses of Bhutan, he was entertained to tea: 'presently a servant came, bearing a large tea pot ... and then giving a circular turn to the tea-pot, so as to agitate and mix the contents, he poured a quantity into the palm of his hand'.

There followed an elaborate tea-drinking ceremony in the presence of the local ruler. When Turner moved on to Tibet, he found that such rituals were different, but no less important in governing circles. In so bitterly cold a country as Tibet, tea had its practical side. After a long journey, hot tea was always available to warm and comfort the numbed travellers.[2]

By the time Europeans made direct maritime trading contact with Asia, tea itself had moved westwards, spreading into countries of 'Asia Minor'. Travellers to Persia in the seventeenth century told of local tea shops and taverns serving the boiling drink in brass and earthenware pots. It was a beverage which had widely acclaimed properties:

> The Persians, Indians, Chineses and Japaneses assign thereto such extraordinary qualities that, imagining it alone able to keep a man in constant health, they are sure to treat such as come to visit them, with their Drink at all hours ...

European expansion to the east brought them into direct contact with that rich diversity of human societies which both amazed and seduced them. And wherever they traded or settled in the East, there they found tea. Early settlers in India found tea-drinking commonplace. Writing from Surat in 1638, one man described how,

> we took onely The, which commonly used all over the Indies, not onely among those of the Country, but also among the Dutch and the English, who take it as a Drug that cleanses the stomach, and digests the superfluous humours by a temperate heat particular thereto.

Tea-drinking quickly established itself among Europeans in India. Among the Dutch 'the Tea-pot's seldom off the Fire, or unimploy'd'. Despite the hot climate, one traveller wrote of India in the 1690s, 'yet we find [tea] very convenient for our Health, and agreeable to the Habits of our Bodies.' They soon came to accept that tea had wide medicinal qualities. It had, said this same traveller,

> the repute of prevailing against the Headache, Gravel, and griping in the Guts ... The frequent use of this Innocent Tea, and the perpetual perspiration caused by the Heat, which is augmented by this Liquour, are the reason why the

> Gout and Stone, Agues, Rheumatisms and Catarhs are rarely heard of in these parts.[3]

Similar exaggerated claims were to form a refrain to the history of tea-drinking when it spread to Britain in the course of the eighteenth century. Equally it was part of the West's incorporation of exotic ingestibles into contemporary pharmacology. Tea – like other subsequent commodities – was promoted for its medicinal virtues. Doctors, apothecaries and scientists turned to the newly discovered products of the distant world, finding in them antidotes, cures and restoratives of the most fundamental kind.[4]

Time and again, as adventurous Europeans penetrated the most exotic corners of lands to the east, they were impressed and entertained by local tea-drinking. Returning overland to India in 1828, Captain Mignan interviewed a Persian prince: 'I was much surprised at having tea handed round to us in place of that universal beverage of the East coffee. All who can afford it are now in the habit of drinking it throughout the day'. Costly, and therefore exclusive, tea had reached Persia via Russian merchants, affording, thought Captain Mignan, a great commercial opportunity for enterprising British merchants.[5]

Naturally enough, tea soon found its way back to Europe; one of the exotic, costly luxuries of the East which were desired initially for their exclusivity and curiosity value, but came loaded with that accumulation of qualities and benefits alleged by traders and travellers. Good for the health, stimulating and a token of social exclusivity, tea began to arrive in Europe in bulk in the seventeenth century.

Tea became a feature of social life of the two major European trading nations in Asia – Holland and England – in the mid-seventeenth century. In both places it was promoted by similar arguments. Dutch 'moral physicians' recommended tea as a restorative against a host of complaints. But there, as in England, it remained the drink of the prosperous for much of the seventeenth century. Unlike other tropical commodities, it failed, initially at least, to attract the ire of religious and social orthodoxy. When it became popular among the poor, however – when privilege had been breached and polite conventions overturned by popular usage – complaints about tea began to surface. But for much of the seventeenth century, tea drinking in Europe remained costly and fashionable, at worst the object of cartoons and literary caricature.

> Tea that helps our head and heart
> Tea medicates most every part
> Tea rejuvenates the very old
> Tea warms the piss of those who're cold.[6]

Still, the fundamental question remains – why tea?

Tea came to Europe as an accidental by-product of the maritime and trading speculations of Holland and England. Like so many other man-made and natural commodities greedily adopted by Europeans, tea was one of the accidental fruits of empire. As always, rumours preceded the product. Travellers' tales, memoirs and letters of early missionaries, all told of voyages and overland travels, entertaining literate Europeans with accounts of the extraordinary cultures to be found beyond Europe's traditional pale. As early as the mid-sixteenth century, Venetian and Portuguese reports first told of the widespread Chinese attachment to tea. The establishment of Portuguese trading bases in India, with their onward links to China and later Japan, forged direct maritime contacts between Europe and the customs and commodities of Asia. Here were social and commercial attractions which soon proved irresistible to other European trading nations. But the extraordinary rise of the tea industry was not merely an accident of empire. Though its origins may have seemed capricious – like most discoveries from the edge of the known world – its development and exploitation were deliberate and well-organized. The urge to profitability brought together distant producers and an expanding army of European consumers. It was a pattern which was often to be repeated between the seventeenth and nineteenth centuries.

Though the first European traders in the east were Portuguese, it was aggressive Dutch traders who awakened Europe to the commercial attractions of Asian commodities. When they – and later the British – insinuated themselves into the existing trading systems which straddled the Indian and Pacific Oceans, they discovered a veritable treasury of valuable goods, staples and markets. Thanks to the invention of the joint stock company, the merchants of Amsterdam and

London accumulated unprecedented levels of commercial power and wealth. And in the process they seduced the consumers of the western world with a galaxy of goods which had previously been the preserve of Asian consumers. The most attractive, most sought-after and eye-catching initially were goods from China.

Early trade with the Chinese was indirect, but after complex negotiations the Chinese granted limited but direct access at a small number of ports. Symbolically, when the Europeans paid court to the Chinese in search of direct trade, they were entertained to tea. Negotiations between representatives of the East India Company and the Chinese Emperor began thus:

> At the beginning of dinner, there were several bottles of Thea served to the table, whereof they drank to the Embassadours, biding them welcome; this drink is made of the Herb The or Cha ... The Chinese boast as much of the excellence of this infusion, as the alchymists of the vertues of their expected Elixir.[7]

Not surprisingly, Europeans quickly accepted similar claims for tea. Educated, and especially medical, opinion lauded its qualities to a reading public keen to combine fashionable tastes with the dictates of good health. A Dutch doctor, simply repeating older claims from Asia, assured his readers that: 'Nothing is comparable to this plant. Those who use it are for that reason alone exempt from all maladies and reach an extreme old age.'

Some, notably French doctors, took against tea: 'The impertinent novelty of the century', one called it. In fact medical opinion was divided. Some thought that tea explained Chinese longevity; others thought it merely a passing fad. Slowly however the custom took root. Even Cardinal Mazarin drank tea – to relieve his gout.[8]

In 1659 a London newspaper reported that:

> Theire ware also att this time a Turkish drink to be sould, almost in evry street, called Coffee, and another kind of drink called Tee, and also a drink called Chacolate, which was a very hearty drink.[9]

At the time, tea was much less popular than the other two drinks; more a source of fashionable and medical debate than an object of widespread consumption. Indeed tea had already been discussed in England in a number of early seventeenth-century travel accounts which described its benefits and reported its widespread consumption in China. But the habit did not take root in England until the 1660s. Symbolically, the East India Company made an offering of their first formal import of tea – a mere two ounces – to King Charles II in 1664. Curiously, it was in London's coffee houses, which rapidly increased in number after the Civil War, that tea found its most popular outlet. In fact the coffee houses proved crucial in the dissemination of the popular cultural habits of drinking tropical drinks and smoking tobacco. From those centres of metropolitan, male social life, the new habits – of drinking and smoking together – spilled out across the country, and into domestic life.

Initially the coffee houses provided a forum for fashionable sociability. The drinks they offered were, at first, faddish and exclusive; those promoting them appealed to the fashionable instincts and stylish ambitions of the capital's prosperous men. Tea, proclaimed a handbill in 1660, is a drink 'of such known vertues, that those very Nations famous for Antiquity, Knowledge, and Wisdom, do frequently sell it among themselves for twice its weight in silver'. After listing tea's many qualities, this broadsheet concluded with the resounding claim that the virtues of 'this Leaf and Drink are many and great is evident and manifest by the high esteem and use of it (especially of late years) among the Physitians and knowing men in France, Italy, Holland and other parts of Christendom.'[10]

Tea-drinking began to make a swift impression on the English elite. On 25 September 1660, Samuel Pepys, clerk in the Admiralty, told how, after discussing the prospects of 'a peace with Spain and a war with France and Holland' his colleagues 'did send for a Cupp of Tee (a China drink) of which I never had drunk before.' Seven years later, in June 1667, Pepys returned home to 'find my wife making of Tea, a drink which Mr Pelling the pothecary tells her is good for cold and defluxions'.[11] By then, tea drinking had been given the seal of Royal approval. When Charles II married the Portuguese princess Catherine of Braganza in 1662, his bride introduced the English Court to the tea-drinking habit which was well entrenched in her home Court. The English royals adopted the custom – the surest and quickest way to spread any social fad among English elites. At much the same time (1666), royal emissaries to Holland returned not merely bringing tales of the fashion for tea in Holland, but importing tea for their wives and friends. Slowly but surely the Court and its entourage began to drink tea.

The East India Company, alert to the growing popularity of this exotic fashion, began to import more tea. Though mentioned in Company papers in the 1660s, it was not imported in bulk until 1678. From the 1680s the volume increased markedly. In 1685 a Company letter instructed its agents:

> Thea is grown to be a commodity here and we have occasion to make presents therein to our great friends at Court; we would have you send us yearly five or six canisters of the very best and freshest Thea. That which will colour the water in which it is infused, most of a greenish complexion is generally best accepted.[12]

It is significant that the Company needed tea for gifts to friends in high places; to flatter and please its contacts in and around the Court. This corporate generosity would of course help secure the interests of the Company in any future difficulties. But this liaison between Company and Court also serves to confirm the importance of tea in the Court itself. Here, at the apex of English society, fashion was shaped, confirmed, and then disseminated. Or rather, it was copied by those closest to the Court, in the hope that they might afford their own social behaviour the veneer of courtly style. This was to be an often-recurring pattern in succeeding years; royal and aristocratic fashion and patronage, adopted by the well-to-do, later still passing down the social scale into the world of the humble. In the 1680s tea was a courtly ritual and a source of flattery and persuasion between major traders and the Court. By the 1780s tea was the drink of the British common people.

Throughout the late seventeenth century, the main problem facing the companies trading to Asia was the uncertainty of tea supplies from China. Transhipping in India or Indonesia – and that after the uncertain deliveries by Chinese shippers – was a much less satisfactory system than direct trade to and from China. As tea grew in popularity – and profit – it was increasingly apparent that direct trade to China was the key to a boundless and unimaginably lucrative market.

Not surprisingly, the tea trade remained uncertain and sometimes haphazard, and to add to the East India Company's financial woes, duty on tea was charged at 5 shillings per pound, making it available only to the prosperous. It was a costly import, subject to the incalculable dangers and problems of long-distance trade, the disruptions of warfare, and finally the punitive exactions of the English excise system.

It was however the uncertainty of supply which caused most trouble in that first generation of tea imports. The breakthrough came in 1713 when the Company secured agreement to trade direct to Canton. From 1717 English ships began a regular cycle of trade direct to China. Even then, business was difficult. The Chinese imposed severe limitations on the trade, and insisted on silver in return. But the rewards were enormous. English ships began the annual voyage home packed with Chinese silks, porcelains – and tea – creating the fashion for 'chinoiserie', filling the coffers of the East India Company and transforming forever the social habits of the British people.

The East India Company papers show that tea 'took off' as a major commodity in England in the years 1700 to 1710. Thereafter the Company's imports from China registered extraordinary growth. The bare figures tell the remarkable story. In the 1720s almost nine million pounds of tea were landed. In the following decade it grew to 11.5 million, rising to more than 20 million in the 1740s. By the 1750s more than 37 million pounds of tea came to Britain. Over that 40-year period, importations of tea had increased fivefold. Not surprisingly, the cost fell sharply, dropping roughly by a half, from £0.08/0.10 between 1713 and 1721 to £0.05 from 1741 onwards. The Company reaped enormous profits from this burgeoning trade.[13]

Like all long-distance trade, the tea trade was subject to periodic, unpredictable blips: freaks of weather, warfare, years of glut. No less worrying for the East India Company was the success of European rivals in penetrating the Canton market and returning with their own cargoes of tea. Other European companies flooded the European market with Chinese tea, a growing amount of which found its way to England illegally, by smuggling. The French company was especially adept at steering tea into the Channel Islands and thence illegally (and without dues) into England. Here was the basis for that other growth industry of the period, the massive development of smuggling, especially along the south coast and in the West Country. The East India Company – forced to pay duties on its imports – watched with rising irritation as ever more English people were able to buy and consume cheaper tea thanks to enterprising smugglers. At times, the East India Company may have provided a mere 25 per cent of all English tea; the rest was smuggled. In North America of course, where a rising sense of local identity fuelled resistance to British imperial exactions, consumption of smuggled items ran at even higher levels.

British fiscal policy was changed from time to time, trying to adapt to the clever stratagems of the smuggling fraternity. The simple truth was that mass consumption of tea had become part of British life, spreading outwards from its initial hold on the upper reaches of life in and around the capital until, by the mid-eighteenth century, it was to be found across the face of the country. By that time some 1.1 pounds of tea per head of population was landed (legally and illegally) in the country. Oddly enough, some idea of how much tea the British consumed by the late eighteenth century can be gauged by the tea imports into mainland Europe, where people tended not to consume it on anything like the scale of the British. By the 1770s and 1780s the European companies were importing an estimated 13.5 million pounds of tea and most of it was re-exported – i. e. smuggled – to Britain and North America.

So great was the demand for cheap tea – and so prohibitive the duties – that smuggling simply got out of hand. Penalties against smuggling tea had become so punitive and counter-productive that the law could not – and should not – be enforced. By the last quarter of the eighteenth century a remarkable phenomenon had emerged. British consumers in their millions were conspiring with armies of British and European smugglers to evade the law – indeed to bring it into disrepute – in order to flood the British market with a cheap product grown at the far side of the globe. It is easy to see why this revolt took place. Duties effectively raised the cost of tea to the British consumer by more than 100 per cent of the cost paid by the buyers in Asia.[14] Yet even this absurd fiscal system tells us a great deal. Here was a clear sign that successive British governments and their advisers appreciated that in tea they had a commodity that was the milch cow of government income. For decades British ministers assumed that tea was the simplest and surest way of generating healthy and rising government income. It seemed that everyone would benefit. Importers and traders, the consumer and the excise man; all could derive benefit from the British addiction to tea-drinking. In reality of course, practice began to diverge from theory, and consumers came together with suppliers to drive down the price by massive, illegal imports, and thus reduce the levels of government income. Even so, here was a convergence of interests between the agencies of long-distance trade and British fiscal policy. The state – in the form of its fiscal policy – had developed a keen interest in and a dependency upon the health and buoyancy of trade in exotic importations. By 1784, when the British government got round to the sensible decision of abolishing most of the tea duties, this massive import of tea enabled the British consumption to reach two pounds per head annually.[15]

Tea deposited in the East India warehouses took traditional routes to reach the teapots of the British people. But the smuggled variety was altogether more circuitous. Small boats rendezvoused with European vessels off the English coast, ferrying their tea-chests into a myriad of coves, inlets and deserted beaches in Kent, Sussex and the West Country. From its landing place, the tea went into hiding, 'into church crypts, underneath homes, to castles (two thousand pounds of tea was confiscated in one day from Hurstmonceux Castle) and into caves'.[16] It was then smuggled onwards in smaller parcels to towns and cities, where it was once again forwarded to other centres of distribution and sale. Curiously, by targeting remote coastline points of entry, smugglers created a more genuinely national system of distribution for tea than that shaped by the East India Company, whose import trade centred on London.[17]

By the mid-eighteenth century a clandestine war was being waged on the south coast and in the West Country, between customs officers and the irregular army of local smugglers. The successes of the excise men were sometimes countered by reprisal raids on Customs Houses, when tea was repossessed by smugglers and dispatched along their own trading system. The headstone of one smuggler, Robert Trotman, killed in an excise raid, records;

> A little tea, one leaf I did not steal.
> For guiltless bloodshed I to God appeal.
> Put tea in one scale, human blood in t'other,
> An think what 'tis to slay a harmless brother.[18]

Determined government steps to repress smuggling (not simply of tea of course) seemed merely to lead to violence, especially in the 1740s. But smuggling was too closely enmeshed in the local economy to be uprooted by physical force and threats. Even exemplary punishments and punitive fines – sometimes of whole communities – failed, for there were tens of thousands of people throughout the country who saw nothing wrong in smuggling. It was part of that 'moral economy' of eighteenth-century life which pitched customary practice against intrusive and penal government intervention.[19] Smuggling became a way of life, even among the respectable classes. Travellers between the Continent and England smuggled tea in humbler fashion: ladies had their coats and petticoats adapted to enable them to carry secret pockets filled with tea.[20]

Here was a simple, but curious fact: the rise of mass tea-consumption by the mid-eighteenth century depended heavily on the smuggled commodity. The official imports, i.e. tea with duty paid, could have satisfied only a small part of the demand of the drinking public. The smugglers had justice, if not law, on their side. Their activities helped to force down the price and ensured that tea became ever more popular and diffused throughout British society. They were in effect instrumental in consolidating tea-drinking as one of the most important cultural habits of the British people:[21] illegality and massive crime lay behind the most popular and universal of British customs. The absurdity of the situation was slow to dawn on the official mind but finally, in 1784, the government slashed the duty on tea from 120 to 12.5 per cent.

The East India Company's orders to its purchasing agents specified the types of tea best suited to British taste. As the eighteenth century advanced, it was the ordinary, cheaper types of black and green tea that increasingly filled the holds of returning ships. The more costly black teas formed only 2 per cent of imports; the great bulk was Congo or Bohea. Among the green teas, the costly versions formed a small part of imports, the bulk being Singlo. There were other, more exotic brands which the Canton merchants knew about, and which they tried to buy. But the Europeans were not able to penetrate beyond Canton to the regions which produced these various teas, and, in any case, they were obliged to compete with the internal Chinese demand – especially at Court. Despite – perhaps because of – the massive European demand for tea, the Chinese were insistent that Europeans should not visit the tea-growing regions, or learn anything about the gathering and processing of the leaves. This was one aspect of the broader Chinese distrust and suspicion of outsiders. But it also reflected a healthy economic defensiveness – preservation of the secrets of their remarkable commercial success and wariness of outside interests; were the Europeans to learn the secrets of tea-growing and processing they might simply set up their own systems elsewhere. In time, this is precisely what happened.

The only permanent European presence in Canton was the French missionaries, and they proved an enormous help to all other traders. Such help was needed there, year after year, in protracted and sensitive dealings with Chinese officials who struck a tough bargain in permitting the profitable tea trade. Europeans had to hand over their guns, powder and sails for the duration of their visit, pay a series of taxes based on the size of their ships, and could only deal with specified groups of Chinese merchants, the Hongs. There was enormous suspicion and distrust between the two sides (though the Europeans, united for collective self-interest and preservation, were fissured by their own national and trading rivalries).

Those who negotiated for the tea were experienced judges not only of the minutiae of that particular trading system but also of tea itself. They landed each year in Canton with specific instructions from the Company about the volume and types of tea required, and every year brought a fresh round of delicate negotiations to discover the reliable and financially sound merchant houses. There were, inevitably, periodic problems and disputes, but on the whole mutually beneficial trading relations developed between the Europeans and the Chinese merchants. When the deals were struck, the final – and vital – task was the careful packing and loading of the produce. Tea is easily ruined, its flavour and taste quickly destroyed by contact with a host of other items. Safely packed in chests, loaded in the holds away from other contaminating commodities, it could survive the long haul to European markets.

With the cargoes of tea travelled another Chinese product vital to the European appetite for tea-drinking: the porcelain ware used to brew and serve the tea. Unlike other cargoes, these exquisite products could not contaminate the tea; they added ballast to the ships and established a demand for luxury tableware – for 'China' – which was quickly copied by craftsmen throughout western Europe.

Chinese porcelain had been imported in the seventeenth century, normally transhipped via European trading posts elsewhere in Asia. But the emergence of tea-drinking in the eighteenth century confirmed Chinese porcelain both as a fashionable necessity and, in its cheaper, imitated form, as an increasingly popular artefact on European tables. Europeans bought the whole range of Chinese wares, but overall the greatest demand, specified in the orders accompanying the ships bound for Canton, was for drinking-ware; for tea and chocolate cups, for milk and sugar bowls. It is now recognized that Chinese ceramics had by the early eighteenth century 'reached a new stage of refinement and invention', and European demand could be satisfied thanks to a remarkable industry, based in the ceramic factories of Chin-te-Chen, near Nanking, a city of a million people and 3000 kilns.[22]

Chinese tea and ceramics thus found their way to Europe in quite amazing quantities. It was a trade which enriched and empowered the great European trading houses, and proved a rich source of taxation for European governments. It was a source of employment for armies of people, from the humble sailors below decks to the harassed servants plying customers with hot beverages in homes and coffee houses across Europe and North America. Yet there were more subtle forces at work. Behind the obvious figures, the statistics, the mountains of tea, there lay a subtle change in the way millions of people behaved. British sociability itself had changed, revolving, at certain key times of the day and for particular occasions, around the serving of tea. Tea insinuated itself into every walk of life: into the most fashionable of homes (where tea-drinking formed the centre of female entertainment and discussion) through to the coarsest of work-places, where men broke their labouring routines for the strengthening refreshment of hot, sweet tea.

By the 1780s, tea drinking had spread through all classes and all regions in Britain and become an element in the daily diet of the poorest (a fact loudly denounced by a host of commentators who worried about what they took to be the rise of 'luxury' among the common people). Thomas Turner complained in 1758 of the 'too frequent use of spiritous liquors and the exorbitant practice of tea-drinking [which] have in such manner corrupted the morals of people of almost all ranks'.[23]

The poor seemed especially keen on 'vieing with their superiors, and imitating their luxuries, [and] throw away their little earnings upon this fashionable herb'.[24]

The national addiction irritated a number of mid-century observers.

> The young and the old, the healthy and the infirm, and the superlatively rich, down to the vagabonds and beggars, drink this enchanting beverage when they are thirsty, and when they are not thirsty. It is a foolishness of folly.[25]

Few people drank quite as much tea as Dr Johnson, who consumed it by the pint (not surprisingly he was a notorious insomniac). He described himself as 'a hardened and shameless tea-drinker, who has for many years diluted his meals with only the infusion of this fascinating plant; whose kettle has scarcely time to cool ...' But by then everyone seemed to drink tea. It was, thought Jonas Hanway in 1757, a vice of the English that 'the laborer and mechanic will ape the lord'. It infuriated him that 'your servants' servants, down to the very beggars, will not be satisfied unless they consume the produce of the remote country of China'.[26]

There was however a curious paradox here, for low income groups in Britain were now wedded to two items – tea and sugar – grown and transported great distances:

> it appears a very strange thing, that the common people of any European nation should be obliged to use, as part of

their daily diet, two articles imported from the opposite sides of the earth.[27]

At one level, what made this possible was the dramatic fall in price. But tea had the added attraction, for low income groups, of ease of preparation. All that was required was hot water, and the simplest of dishes or jugs, for brewing. Tea could also be adulterated easily (a virtue in a world where food adulteration was commonplace among retailers). Yet tea had a naturally bitter flavour which, to satisfy British tastes, required the addition of sugar. In its native region, tea was consumed unalloyed by sugar or milk. But the British variant depended for its success on sugar. And here, yet again, the existence of empire proved crucial. At precisely the time tea began to flood the British market, sugar from the slave islands of the British Caribbean arrived in equally amazing volumes, to sweeten the tastes of the British tea-drinking public. Tea from China, sugar from the West Indies (courtesy of the labour of Africans), came together in a hot brew to satisfy a newly-created taste of British people. And both products were made possible by the power of Britain's military and commercial strength. Its companies could strike hard bargains, its navy (and soldiers) command peace and obedience. From such complex but potent forces, the British consumer was won over to the sweetened delights of exotic produce.

Tea had even entered institutional life. In 1776 the matron and the apothecary of Leeds General Infirmary were allowed £6 a year for tea and sugar; twenty years later the nurses asked for the same benefit.[28]

At first glance, propertied complaints seemed justified; the poor were spending what seemed, to outsiders, to be their spare cash on the consumption of exotic goods, imported from the far ends of the earth. The Scottish theologian, Duncan Forbes, could remember a time before the 'opening [of] a Trade with the East Indies … [which] brought the Price of Tea … so low, that the *meanest* labouring Man could compass the Purchas of it …' and when '*Sugar*, the insepearable Companion of Tea, came to be in the possession of the poorest Housewife, where formally it had been a Rarity'. In Scotland, the lowering of the duty on tea in 1784 hit the local whisky industry; thereafter it was claimed that tea 'has become an economic substitute to the middle and lower classes of society for malt liquor'.

Tea was the cheapest of drinks. It was adaptable, could be made strong or weak, its leaves could be dried and used again and, when taken with (cheap) sugar, it provided an instant shot of refreshment. Many critics complained about the cost of tea, assuming that the poor drank the costly varieties enjoyed by the rich. In fact, the poor consumed the cheapest of cheap varieties, often adulterated, often using only a few leaves, and often too reusing the same leaves. As one man remarked, in the early nineteenth century, 'If any body will point out an article that is cheaper and better, I will venture to answer for the poor in general, that they will be thankful for the discovery.'

At one level, this seemed a simple matter of taste, but there was another, more complex explanation. This collective dependence on tropical staples was a function of the rise of a powerful trading economy, able to conquer or overawe distant regions of the world and command them to bring forth, for domestic pleasures and taste, the fruits of the region.

In the last years of the eighteenth century, Europe was convulsed by the warfare and ideological struggles spawned by the French Revolution. The 1790s were a decade of encroaching privation for the British labouring poor. But even in the hardest of times, especially in 1795 and 1797, they clung to their recently found addiction to tea – a fact which both bemused and irritated Sir Frederick Eden in his investigation of the lives of the poor. Those families who, he claimed, were unable to afford 'malt liquor' were now addicted to 'the deleterious produce of China' for their main drink. The amount of water '(which, with tea, forms a deleterious beverage, that is seldom qualified with milk or sugar,) [and is] poured down the throats of a labourer's family, is astonishing.' Anyone visiting a labourer's home in Middlesex and Surrey at meal-times 'will find that, in poor families, tea is not only the usual beverage in the morning and evening, but is generally drank in large quantities even at dinner.'[29]

Plebeian tea-drinking continued to inspire the disapproval of critics who, concentrating on the exotic nature of the produce, and the distance it had travelled, could not bring themselves to think of it as anything but luxury. Nor was this simply a matter of cost. For decades, tea had borne the stamp of luxury and the social cachet of fashionable life and style, to the extent that many found it hard to accept that sugar also had fallen into the hands of the lower orders. This was to be a recurring pattern in succeeding centuries. When the habits and the possessions of the well-to-do became the fads of the masses, hostile critics complained of the way groups spent their time and money on pursuits best left to others. In the nineteenth century, similar complaints could be heard about the rise of popular seaside holidays; in the twentieth century, that myriad of material artefacts which found their way into the homes of the common man provoked similar squeals of outrage from critics who sought to preserve the exclusivity of access to certain pleasures.

By the early nineteenth century, when the process of industrialisation was clearly under way, the diet of British working people became a subject of acute contemporary interest. More recently it has formed the basis for a continuing debate among historians about the standard of life of working people. However we analyse the statistics, there is no denying the ubiquity of tea among the British people. The criticisms of the late eighteenth century simply faded from view under the weight of British consumption. In the years 1801 to 1810 almost 24 million pounds of tea were consumed in the United Kingdom. By mid-century it had almost doubled again, and stood at $44\frac{1}{4}$ million pounds. The average *per capita* consumption was about $1\frac{1}{2}$ pounds.[30] This picture would be familiar to anyone brought up in modern Britain, a nation collectively committed to tea, consuming it at special moments throughout the day; waking to breakfast tea, and retiring with a late night cup of tea – with the intervening hours punctuated by regular, ritualistic drinks of the same.

Other countries however did not follow the British. Of all the tea imported into France in the eighteenth century, only one-tenth was consumed locally, the rest was re-exported. German-speaking states, from the first, preferred coffee. Spaniards scarcely drank any tea at all.[31]

To brew and drink their tea, the British bought the appropriate tableware in vast and ever increasing volumes. Long before tea became a European fashion, Chinese porcelain – the basic equipment of drinking – had helped to transform aesthetic tastes in widely scattered regions of the world. An ancient maritime trade had linked China, India and the Gulf; from there the most delicate and sought-after items of Chinese manufacture had found their way by overland caravan routes to the Mediterranean. In recent years, archaeologists have found remains of Chinese pottery throughout Central Asia, in the Middle East, East Africa, India and South East Asia.[32] Above all, it was the delicate beauty of those Chinese manufactures which caught the eye and established a demand. Wherever the complex pre-modern trading routes finally came to rest, there could be found the finest of Chinese goods. It was in large part a luxury trade, but it also had the effect of raising the standards and skills of local crafts and industries. In Persia, for example, skilled men sought to copy the most beautiful of Chinese porcelain. But no one quite managed to achieve the quality and the finesse of the originals. This demand for Chinese goods, on the very edges of trade to China, began in the eleventh century; at the time of the Norman Conquest, complex Chinese industries and trading systems were supplying markets far beyond the ken of northern Europeans.

Soon after they encountered Chinese porcelain, European potters tried to imitate it, but they were unable to capture the appropriate mix of materials and processes until the eighteenth century. Curiously, despite its much-sought-after beauty, Chinese porcelain was initially imported into Europe in bulk not for its own sake, but as ballast; as crude dead-weight necessary for the safe handling of contemporary sailing ships. Since the most valued of Chinese cargoes – tea and silks – were loaded in the centre of the vessel (as far away as possible from damaging contact with water), the ship's trim was all the more important. For every ton of tea imported, six tons of porcelain were added as ballast. In this fashion, it has been calculated, some 240 tons of Chinese porcelain were imported into England each year.

The amount of porcelain ordered and packed by the traders in Canton was extraordinary. They wanted volume and bulk, and were able to strike hard bargains with their Chinese counterparts. The result was that the price paid for porcelain was very low. In 1712 a 216-piece dinner service cost £5.10s.; 5000 teapots imported in 1723 cost 1½d. each. Something like

5 million pieces were imported each year. In 1718 a 29-ton lot contained 250 000 pieces; six years later a 40-ton lot had 332 000 pieces.[33]

These items, however beautiful and delicate, were imported into Britain in such profusion that they prompted a revolution. Like tea itself, Chinese porcelain soon changed from exotic rarity to commonplace and ubiquitous artefact, to be found on tables throughout the land. Rich people, the pioneers as we have seen of tea drinking, passed their possessions on to their inferiors; chipped plates and cups, too damaged or unsightly, passed down the chain of ownership, generally via servants, to poorer groups. But on top of that, the sheer volume of imports, and consequent price reductions, enabled more and more people to acquire their own tableware. By 1791, when the Company decided to stop further imports of porcelain, some 215 million pieces had been imported. Millions of British homes contained domestic items which had been shipped half-way round the world.

The English pottery industry, inspired and nurtured by the Chinese imports, began to catch up, prompted by demand, by the example of Chinese craftsmanship, and by the inspired leadership and initiative of a handful of manufacturers, notably Josiah Wedgwood. At first their products were much coarser, less durable and easily broken. British manufacturers soon began to adapt their products to the peculiarities of local taste. Tea-drinking in Britain had taken quite a different direction from tea-drinking in China. There, tea was made direct in the kettle and drunk when cool. The British liked their tea brewed in a pot, and served hot; hence the need for a teapot, itself adapted from the shape of Chinese wine flasks, but with a handle to facilitate handling. A similar change took place with the teacup. Hot tea required a vessel with a handle, but cups with handles were more difficult to store and ship great distances, though easier to distribute locally.[34] From this fusion of Chinese styles and British usage, there emerged the distinctive apparatus of British tea-drinking.

The best Chinese porcelains prompted a number of European industries, encouraged by royal patronage, to match and even to surpass the quality of imported ware. Meissen and Sèvres were perhaps the most notable and best-remembered, but it was widely accepted by the mid-eighteenth century that any self-respecting royal court required its own local manufacturer. In the words of the Duke of Wurttemberg, 'A porcelain factory is an indispensable accompaniment of splendour and magnificence.'[35]

From this royal and aristocratic involvement (which involved financial losses, subsidies and extravagant waste) there evolved fashion, publicity – and the prospects of a bigger market for European porcelains.

The desires of the British upper classes mirrored their European peers, but British tastes were satisfied by commercial rather than royal patronage. Above all others, it was the brilliant enterprise of Josiah Wedgwood which catered to the fads of the rich. In doing so he became the most successful of all English pottery manufacturers and salesmen. In the process he transformed the tastes of the British people at large. Wedgwood popularized items of trade which were initially exclusive. Like tea itself, the pots and cups from which it was served (and a much broader range of pottery) were transformed from the exclusive to the popular.

All this was made possible by Wedgwood's innovative marketing campaign. His goods were manufactured in new workplaces, to a standard rarely achieved before in England, but it was his marketing which elevated his goods above all others. Before his death in 1795 (when he was worth a fortune of £500 000) his good were sold, like Chinese pottery before them, throughout the world; in China, America and India. Using bilingual clerks and agents, Wedgwood marketed across Europe, though aristocrats helped, unknowingly, by sending his wares as gifts to friends in Europe. Wedgwood's pottery was regularly shipped to the colonies. Indeed the bulk of his trade by the 1780s was for export. His wares were inescapable. One contemporary noted that in travelling from Paris to St Petersberg, from Amsterdam to the farthest point of Sweden, from Dunkirk to the southern extremity of France, English earthenware was produced. Similar items appeared throughout the Iberian Peninsula, in North America and in the slave colonies of the Caribbean.[36]

Although it is true that Wedgwood's potting techniques and system of manufacture, and the skills of his craftsmen, created the finest of pottery, it was his marketing which proved crucial. Rather than sell to a mass market, he initially aimed at the prosperous; at those upper reaches of English life for whom the fashion of tea-drinking had become so marked a feature of contemporary domestic sociability by the mid-eighteenth century. What he aimed for, and achieved, were high prices and a mass market. Wedgwood carefully targeted his markets; aiming first to sell to and please royalty and aristocrats, the pacemakers of fashion. Once they had adopted a particular fad, others quickly followed. That, after all, was what happened with tea itself.

Wedgwood opened showrooms in London to appeal directly to the capital's most fashionable and elite groups, taking pains to exclude lower income groups. In the capital, he built up an 'aristocratic clague'. Unwittingly, they served as his most influential agents: 'They praised his ware, they advertised it, they bought it, and they took their friends to buy it.'[37] Wedgwood appreciated a central fact which recent historians have sometimes doubted; that fashion came from the top and percolated downwards.

Fashionable life, especially for women, revolved around the tea-drinking ceremonies. Visitors from abroad were impressed. A German lady wrote in 1786 about 'a first class English tea-party' she attended at Windsor:

> The tone was intimate and refined: the hostess busied herself delightfully and fast enough to allow grace and deftness. While Madame La Fite prepared the tea, the ladies continued their fancywork, sewing bands of fine muslin. While we sipped our tea, pretty and practical discussion took place.[38]

With Wedgwood's goods secured as the playthings of London's great and good, it was but a matter of time before more humble folks emulated their superiors. Throughout, Wedgwood remained acutely sensitive to fashion, changing designs, colours and production systems to accommodate fashionable change of moods. Black teapots, for example, were perfectly suited to highlight the beauty of fashionable ladies' bleached hands. It was testimony to his remarkable success that his London showrooms themselves became a fashionable meeting place where the wealthy could parade and be seen at the forefront of contemporary taste. He then replicated the process elsewhere, with warehouses and showrooms in Bath, Liverpool and Dublin.

Having secured a niche among the upper classes, Wedgwood proceeded to target less exalted groups – 'The Middling Class of People, which class we know are vastly, I had almost said, infinitely superior in number to the Great'. To appeal to this new group, Wedgwood pitched his sales at contemporary fads and passions among the middle class: 'begin at the head first, and then proceed to the inferior members.'[39] It was a tactic which worked brilliantly and his tableware soon appeared in the dining-rooms of the middle classes.

Before 1720, the new items of tableware were unusual among lower income groups. Perhaps only one person in ten owned the crockery needed to make and serve the exotic drinks so fashionable in upper reaches of English life. By the mid-eighteenth century, all this had changed (on both sides of the Atlantic), as ever more people were able to buy the new tableware and more and more people made tea in their homes.[40] Tea-drinking had become thoroughly domesticated, part of those rituals of domestic sociability – especially important for women – which provided an alternative form of refreshment and entertainment to the publicly based consumption of alcohol (and coffee).

By the early years of the industrial revolution, the British, of all social classes and regions, were keen tea-drinkers. Moreover all of that tea came from China. By 1820 perhaps 30 million pounds of tea were consumed in Britain. As much as 5 per cent of the English gross domestic product was involved in tea. Yet no European had yet penetrated beyond the merchant houses of Canton. No one really knew how tea was grown or manufactured. The Chinese had, so far, kept their secret intact – despite the fact that tea production had seeped into Japan and Java.[41]

The East India Company had maintained its grip on tea supplies for more than a century but its days were clearly numbered. It had emerged and flourished in an age which promoted the ideal of monopoly trading. In Africa, in Asia, and by the Navigation Acts throughout the Americas, trade was tightly controlled and manipulated to the benefit of the mother country. But times were changing. What had appeared unquestionably clear in the late seventeenth century – that restriction and monopoly was the stuff of national well-being – was in doubt a century later. Monopoly had begun to give way to freer trade (nudged in that direction by Adam Smith in 1776). The once-great trading companies, rooted in monopoly, seemed dated. Like slavery – itself a function of a closely controlled mercantilist imperial system – the monopolistic habits of the East India Company belonged to another age. In fact both the monopoly of the company and the existence of chattel slavery were ended in the same year – 1834. Henceforth, free trade – backed by the power of the Royal Navy – was thought to be the most appropriate way forward for British economic well-being. The British were consuming ever greater volumes of both sugar and tea. But by the 1830s a new economic orthodoxy demanded that these and other staples should find their way to Britain via new, more open routes. Popular taste however remained unchanged, and so did public demand. The British could not imagine life without their tea. Indeed tea was part of their essential Britishness.

The years of massive population growth and encroaching industrialisation simply confirmed the British addiction to tea. But from the 1830s, with the introduction of tea into India and Ceylon, the British turned their back on their traditional supplier of tea, China, consuming instead the new teas cultivated within the bounds of their own empire. The appetite remained as insatiable as ever; only the suppliers had changed. The advantage to the British of producing their 'own' tea within the confines of their own empire, were enormous. Henceforth they could ensure cultivation, production and distribution through their own companies – from Indian producer to British consumer. The demand – the taste – for tea among British people had been nurtured and satisfied by a different economic arrangement. But both cases – the trading company and colonial control – were functions of British power and dominance.

# 3 Coffee

Coffee-houses were to be found in most corners of mid-eighteenth century London and had also crept into a growing number of provincial towns. In London (where there were about 550 by 1740), they were centres of conviviality, and places to discuss business, the arts and politics, and whatever passed for current gossip. Men tended to drift to what became their chosen coffee house. There they could guarantee to find friends, sympathetic souls, news, gossip; they might even collect their mail at the coffee-house, and get the latest news there from the most distant parts of Britain and from far-flung colonies. But the houses' main and abiding purpose was to refresh their customers (who were, from first to last, male) with bowls of strong black coffee. This was coffee as Europeans first encountered it. Long before the drink took hold in Britain, merchants and traders met it in Turkey and the Middle East. Readers were told that the Turks liked their coffee 'in little China Dishes, as hot as they can suffer it; black as Soot and tasting not unlike it'.[1]

It was precisely this strong drink which became widely available, in a very short time, through London's coffee houses from the 1660s. But it was a drink with a remarkable history long before Europeans acquired their taste for it. Originating in Ethiopia, coffee was transplanted to Arabia, notably to the Yemen. There the Sufi seemed to have perfected its concoction, and its fame as a popular beverage quickly spread to other Arab countries. Gradually, the habit and the commodity were adopted throughout the region via traders and merchants. By the sixteenth century, coffee-drinking had become a prominent social habit in Cairo. From there the custom spread to Syria and on to Constantinople. But in the process of geographic diffusion the drink had broken free of the religious world of Sufism, to become an important feature of urban male sociability. Here was a drink which offered refreshment but also provided an occasion and place to meet, for business, for pleasure and for politics.[2]

Like other social innovations, particularly when exotic and luxurious, coffee provoked disapproval. From the first, Islamic clerics disliked coffee's intoxicating effects, viewing it much as they did alcohol.[3] Coffee also displeased local religious elites by providing a focus for social and religious debate; wherever men gathered to drink coffee, it was inevitable that they would discuss matters of mutual interest. The drink was, however, hard to ban or control, not least because it swiftly insinuated itself into the social (especially urban) fabric of Islamic societies. Coffee was more than a stimulating drink; it provided a forum and opportunity for male social activity – a pleasant, time-consuming (and harmless) forum for male society. Transplanted into Europe, coffee soon adopted a similar role. By the late seventeenth century, coffee-drinking had become a feature of male social life from Cairo to London.

Coffee's success was carried forward by contemporary science as well as by fashion. Like a myriad other exotic products, coffee became part of the apothecary's equipment, joining the expanding list of exotic medical produce used in a range of medical prescriptions. Again, Europeans were merely following a much older Arab tradition. As early as the fifteenth century, coffee had been an object of intellectual curiosity in Arabic medical and theological literature. Moreover we need to recall that much of that Arabic medical literature was crucial in shaping early modern European medicine. When Europeans were first introduced to coffee-drinking, there already existed a literary and medical debate about coffee to which Europeans could turn for evidence about this new exotic commodity.

Early proponents of coffee in Europe proclaimed its alleged physical benefits to promote its adoption. There was plenty of medical/scientific evidence to turn to and, not surprisingly, they found repeated proof of its medical virtues in this older literature. To those who urged coffee-drinking, its virtues seemed boundless. It was, claimed an early medical authority, 'of an excellent drying Quality, [which] Comforts the Brain, and dried up Crudities in the Stomach'.[4] It was good for:

> Rickets and Swooning-Fits; it helps Digestion, eases Pains of the Head, raises the Blood, suppresses Vapours, gives Life and Gaiety to the Spirits, hinders Sleepiness after Victuals, provokes Urine and the Courses, and contracts the Bowels...

Its benefits seemed boundless. Good for worms in children, for 'Green-Sickness' among young girls, coffee also helped

'Abortion, and confirms the Tone of the Parts drunk after Eating'.[5]

Such claims, often derived from earlier writers, were repeated and asserted by a string of eighteenth-century authors. One alleged that coffee:

> supports the vital Flame, and defends the Body from Pestilential Infection. And as such it is generally recommended as a necessary Drink, at least twice a day; the first thing in a Morning, and at four in the Afternoon.

It was even argued that among coffee-drinkers 'in the Countries of the East' locals were rarely troubled 'with the Stone, Gout or Dropsy...'[6]

Here was a drink which, if what its defenders said was true, seemed a virtual panacea – socially acceptable and physically restorative. Coffee could be used to effect the difficult tasks of living and trading in exotic locations overseas. Many of the ailments of tropical life could be eased by coffee. It was claimed, for instance, that among slaves in the Americas, coffee helped 'languid circulation'. Among slave women, 'obstructed menses' were common and 'strong coffee is often employed as a deobstruement'. On the plantations, the slave overseers 'find great support from a cup of coffee before they go into the fields'. Knowing their frequently dissolute life-style, this was most likely an early example of the use of coffee for a hangover. More seriously, it was argued that sufferers from smallpox could secure relief from their 'tickling vexatious cough' by drinking coffee. When served with milk and sugar, coffee was 'a highly nutritious and balsamic diet'. Good for consumption, it also helped those who had taken too much opium.[7]

Such comprehensive wonders claimed for coffee (and other tropical staples) understandably attracted a fair share of criticism from sceptics and opponents. Each and every claim was dismissed, for example by men keen to promote home-grown produce rather than costly imports. One of coffee's most severe critics, Dr Simon Pauli, alleged that, along with tea, coffee 'so enervates the European Men, that they become incapable of propagating their Species like Eunuchs'. He made precisely the same accusation against Persian coffee-drinkers, who 'though salacious, are nevertheless generally impotent'. Coffee, claimed Pauli, produced 'Effeminacy and Impotence'.

He thought that: 'all these Things are unfit for fecundating the Semen...'[8]

Coffee and other exotic goods were often discusssed – at least in its early days in Britain – in two contradictory ways. For some, it was a threat to contemporary masculinity both in its physical side-effects and in its social consequences (of generating 'effeminate' social habits). Such extreme criticisms provide an important insight into coffee's sudden pre-eminence. Its rapid rise and popularity could be gauged by the threats this new-fangled habit was deemed to pose to contemporary life and values. It seemed to upset the delicate social balance.

As coffee's popularity increased, as imports rose, the debate about its virtues and vices became more intense. The rise of this new social habit taking place alongside a convoluted, arcane debate which itself drew upon the older Arabic literature, but the whole affair was infused with contemporary mythology. What influence these conflicting claims played in shaping social habits is, however, hard to tell.

By a freak of circumstance coffee came to England shortly before the devastating plague of 1665. It was even claimed that the drink offered protection:

> It is remarked by several Learned Men abroad, that Coffee is of excellent Use in the time of Pestilence, and contributes greatly to prevent the spread of Infection...

In Turkey it was argued the plague rarely struck families 'who are rich enough to enjoy the free Use of Coffee'. The poor, on the other hand, who were unable to afford coffee, suffered.[9] Today, a more complex explanation would be put forward. But the argument is revealing, for it exposes the broader intellectual and social debate prompted by the impact of new, exotic commodities. Coffee and other staples provided pleasure and sociability, but they also drew upon and in their turn stimulated an intellectual debate which was partly scientific/medical and partly social. The arguments about tropical staples were in essence one aspect of a much broader intellectual discourse prompted by the collision between the West and the wider world. The West was slowly coming to terms with exotic peoples, produce and habits, and needed to find intellectual justification for incorporating them into the mainstream of western life.

Coffee-drinking in Islamic societies had thrived in and around urban coffee-houses, becoming especially important in the course of the sixteenth century. Coffee-drinking rituals helped to shape the pattern of the day, bringing men together in routines of male companionship. The coffee-houses also emerged as important venues for business, religious and political transactions. The Arabic and Turkish coffee-house (much like the English ale-house) was not solely a place to drink. They attracted more and more men, of all social levels, to their doors. Those who were unable to attend the coffee-house could have coffee delivered (an early 'take-away' service) to their place of work in the neighbouring commercial area. Young boys delivered fresh coffee to shops and offices throughout the working day. Thus, coffee-drinking and its associated rituals spread from the coffee-house to the place of work. Today, coffee-drinking in the workplace is so universal that it is hard to imagine most western enterprises being able to function without regular and ample provision for its accessibility. Yet here is a custom with a remarkable history – a habit pioneered in the Yemen, in Cairo, Constantinople and Damascus in the sixteenth century.

In all those cities there was an remarkable profusion and variety of coffee-houses. Some were mere benches on the street. Others were lavish emporia; rich displays of contemporary style and architecture, places of luxurious fittings and sumptuous facilities. From Baghdad to Constantinople, the best of coffee-houses were handsome institutions; close to rivers, sheltered by trees, often with their own fountains and cooled by breezes which passed through their open-plan structures. Visitors to such attractive places were always impressed by their peaceful beauty; by the calming ambience of these, the most costly of coffee-houses. One major complaint was that men spent too much of their time there. Sir George Sandys thought that, in the coffee-house, 'the Turks sit chatting most of the Day, and sip a Drink called Coffa'.[10]

The equipment for preparing and serving coffee was developed in such coffee-houses. Like the drink itself, this was later copied and used in western Europe.

Arab and Turkish coffee was served fresh and extremely hot. If allowed to stand, the drink deteriorated. It was difficult for casual street vendors to sell cups of coffee as they sold most other items. Thus, the coffee-house was established as *the* main supplier of coffee. But there was an added reason for the popularity of the Islamic coffee-house. Quite simply, they provided an opportunity and excuse for men to leave their homes. They could leave behind domestic noise, confusion and friction, the babble of children, of disputative wives, of quarrelling servants. Even the poor man liked this haven, for it enabled him to quit the misery of crowded conditions and to find comfort and relief in the masculine world of his favourite coffee-house. Doubtless womenfolk too would dearly have liked to find a similar escape. As it was, coffee-houses became, and remained, a male preserve.

When coffee came to Europe, it seemed natural that the coffee house would quickly follow. After all, this was where Europeans familiar with Turkey and the Levant first came to know of coffee. Trade between Europe and the Levant had, for many years past, spawned stories about exotic life in Middle Eastern countries. In 1624 Sir Francis Bacon wrote,

> They have in Turkey, a Drink called Coffa, made of a Berry of the same Name, as Blacke as Soot, and of a Strong Sent. ... And they take it, in their Coffa-Houses, which are like our Tavernes.[11]

London's coffee-houses had direct Middle Eastern origins. When David Edwards returned from his merchant days in Smyrna he came home with a Greek servant, trained in the preparation of morning coffee. In 1657,

> The Novelty of it drew so great Resort to his House, that he lost all the Fore-part of the Day by it; insomuch that he thought it expedient to rid himself of this Trouble, by allowing his Greek servant (in conjunction with his son-in-law's Coachman) to make and sell it publically. They set up their Coffee-House in St Michael's Alley in Cornhill, which was the first in London.[12]

Though an earlier coffee-house may have opened in Oxford, it was the London venture which proved most influential. Within a decade coffee-houses had sprung up throughout the capital, many of them clearly marked by the distinctive signs of the Turkish coffee pot or a Turk's head,[13] and thereafter Turkish images of the coffee business betrayed the popular association between coffee and its Middle Eastern homeland.

An early English convert to coffee was William Harvey, famous for discovering the circulation of the blood. Long before London had its own coffee-houses, Harvey owned his own coffee pot. According to Aubrey, 'he was wont to drinke coffee; which he and his brother Eliab did, before Coffee-houses were in fashion in London.[14] Harvey's access to coffee was simple; his brothers were 'Turkey merchants', though he may also have been attracted by the alleged medical benefits of coffee. But he could scarcely have imagined that his own taste, unusual for the time, would, within a mere decade of his death, become so popular across the capital.

By the end of the seventeenth century, the London coffee-house, like its predecessors in Cairo and Constantinople, had become an important social and commercial forum for men in the capital. A number of business enterprises emerged from informal gatherings in a coffee-house. Others provided a centre for up-to-the-minute information – about insurance, banking, maritime trade and the minutiae of colonial life. Elsewhere men learned to perfect their social or political styles in these 'penny universities', imbibing ideals and views in the partial political or social atmosphere which developed in certain coffee-houses.

Men of like minds gravitated to particular coffee-houses. Some, for instance, provided rich pickings for the medical fraternity. Surgeons and apothecaries gathered in particular ones 'to discuss the diagnosis and treatment of patients' diseases'. Physicians and apothecaries tended to meet in their own coffee-houses: they were divided by politics as much as by professional rivalries. Physicians complained that the apothecaries spent their time 'hunting for more [patients] in Coffee-houses or other Places of Concourse'.[15] Whatever their particular professional interests or views, men of all sorts were drawn to the coffee-house. It was the one institution which offered a public meeting-place that was less raucous and disruptive than the ale-house.

In London, the coffee-house soon rivalled the tavern, providing most of its social conveniences without the drunken irritations. Its distinct mix of pleasure, business and sociability was infectious, and the coffee-house quickly proliferated across the capital, thriving with the pulse and pattern of the London season. An early coffee trader, John Farr, had been prosecuted in 1657 for irritating his neighbour with the smell of coffee night and day.[16] Soon however the aroma was ubiquitous. By 1663 there were 83 coffee-houses, most of them close to the Exchange, all paying for a licence and offering guarantees of good behaviour. By Anne's reign, there were perhaps 500 of them in London.[17]

Many offered much more than coffee. Chocolate, sherbet, tea, sometimes ale, all and more were available in London's coffee-houses. Each establishment developed its own style, its own conventions and rules. In a clear departure from tavern life, some forbade swearing or quarrelling. Others allowed no gambling, no blasphemy and no speaking of 'affairs of the State "with irreverent tongue"'[18] Political factions made their home and headquarters in a particular coffee-house and their own brand of politics shaped the tone of local business. Customers at certain coffee-houses were provided with newspapers, broadsheets and tracts, and gradually coalesced into distinct political clans. In a reprise of the earlier Arab experience, the coffee-houses offered a natural forum for political (sometimes subversive) debate, but attempts to suppress them (in 1675) as a bed of sedition were bound to founder on their well-entrenched popularity. The Rota Club, which met to discuss republicanism just after the Restoration, gathered in a coffee-house. In 1677 for instance a former Cromwellian captain, now keeper of a coffee-house, was arrested for 'publishing and dispercing' false news. Yet they also had their value for the government. They could be used for example to plant and spread governmental rumours. In 1665 Pepys – a government official – was urged to visit coffee-houses to fan rumours that the Dutch were mistreating British sailors. Once placed in the coffee-house, a rumour would 'spread like leprosy'.[19]

The coffee-house was all things to all men; a forum for the famous (the Royal Society was founded in a coffee-house), and yet a cheap, warm meeting-place for poorer men. Despite such variations, coffee houses had important features in common. They were clearly important venues for (and expressions of) male sociability and cameraderie. For that very reason some women disapproved. *The Women's Petition against Coffee*, published in 1674 railed against what it took to be the emasculating effects of coffee.

> Never did Men wear greater Breeches, or carry less in them of any Mettle whatsoever... The Occasion of which Insufferable Disaster, after a serious Enquiry... we can Attribute to nothing more than the Excessive use of that Newfangled, Abominable, Heathenish Liquor called COFFEE, which Riffling Nature of her Choisest Treasures, and Drying up the Radical Moisture, has so Eunucht our Husbands, and Crippled our more kind gallants, that they are become as Impotent, as Age, and as unfruitful as those Desarts whence that unhappy Berry is said to be bought.[20]

It was the male exclusivity of the coffee-house which seemed to cause offence. They were places which seemed to exclude women, attracted men of all social classes and persuaded them to dally throughout the day, and long into the night, over pleasures denied to women.

Pepys was one of the more famous habitués of the coffee-houses, recording some 80 visits in his diary. He ranged from the Turk's Head on the waterside at Westminster (where customers sat round a large oval table 'with a passage in the middle for Miles to deliver his coffee') to a number of coffee-houses near the Royal Exchange, where merchants discussed business, and to Covent Garden to listen to Dryden and other contemporary wits sharpening their brilliance in public.[21] On 3 February 1664, Pepys stopped off at 'the great Coffee-house' in Covent Garden,

> where I never was before – where Drayden the poet (I knew him at Cambridge ) and all the wits of the town, and Harris the player and Mr Hook of our college; and had I time then, or could at other times, it will be good coming thither, for there I perceive is very witty and pleasant discourse.[22]

By the time of Pepys's death, coffee-houses were so commonplace, so ingrained a feature of London life that it was impossible to imagine metropolitan life without them.[23]

Banks were founded, deals struck, debts paid and orders placed in a coffee-house (when conventional business hours had ended). One in Sweetings Alley became known as the Stock Exchange Coffee House. Lloyd's Insurance Company and the Commercial Union took modern shape in a coffee-house. In addition to providing such business opportunities, the London coffee-houses of the early eighteenth century had come to dictate the pattern of daily life for thousands of men. The keenest began their day there, taking breakfast and catching up with the latest morning gossip or reading the newspapers. Better, more fashionable coffee-houses became a stage for the leisured life of the well-to-do. The favoured house was, at once, a public place where one could be seen, and yet, by dint of local convention or cost, exclusive enough to keep out undesirables. Foreign visitors sometimes caught the mood.

> At 12 o'clock the *Beau Monde* assembles in several coffee and chocolate houses... and all these are so near to one another that in less than an hour you can see the company of them all.[24]

Ten years later, Baron Pollnitz described the day of the coffee-house habitué. After a walk in the park, the English gentleman,

> saunters to some coffee or chocolate house frequented by the persons he would see, for 'tis a sort of rule with the English to go once a day at least, to houses of this sort, where they talk of business or news, read the newspapers, and often look at each other without opening their mouths...

Each coffee-house developed its own particular etiquette; conventions of behaviour which sometimes bemused outsiders. Conversation flowed, but when it stopped, long periods of silence often ensued, silence which the English found normal but which struck outsiders as remarkable;

> they are often separated by an interval of silence, more or less considerable, all persons present looking at each other and reflecting upon what they have heard.[25]

For men new to London and for the ambitious, coffee-houses were ideal: a starting point to begin to make sense of (and to forge contacts in) the bewildering confusions of London life. When Francis Lockier first arrived in London at the age of 17, 'an odd-looking boy, with short rough hair and that sort of awkwardness which one always brings up at first out of the country', he made for a coffee-house to establish himself.[26]

The houses were in effect the centre of much of London's public social life. They were also places where the ambitious could flaunt their potential:

> where they may in a very little time be known; their Character likewise may be partly discovered, even by People that are strangers to the Language, if they appear cool in their Discourses, and attentive to what they hear.

Some however disliked the coffee-houses. Not only were they 'full of smoak, like a Guard-Room, and as much crowded' but they were centres (and cause) of tittle-tattle: 'I believe 'tis these Places that furnish the Inhabitants with Slander, for there one hears Accounts of everything done in Town, as if it were but a Village.'[27] There were however advantages. Simply to frequent a coffee-house provided a man with a fixed abode and an address. ('Sir, I am to be found at such a place.') and, for the impoverished but ambitious, avoided the need to confess to more humble surroundings. A man could 'behave as if in his own house, make appointments, and have his letters delivered there'.[28]

In time, the exclusiveness of certain coffee-houses, rooted in politics or social refinement, solidified into new select clubs, forerunners of some of London's modern clubs. Reputations and styles of coffee-houses waxed and waned. By the mid-eighteenth century the 'wits' had moved to the Bedford:

> Almost everyone you meet is a polite scholar and a wit. Jokes and *bon mots* are echoed from box to box; every branch of literature is critically examined and the merit of every production of the press or performance of the theatres weighed and determined.[29]

Visitors, especially foreigners, were struck above all by the coffee-house addiction to politics and newspapers. In fact coffee-houses proved to be the breeding ground for embryonic newspapers, providing the press with news and with a ready-made network of readers who devoured the printed word. Those early newspapers depended upon advertisements for income, and keepers of coffee-houses felt, in time, abused by the newspaper owners. By 1728 they complained of being used as pawns in the fight between rivals.

> The *Coffee-Men* are the Persons who do the Business of the *Advertisers*. The Coffee-Men are they who *circulate* Advertisements, and direct them to their proper Ends. The *Coffee-Men* pass them from Hand to Hand, and make them known to the whole Town. And if the Coffee-Houses were to shut up... what would become of *Advertisements*?[30]

As newspapers proliferated in the eighteenth century (London had four dailies and five or six tri-weekly evening papers by 1760)[31] the coffee-houses became, in effect, libraries – especially for men who could not afford to buy a newspaper (tradesmen, mechanics, artisans of the self-improving kind). They and many more found refreshment in a bowl of coffee and discovered knowledge in the free newspapers.

Yet despite coffee's public success, it failed to make a comparable impact within the home. However, the price of coffee went down, driven by the demand of the coffee-houses. By the late seventeenth century, a bowl of coffee could be had for a mere penny.[32] Some houses sold raw coffee. The Turk's Head in Change Alley advertised 'the right Coffee-powder at 4s. to 6s. 8d. per pound. By the mid-eighteenth century, coffee-drinking had spread beyond the coffee-houses. Coffee was now consumed in prosperous homes (generally as an after-dinner drink), though only on a small scale. It was also available, by the cup, from street vendors at night coffee-stalls at appropriate points on the streets of London.[33] In general, however, it was in the coffee-house that coffee-drinking acquired its popularity. 'The cheapness of it, with the Convenience of this Way of Meeting (being prefereable to those in Taverns and Ale-Houses) soon increased its Drinkers...'[34]

In the early years of the eighteenth century, the British consumed more coffee than tea and, until about 1720 the coffee-pot was a more common domestic item than the tea-pot. Thereafter however tea consumption rapidly and vastly outstripped coffee. Though more and more coffee was imported, by the East India Company from its Yemeni factory in Mocha, the very great bulk was re-exported to Europe. The English retained most of their tea imports – but re-exported most of their coffee.[35]

The rise in the European consumption of coffee, in common with other staples, prompted massive changes in its production and shipping. As demand for ever more coffee began to place great pressure on the original markets in the Yemen, Europeans were able to shift coffee production to new regions. The British like everyone else were initially dependent on imports from the Middle East. Gradually however they began to develop their own coffee industry. As Europeans came to secure distant regions of the globe to their tightening imperial and settler control, they acquired territories on which they could transplant crops from distant reaches of the world. Their tropical colonies provided a test-bed not merely for the transplanting of population – black and white – but for agricultural experimentation on a global scale. To be able to transplant, nurture and develop produce within their own territories (where strategeic and economic control could ensure effective national monopoly) was to short-circuit the problematic dependency on indigenous producers, be they Chinese tea-growers or Yemeni coffee farmers. Again, this was no simple accident – the accidental global transfer of plants, roots or shoots – but a calculated imperial and economic policy whose prime aim was the material betterment of the metropolis. Coffee is a case in point.

All the major European colonial powers introduced coffee into their tropical settlements. The Dutch planted in Sumatra, the Celebes, Timor, Bali, Ceylon and Java, (which produced five million pounds by 1725). The French grew it in Martinique, later in St Domingue, the British in Jamaica and then along a string of islands through the Caribbean. The Spaniards introduced coffee into Puerto Rico and Cuba. Finally, and most spectacularly of all, it was planted in Brazil. From these and a myriad other colonies there flowed that array of coffees so beloved of the drinker.

These changes marked the beginning of a rapid decline for the original Yemen industry. As coffee production thrived in the new regions, the original Arab industry found it impossible to keep up with the competition and by 1901 only 400 people worked in it.[36] Among the many factors which gave the new European-inspired developments their competitive edge was the fact that coffee was henceforth grown on plantations: bad news for plantation workers, but excellent news for European consumers. Production was henceforth under direct European control and the vagaries of distant, alien production and initial distribution were replaced by that intrusive direct management which characterized the mercantilist system. But slavery on coffee plantations was different. Unlike sugar plantations, coffee plantations were relatively small, employed more white people and had a generally 'better' black/white ratio. By the end of the eighteenth century, at a time when the West Indies were under severe attack in Britain, coffee production was seen as a potential saviour for the islands. Proponents of coffee in the islands also wanted to encourage increased production, partly to undermine the role of tea: 'it might be afforded here at a price to render it a cheap substitute for those enervating teas and beverages which the inferior classes of people adopt from necessity'.[37]

The dramatic success of the British settlements in the Caribbean was of course based on sugar. So dramatic were sugar profits – quick, easy and apparently endless – that more and more West Indian settlers rushed into sugar production. But coffee cultivation remained important throughout the islands, dominating the lives of a large number of slaves. Wherever the British acquired new lands (as they did most spectacularly at the Peace of Paris in 1763, taking Dominica, St Vincent, Tobago, Grenada and the Grenadines) they tended to convert the diversified economies of those islands into sugar. But sugar could not be grown everywhere, and coffee remained an ideal crop, grown at higher altitudes, in a large number of British islands. On the eve of slave emancipation, for example, 14 per cent of Jamaica's slaves worked in coffee. At much the same time almost half of Dominica's slaves (7700 of them) worked on coffee plantations. On St Lucia in 1815 coffee employed 20 per cent of the slaves.[38] This shift in coffee production to the Caribbean also undermined London's early monopoly, and Bristol, Liverpool and Glasgow began to take a share of the import (and re-export) of coffee.[39]

By the late eighteenth century coffee was a major industry which employed a substantial number of slaves, benefited a number of major British ports and shaped key areas of British sociability. But its potential as a drink within Britain seemed thwarted by the dominance of tea. The British, quite simply, had become a nation of tea not coffee-drinkers. Planters and their backers tried hard to reverse the trend, to point out the benefits and simplicity of coffee production and consumption.[40] But, by then, they faced an impossible task. On the eve of the French Revolution – only years after the Americans had tossed their own highly taxed tea into Boston harbour – the British were addicted to tea, not coffee.

Nonetheless, there was a massive increase in coffee importation into Britain. In 1700 official coffee imports were valued at £36 000 (compared to sugar's £668 000). There were periodic ups and downs in the eighteenth century, but from mid-century the value of coffee imports went progressively upwards. The £75 000 of 1750 had increased to £257 000 ten years later, reaching £451 000 in 1775 and £1 396 000 in 1794.[41] But the very great bulk of these coffee imports were promptly re-exported to coffee-drinking Europeans, especially the Germans.

Coffee had obviously established itself as a characteristic of British society and diet. It was not however strictly necessary for everyday life. It was one of those luxuries railed against by critics of unnecessary consumption and by critics of empire and mercantilist policy who viewed the creation of trade in luxuries as the basis for Britain's pernicious global power. Benjamin Franklin was only one of many critics who saw, in the rise of Britain's attachment to the coffee and other similar trades both cause and occasion of an imperial power he detested. Yet such criticisms must have seemed incomprehensible to the mid-century coffee-drinker. Large numbers of men could not imagine social life without it: coffee in itself, coffee as a stimulating drink which revived, refreshed and reinforced; coffee as the centre of male sociability. Coffee-drinking had also become part of the dining habits of the well-to-do. Though never consumed on the same lavish scale as tea, coffee had its own unquestioned role in the routines of fashionable dining and entertaining. Moreover a similar story could be told for much of western Europe and for the North American colonies. Within less than a century, a crop which had originated in a remote corner of the Arabian peninsular was now grown in the highlands of Java and the Blue Mountains of Jamaica. It was drunk by the gallon throughout the western world. Its production was scattered to the far reaches of European settlement and colonization, grown by indigenous peoples and by imported African labour in conditions of abject bondage and dependence. But who, in the convivial comfort of their smoky London coffee-house, gave so much as a thought to that ironic fact? Who stopped to ponder the human cost of those pleasurable fruits of empire which had, by the late eighteenth century, so transformed the face of the western world?

# 4 War, Disease and Settlement: the Americas

The British enjoyed their cups of tea and coffee courtesy of massive changes in relations between Europe and the wider world. Though supplies of tea continued to arrive from Asia, both tea and coffee were made palatable by the addition of sugar from the New World. The British – and other Europeans – cultivated sugar in the Americas and grew coffee in the mountains of their West Indian islands. The tobacco available in London's coffee houses also came from the European colonies in the Chesapeake. In all these cases, European settlement and economic development had taken place in the teeth of, and at the expense of, the native peoples of those regions. What happened to those peoples was yet another (in this case catastrophic) consequence of the European encroachment on distant lands and people. But, once again, it was no mere accident. The disasters which befell the Indian peoples (and which eased the European development of key areas of the Americas) were but another aspect of Europe's predatory assault on the wider world.

The voyages of discovery which pushed out from Europe in the fifteenth and sixteenth centuries brought Europe into direct maritime contact with Asia, Africa and the Americas. Both sides in those contacts (though the process was much too complex to be described so simply) were transformed utterly by those meetings. Europeans were changed fundamentally by the people and lands they encountered at the far side of their oceanic journeys. So too in time was domestic life in Europe. Even more convulsed however was the fate of indigenous peoples in distant parts of the world. Europeans, and the unknown microbes they harboured, threw their lives into turmoil. In origin however, this age of exploration seemed straightforward enough.

As sailors and merchants headed out from their more familiar home waters, they were inspired by a host of forces, but most shared two related inspirations: the desire to expand the

Christian world – to bring Christianity to benighted pagans (and to outwit and outflank the assertive world of Islam), and the urge to profit from trade with the wider world. No explorer worthy of the name could forgo the chance to spread the Christian message. They were, in effect, latter-day maritime crusaders, launching their faith in unknown quarters of the world. Of course they also lusted for wealth and trade, though this rarely dimmed their religiosity. The missionary instinct, basic to Christianity from its earliest days, was from the fifteenth century onwards projected onto the wider world, aided by powerful new clerical orders whose main purpose in life was conversion. Wherever Europeans settled, traded or explored, they set out to convert the locals, and sow the delicate seeds of Christianity in environments which were often as hostile to their faith as to their physical well-being. But they also wanted their share of trade, more especially for those luxurious commodities from far away which so dazzled and pleased European elites.[1]

Properous Europeans were delighted and tantalized by that range of exotic goods which trickled through to them from lands far beyond both their ken and their imagination. The spices of India and South-East Asia travelled, normally via Islamic merchants, to the Red Sea and the Persian Gulf, thence to Baghdad or Alexandria. Silks and spices from China came overland on the 'silk route' to the Black Sea. There they converged with other trading systems, from Russia and Ukraine, each bringing products from their own mysterious hinterlands. Along these routes there passed the most exotic of goods, from the most distant of places (often joined *en route* by other goods – carpets in Persia for example). Here then was a complexity of trading systems which fed exotic, costly items into the economy of the eastern Mediterranean. From there, the powerful mercantile dynasties of the Italian city states forwarded the goods to mainland Europe.

These items of trade served to confirm the most fantastic of stories about the wealth of the East told most famously by Marco Polo (who travelled in China and India in the late thirteenth century). In time, the realities of distant lands were to prove even more stunning than the most fanciful of post-Marco Polo story-telling. Dazzling stories – and tangible proof – of wealth did not however come solely from the east. Among

Marco Polo's most seductive tales had been details of fabulous treasures of gold. Yet it was clear enough that gold – that talisman of wealth across the centuries – was to be had in abundance, not only from the east but also from that mysterious continent south of the Sahara. Overland Arab and Berber caravan routes had long delivered gold to Mediterranean merchants; they in turn fed it to European markets. But to trade direct with the African suppliers required a maritime leap in the dark. No one had sailed there and survived to tell the tale. Here then was scope for imaginative and daring seamanship. Africa – like Asia – beckoned those men fired by the Christian and commercial ambitions of the fifteenth century. The Portuguese were ideally placed for such ventures and, thanks to state backing, commercial and personal daring, and the accumulating improvements in shipbuilding, cartography and navigation, they had sailed as far as Benin by 1475.

These incursions on the African coastline were of course part of a much broader shift in European maritime trading interests. In the course of the fifteenth century, groups of new Mediterranean powers and traders – in Italy and the Iberian peninsula – began to push the interests and boundaries of European mercantile communities in other directions, most notably to the Atlantic, in part to outflank the obstacles of an aggressive Islam to the east. Europeans were in effect looking for new ways, new routes, to secure the prizes of the East. Thus did their attention turn to other routes; to ideas of circumnavigating Africa and finding the elusive passage across the Atlantic to Asia. We need to remind ourselves that when Columbus made his first sight of land in the eastern Atlantic in October 1492 he thought he was gazing at Japan. In fact he stepped ashore in the Bahamas. The subsequent explorations and settlement of the Americas by successive waves of Europeans proved as brutal and destructive a story as we might find anywhere.

Unlike Asia and Africa, the Americas were completely unknown – even unimagined. They had for centuries remained in isolation, their inhabitants, natural world and animal kingdoms untroubled by contact with the human and medical problems which had beset the western world. Though nomadic and agricultural Indian societies were scattered throughout the Americas, major civilizations had developed in only three main regions. The Maya civilizations had thrived in the Yucatan and Central America, their pre-eminence eclipsed from about AD 1000 onwards by the Mexica (better known as the Aztecs) whose empire, based in Tenochtitlan, fanned out from the Valley of Mexico to dominate tribes throughout a wider imperial hinterland. On the eve of European contact the Aztecs controlled a thriving but greatly overtaxed imperial system. Much the same was true of the third great American civilization, the Inca empire of the Andean highlands.

Here then were major imperial civilizations, all of whom had held subject peoples in abject dependence, extracting from them lucrative and painful tribute. They were, however, about to meet people no less aggressive and violent, but who came armed with hardware (and microbes) that the Indian people could scarcely comprehend. The Europeans who, following Columbus, were about to launch themselves on these people came, initially, in search of Asia. They soon realized that here in the Americas was local wealth and the prospect of material bounty in abundance. In the short term however the Indian people stood in their way.

Even now, centuries later, it is hard to comprehend what happened to these Indian peoples. The isolation of the Americas would ensure that their inhabitants would suffer like no others in their dealings with the Europeans. To fall in battle, to face military defeat, was understandable. What made the fate of of the Indian peoples all the more unpalatable was that much of it seemed inexplicable and mysterious. So many succumbed, not to the sword, but to a range of devastating illnesses and epidemics which seemed to surge irresistibly through their societies. First in the Caribbean then in Mexico, Central America and in Peru, later in North America, European invaders and settlers brought disease and death on a scale which beggars belief. The precise details have, inevitably, been the source of historical controversy, but recent scholarship has argued that the population of the Americas approached 100 million on the eve of contact with Europeans. Thereafter, from one region to another, populations collapsed. In Mexico, the population dropped from 25 to 17 million in a single decade; within 75 years it had plummeted by 95 per cent. In Peru, the population of nine million fell to 600 000 in a century. In Nicaragua it fell by 92 per cent; in

Guatamala by 94 per cent. The native populations of California and Florida fell by more than 95 per cent, in the century following contact. The diseases which wrought this unparalleled havoc were varied and mixed. Influenza in Hispaniola (contracted from pigs on Columbus's vessels), quickly followed by typhus, measles, chickenpox, diphtheria, scarlet fever, typhoid, whooping cough, bubonic plague and, most virulent of all, smallpox. Millions of Indian peoples died and the havoc inherited by survivors – debility, infertility, collapse of morale – completed the devastation begun by disease.[2]

They began to die soon after meeting the Europeans. From one region of the Americas to another, the indigenous peoples[3] succumbed in numbers and on a scale which amazed and perplexed the Europeans. On the island of Hispaniola a population of perhaps four million Indians collapsed to a mere 100 000 by 1508. Soon after, in Cuba, a similar disaster had taken place: 'once heavily populated with Indians: today there are only Spaniards.'[4] As their numbers diminished, the Indians lamented their fate, cursed (and often abandoned) their gods, and looked with confused distrust at the obvious instruments of their misfortune – the Europeans. An Indian from the Yucatan looked back mournfully to the old days – to the days before the European impact:

> There was then no sickness; they had no aching bones; they had then no high fevers: they had then no smallpox; they had then no burning chest; they had then no abdominal pain; they had then no consumption; they had then no headache. At that time the course of humanity was orderly. The foreigners made it otherwise when they arrived here.[5]

Sometimes the ailments, diseases and viruses even raced ahead of the Europeans, travelling on animals, goods and other Indians, infecting communities even before the white man arrived.

Europeans, prepared for violence from the Indians, were amazed to see local peoples collapse before them. Whole tribes, communities and, in time, whole civilizations crumbled in the face of an invisible army,[6] an army infinitely stronger than anything the marauding Europeans could muster in the field. The most potent of killers were not the arms and organizations of the white invaders – though they were potent enough – but the unknown germs which spread from Europeans, (and Africans) to Indians, with an invisible and malignant power, reducing the Indian numbers, disabling survivors and shattering native belief in local deities. Their gods had left them unguarded and weak against the ravages of their enemies. Indians, said a German missionary in 1619 'die so easily that the bare look and smell of a Spaniard causes them to give up the ghost'.[7]

Here was a horror story which unfolded throughout the Americas. Moreover it seemed to know no end, but continued, from the Caribbean, Mexico and Peru in the sixteenth century, to the Great Plains in the nineteenth. For their part Indians railed against their collective frailty. By the 1580s – less than a century after Columbus first made landfall in the Americas – indigenous people had all but disappeared in large regions of the Caribbean, Mexico and Peru. It was recorded that the Caribbean coastline was 'so wasted and condemned, that of thirty parts of the people that inhabit it, there wants twenty-nine; and it is likely the rest of the Indians will in short time decay'.[8]

It was, above all, smallpox that devastated the Indians. Some time around Christmas 1518, a smallpox epidemic began its lethal journey into the Caribbean and thence to Central America, cutting a path through the native peoples of the islands, Mexico and as far away as Peru. Las Casas, a bewildered onlooker, thought the disease spared only 1000 people in Hispaniola 'of that immensity of people that was on this island and which we have seen with our own eyes'.[9]

In ravaging the natives, smallpox seemed to be in alliance with the Europeans. The Spanish attack on Aztec Mexico, led by Cortés with a mere 600 men – was assisted by disease. One man in Cortés' second expedition from Cuba to Mexico was infected with smallpox. From his coastal posting, the disease spread rapidly among the Indians. It raced ahead of the advancing Spaniards, killing perhaps a third, perhaps a half of the Aztec population. They did not know precisely what killed them, but it was a collective death more diabolical in its suffering than anything the Spaniards could have devised.

> Some it quite covered on all parts – their faces, their heads, their breasts, and so on. There was a great havoc. Very many

> died of it. They could not walk; they only lay in their resting places and beds. They could not move; they could not stir; they could not change position, nor lie on one side; nor on their backs. And if they stirred, much did they cry out. Great was its destruction. Covered, mantled with postules, very many people died of them.[10]

Cortés and his violent band destroyed what was left of the Aztec empire, creating from the ruins the origins of modern Mexico.[11]

The story was repeated in other regions of Spanish invasion and conquest. Even before Pizarro invaded Peru (1530–1), the Incas had been laid low by the epidemic, thinning the population and undermining resistance to the subsequent Spanish onslaught. As Spaniards moved north and south out of Mexico, they encountered societies already damaged by disease. When Hernando de Soto drove north, seeking legendary wealth of the kind discovered elsewhere, he found instead ample evidence of human misery; empty settlements, piles of bodies – all spoke to the earlier passage of irresistible disease. The impact of disease was not, however, uniform, or the same from one place to another. Some Indian peoples were better able to resist or avoid the disease than others. Those living in small nomadic communities (able to retreat to isolated canyons, for example), sometimes avoided the worse ravages. But wherever scholars have looked, there they have found devastation among the Indians. Among the desert Indians of north-western New Spain, Indians were reduced by 30–90 per cent; abandoned sites were everywhere. The damage to local Indian life cannot be counted simply by the numbers of dead, however. The survivors, stunned by what had happened to those around them, were rendered helpless; confused and also exposed to whatever blandishments were offered by Christian missionaries. Thus the priests often completed more peaceably what their kinsmen had begun more bloodily.[12]

In this, the Spaniards were the pioneers, infecting Indians they met or approached, but other Europeans were no less fatal in their contacts. The French and Portuguese intruded smallpox into Brazil, the English took it to Florida; the French scattered new disease among native peoples of Canada. In 1616 Jesuits noted that Indians on the Canadian Atlantic coast,

> are astonished and often complain that, since the French mingle with and carry on trade with them, they are dying fast and the population is thinning out. For they assert that before this association and intercourse, all their countries were very populous and they tell how one by one the different coasts, according as they have begun to traffic with us, have been reduced by disease.[13]

On the eve of the Plymouth settlement in New England (1620), Indians in Massachusetts had slipped into communal decline. One European noted that they

> died on heaps, as they lay in their houses; and the living, that were able to shift for themselves, would runne away and let them die, and let there Carkasses ly above the ground without burial ... the bones and skulls upon the severall places of their habitations made such a specatcle ... it seemed to me a new found Golgotha.

Time and again contemporaries were shocked by the scale and the horror of these deaths. 'They died in heaps, like bedbugs.'[14] Whatever the statistical doubts, however uncertain historians have been to make bold demographic claims about these epidemics, it seems clear enough that the first and most important contribution from the Old World to the New was disease. At least half the populations of the Aztec, Maya and Inca civilizations died, shortly after their civilizations collapsed. This 'great death' raged for the best part of a century. By 1600 some twenty epidemics had surged through the native peoples of the Americas. By then perhaps only *one-tenth* of the initial population remained. A recent historian of the disaster writes: 'Perhaps 90 million died, the equivalent in today's terms of the loss of a billion.'[15]

It is hard, even now, not to agree with those Indians who felt that their gods had fled, leaving them to a ghastly fate.

It is tempting to portray the initial European conquests of the Americas as superior civilizations overwelming less advanced people. Technology certainly played its part: firepower, metal weaponry and horse-borne manpower, all proved too potent for Indian defences. But much of what happened makes little sense without remembering that disease also sapped the vitality of large numbers of Indian peoples. *Even before* the Spaniards made their military forays and attacks, the diseases of the Old World and of Africa had preceded them, killing their foes, enfeebling survivors and making ready the coming of the Europeans. And here was the rub. The governing and military elites of the Indian peoples were sometimes mortally wounded and weakened *ahead* of the conflict with European arms. Governors, soldiers and advisers – all and more were swept away leaving their peoples woefully ill-prepared and manned for the impending attacks and invasions.

It was however an uneven picture. Or rather there were exceptions to this dismal generality. People who lived in inaccessible mountains or jungles – whose land was unattractive to Europeans – were often able to survive the coming of the invaders. After all, pockets of such people survive to this day in parts of Central and South America and the Caribbean. But they survive because their ancestors avoided those destructive contacts so common to other native people in the hemisphere. They survived because they eluded the Europeans (who tried, it is true, in time to bring them to heel). Such people had little to offer the Europeans; their habitat was inaccessible and their possessions scarcely worth noticing. Add to this, their fierceness (soon a legend among white settlers) proved a powerful disincentive to the establishment of contact. Their survival hinged on inaccessibility – and that inaccessibility meant that their habitat was of no real value to Europeans.

Even so, the physical resistance of many Indian peoples was astonishing, and few, today, doubt that the relatively small bands of invading Europeans could have won without their invisible, microscopic allies. One Indian civilization after another exacted a high price from the Europeans in death and suffering. But in their turn as they finally succumbed to military power, they were put to the sword, burned, enslaved and sometimes utterly destroyed. The true temper of the early European incursions into the Americas, the fundamental tone of their conquest, was to be seen in the unrelenting savagery unleashed on the Indian civilizations. The major civilizations of Central and South America fell to set-piece battles which raged through their capital cities, street by street, house by house, in conflicts which matched, for suffering, anything from the twentieth century. The Aztec empire fell in 1521 after a seige of eighty days, leaving only the pyramids. 'The home of the Aztec was again what it had been at its beginning, a muddy island in a lake.' The scribes of the Aztec people mourned their collapse.

> Weep, my friends,
> Know that with these disasters
> We have lost our Mexican nation.[16]

The pattern of subsequent centuries was thus established in those first years of European invasion. Land for European settlement and development in the Americas could only be secured by wresting it from local native peoples. Though the details varied from one region to another, the fundamental fact was clear enough; that the Indian people were the obstacle to European settlement. And though the Indians won the occasional battle, the tide of war flowed irresistibly against them over a period of four centuries.

With Mexico (New Spain) conquered, Europeans poured across the Atlantic, escaping the poverty of Spain for the precarious prospects of wealth in the Americas. Again, the smallpox went ahead of their armies, now undermining the Maya of Central America. In 1520,

> Great was the stench of the dead ... half the people fled to the fields. Dogs and vultures devoured the corpses. The mortality was terrible ...

No less terrible were the subsequent massacres which the invading Alvarado visited upon the Mayan people in a series of battles and butcheries:

> The Indians they killed were so many that they made a river of blood which became the Olintepeque.[17]

Those he did not kill Alvarado enslaved. So harsh was his rule that even other Spaniards began to complain. But their doubts were of no avail to the Mayan people.

By 1530–31 the Spaniards led by Pizarro had moved on to contact with the dazzling civilization of the Incas, an empire 3000 miles in length and stretching from the Pacific coast to the Amazon forest. It was more complex, more mature and varied than the Spaniards could imagine. But it also possessed an abundance of those valuables that the marauding Europeans lusted after. News of impending Spanish approaches coincided with a smallpox epidemic that killed the king and his heir. Again, its results were devastating, dividing the rulers in a bitter civil war, prompting public unrest and undermining the population. It was at this moment that Francisco Pizarro returned, equipped with 200 men and 70 horses.[18] Numerically it was a puny force which caused the Incas no immediate alarm. But this was to prove a serious misjudgement which cost them dear. That same small band, in 1532, was able to massacre between 5000 and 10 000 Peruvians. Having then secured an unimaginable tribute – seven tons of gold and 13 tons of silver – the Spaniards promptly broke their promise, and killed the Inca king Atawallpa.

> After seizing
> Our father Inca;
> After deceiving him,
> They put him to death.
>
> He with the heart of a puma,
> The adroitness of a fox,
> They killed
> As if he were a llama.
>
> Hail fell,
> Lightning struck,
> The sun sank,
> Night came.[19]

It was a long, dark night, which in time was to envelop all the Indian peoples of Central and South America. Each resisted in their own way. Each came to terms with their reduced circumstances. And of course, in recent years, Indian people have begun to seek redress for the manifold wrongs done to their people. But, in the short term, there could be no doubt that the Europeans had triumphed. They had, within less than half a century, established thriving bases and societies in the Caribbean, and used those bases to launch an even more dazzling conquest of Central America and Peru. The region began to open up to European settlement and exploitation. Though the conquests had been hard won – in places even fortuitous – few doubted their value. The wealth which flowed back to Europe – initially to Spain – the prospects of still more bounty (to say nothing of exotic goods as yet scarcely comprehended) soon alerted other European maritime nations. The Americas began to beckon the daring and the adventurous much as Asia once had done. When other nations made their own tentative settlements in North America a century later, it heralded a reprise of the same disasters for the Indian peoples of the north.

Viewed from the Americas, the initial invasion of these bearded and savage Europeans heralded more than a major physical and military threat. The Spaniards came as unfathomable beings, different from any people known to the Indians, astride beasts (horses) unknown in the Americas, borne to the shoreline by vessels more fanciful than real, and emboldened by weaponry of unimaginable ferocity and power. And, as if to cap it all, they were heralded by fatal diseases of ugly and agonizing terror. Try and fight as they might, the Indians could find no way of surmounting these overwhelming odds.

No single factor reduced the Indian peoples; no one factor rendered them prone to European assault (save of course the European presence itself). But one disease in particular – smallpox – had devastating consequences. It has been described as 'a disease with seven league boots'.[20] It was (is) a fiercely communicable disease, of long standing in the Old World but utterly unknown in the Americas until the Europeans arrived. In Europe itself between the fifteenth and late eighteenth centuries it accounted for perhaps 10–15 per cent of all deaths, notably among the young.[21] It was, in every respect, a terrifying, agonizing illness. Fever and pain were followed by eruptions of pustules 'that sometimes destroy the skin and transforms the victim into a gory horror'.[22] Those who thought themselves healthy fled, abandoning the sick and the dying. But since the incubation period was 10–14 days, fugitives simply took the mortal illness with them, spreading it ever further. In this way, the Indians of the Americas, fleeing in horror, cast their infection further and further away from the initial point of contagion with Europeans.[23] Smallpox flared among the Indians, from the first outbreak in 1518 through to those last brutal contacts on the Great Plains in the late nineteenth century. From the

Great Lakes to the Rio de la Plata the story of smallpox was the story of American Indians.[24]

When, in the early seventeenth century, the British and the French put down their tentative colonial roots in North America, smallpox once again spilled out from their settlements to assail and reduce neighbouring Indian communities. As had happened in Central and South America a century before, disease lapped ahead of the white man, and Indians everywhere succumbed to a range of ailments but, above all to smallpox.[25] Close to the founding Plymouth Plantation, the Algonquin Indians were devastated; they 'fell down so generally of this disease as they were in the end not able to help one another, no not to make a fire nor fetch a little water to drink, nor any to bury the dead'.

Whole communities died, 'in some not so much as one soul escaping Destruction'. The disease swept through New England and on to the Great Lakes. The Iroquois and Huron may have declined by 50 per cent.[26] The pattern was similar from one Indian nation to another. The Patuxet tribe near Plymouth was virtually destroyed. By 1631 the Massachusetts tribe was reduced to 750 (from 24 000). And of course as they declined the Europeans increased.[27] Survivors knew the source of their problems: 'They have a superstition that as many Indians must die each year, as the number of Europeans that newly arrive'.[28]

By 1705 an Englishman in Carolina wrote that there was 'not the sixth Savage living within two hundred Miles of all our Settlements, as there were fifty Years ago'.

To make matters worse, traditional Indian medicines and treatment may have exacerbated the initial problems. The healthy crowded into the tents of the sick and were promptly infected in their turn. When diseases – especially the smallpox – entered their horrifying stage, the healthy fled, taking infection with them and leaving the sick to die a lonely death.[29]

In North America, as in Spanish America, the cost was counted not simply in the mounds of corpses or in the pitted faces of the survivors. The catastrophes around them reduced surviving Indians to dire levels of depression and hopelessness. In the words of one Englishman, writing in 1622: 'Those that are left have their courage much abated, and their countenance is dejected, and they seem as a people affrighted'.[30]

Survivors who caught sight of the disfigured faces could not bear to live with such horrible afflictions: 'For being naturally proud, they are always peeping into their looking glasses, by which means, seeing themselves disfigured, without hope of regaining their former beauty', many took their own lives, 'with sullen madness'.

Skills, technologies, leadership, military strength, economic prowess, wisdom – all vanished among the heaps of dead Indians. Political succession, land management and, in the words of James Axtell, 'most important, the natives' religious beliefs, cosmological assumptions, and social morale were battered'.[31] Here, as before in Spanish America, the Indians' own gods had deserted or betrayed them. Not surprisingly they were now predisposed to turn to other gods – one reason why they accepted the spiritual approaches of the white man. The Christian God might prove more helpful and steadfast to peoples whose traditional faiths, no less than their bodies, had been found wanting in the teeth of the white man's ailments. Thus was the circle completed; what disease had torn asunder, a Christian God sought to repair.

This dismal litany of disasters visited on the Indian peoples of the Americas continued, as white incursions and settlements pressed westwards across North America. One half of the Cherokee were destroyed in 1738; twenty years later it was the turn of the Catawbas; almost half died. Two-thirds of the Omahas died in the early nineteenh century and perhaps 'half the entire population between the Mississippi River and New Mexico'. Worse still, in 1837–8 practically all the Mandan Indians were swept away. Wherever the Europeans settled in North America, there they unleashed pestilence on the local Indians on an almost medieval scale. Some of the most remote groups of Indians lived in the Pacific Northwest but not even that isolation could spare them. In 1793 when George Vancouver sailed into Puget Sound, he found the shoreline littered with human skeletons; the survivors had pock-marked faces.

Nor were epidemics a unique one-off event, for disease periodically returned to attack the Indians with renewed vigour. In South America: 'From the last decades of the sixteenth century and into the second half of the nineteenth century, smallpox swept the southern steppes and adjacent areas again and again...'[32] It also attacked newly imported

Africans with equal ferocity, though never with the catastrophic consequences to be found among the Indians.[33] Slaves with pock-marked faces were especially valuable in the Americas because it meant they were guaranteed immunity against further attacks.

We need to recall, through all this doleful tale, that Europeans too were afflicted by smallpox. It lurked in European cities, periodically swept away large numbers of people in Europe and the Americas, and remained a worrying threat until the rapid advance of vaccination in the late eighteenth century. But it was quite different for the Indians. Many Indian peoples simply died out, leaving behind a few of their words and place names – and the amazed descriptions of contemporary Europeans who saw them vanish in a brief convulsion.

The early settlers in North America, curious about the Indians' decline, were told the same story from one tribe to another:

> 'reduc'd to very few Men.'
> 'a small number yet living.'
> 'almost wasted.'
> 'Wasting.'
> 'but three men living, which yet keep up their Kingdom, and retain their Fashion.'

The process differed enormously. Sometimes tribes were utterly destroyed by a single epidemic; elsewhere they were reduced by successive onslaughts. But, whether 'disease struck in one blow or over several generations, the end result was the same. At the close of the colonial period there were only 150 000 Indians left in the East'.[34]

Even when they survived, many Indians felt compelled to move away; to scatter and drift westwards, away from the dangerous Europeans. For their part, the Europeans often viewed Indian decline as God's way of clearing the land for European settlement. Of course not all Indians declined or fled. Many survived, adapted, re-formed and resettled. But it would be false to claim that the Indians suffered anything other than defeat in their dealings with the Europeans. And in that long-drawn-out defeat the 'three horsemen of the Indian apocalypse' were war, disease and settlement.[35]

Settlement came on a grand scale. Spanish settlers flooded into a Spanish empire which covered Meso-America, the Andes and the Caribbean. Up to 1600 some 2583 Spaniards emigrated each year; in the years 1650–1810 almost 4000 crossed the Atlantic annually – most of them young and male. The Spanish settlers were above all else town-builders. As early as 1574, they had founded 121 town in Spanish America. By 1628 the number had risen to 331. From these bases the conquest and commercial harvesting of the Americas was launched.[36]

Here was an example – and here were the rewards – which other Europeans were quick to follow. In time, the relative newcomers were to outstrip the Iberian pioneers, in numbers and rewards. But nothing can detract from the stunning success of those first pioneers. But it had a price, not merely in their own sufferings, but especially in the horrors visited on the heads of the Indian people, and upon the Africans subsequently imported to provide the muscle power for European major economic enterprises.

The devastation caused by imported disease was basic to the history of European settlement and conquest in the Americas. What Europeans were unable to achieve by violence and aggression, they accomplished by disease. More accurately, the two worked together. Sickness, death and resulting demoralization among Indian peoples exposed them to defeat and conquest. Reduced in numbers, Indians everywhere found their lands expropriated by invading Europeans – and Africans. It was be another curiosity – a further irony of the conquest of the Americas – that Europeans needed to turn to another continent, Africa, to find labour to develop those regions they had so recently taken from the Indians.

The migrations across the Atlantic to settle the promising lands of the Americas seemed a mere trickle at first. But throughout the hemisphere, Europeans and reluctant Africans headed for settlements and lands wrested from their indigenous owners or controllers. This simple fact is central. There could have been no profitable European settlement without direct or indirect collisions with Indian peoples. Europeans sought whatever lucrative offerings were to be had. In time it became apparent that the land itself – if carefully conquered, planted and cultivated – could yield prosperity.

But at first, the Europeans needed the help of the very people their presence had dislocated; the Indians.

It is one of history's remarkable ironies that the Europeans began to adapt to a number of important Indian habits. Indeed Europeans found, initially, that they simply could not survive without the help, the foodstuffs – even the pleasures and the advice – of the Indians. No one realized it at the time, but it was the beginning of what historians came to call 'the Columbian exchange'.

From one region to another, Europeans adopted a number of local Indian crops – out of necessity initially but, in time, from preference. Along with a host of other local foodstuffs, the potato, maize, chocolate and tobacco entered the diet of the western world almost like tribute from defeated people. At first they were unexceptional. Europeans in the Americas simply consumed – and then cultivated – what seemed appropriate or necessary. But in some cases, these exotic items (exotic to the Europeans that is) proved even more valuable as export crops. There was, as we have seen, a European appetite for new, unusual goods from the edges of trade and settlement; from Asia and now, increasingly, from the Americas. Within a matter of decades, fashionable European society adopted – and then demanded in ever greater profusion – produce from the Americas, much as they devoured the luxuries of Asia and Arabia. In time, as the initial trickle of American produce became a flood (thanks to the intensification of cultivation in the Americas), the produce began to lose its luxurious image. Eventually, these goods were to be regarded as necessities by millions of people on the other side of the Atlantic.

It was a bizarre formula. Having brought about the near-destruction of the Indian peoples, having expropriated their lands, Europeans found that the Indians nurtured produce which, in refined format, Europe craved. Simple Indian crops were to become so basic to European (later global) life, that is easy to overlook the extraordinary historical change they represented. These, the crops of defeated and subjugated Indian peoples, quickly became the necessities and pleasures of their conquerors, later still of the wider world.

Thus did the western world begin to transform itself – to become in effect recognizably modern – by its rapacious dealings with and domination of the native people of the Americas. Dispatching its conquerors, its merchant adventurers and its varied settlers (whose motives differed greatly), Europe took in return the exotica of the Americas. But who, today, can imagine the potato or tobacco as exotic?

It was however an unequal exchange, uninvited by the Indians but savagely imposed by the Europeans. And to add to the complexity of this transformation, the process was closely linked to – indeed dependent on – aggressive European incursions in other regions of the globe, none more fundamental or crude than their trading presence in Africa. To slake their thirst, to satisfy their luxurious appetites – to line their pockets – Europeans were slowly but effectively creating a global trading and imperial presence. And all for the betterment, the advancement, the enjoyment of Europe itself.

# 5 The Indian Weed: Tobacco

Tobacco was sacred among many native Americans, their prayers and thanks wafting to heaven on tobacco smoke. When Indians first encountered Europeans, they sometimes offered tobacco, or tobacco smoke. Nicolas Perrot, on the Great Lakes, had smoke blown straight into his face, 'as the greatest honour that they could render him; he saw himself smoked like meat'. Much the same happened to Father Paul du Ru, on the Mississippi, where an Indian 'came and blew smoke from his pipe into my nose as though to cense me'. Worse still, the French captain who first encountered the Menominees on Lake Michigan, had tobacco ground into his forehead. When Indians began to worship the amazing items introduced by the Europeans – notably their guns, knives and hatchets – they blew sacred tobacco smoke onto them.[1]

European explorers and settlers quickly picked up the tobacco habit, though not its religious overtones. One of the best Indian fighters in New England in the late seventeenth century, Benjamin Church copied Indian tactics. But his main difficulty was preventing his men from lighting tell-tale fires at night to satisfy their 'Epidemical plague of lust after Tobacco'. Later, Indians were put to more grisly, horrific practical use by American smokers. An English visitor noted that 'Some People have an Indian's skin for a Tobacco pouch'.[2]

Whenever Europeans encountered Indians on their exploratory raids into the Americas, they encountered tobacco. Its use differed from place to place, but it was virtually universal and highly prized. In Mexico, Montezuma smoked a pipe after dinner. The Incas of Peru took tobacco, rather like snuff, for medicinal purposes. Spaniards meeting the Maya were struck by the use of tobacco as an offering to the gods in local baptism ceremonies. As Raleigh sailed up the Orinoco, he described local tribes addicted to tobacco. The story continued wherever settlers and explorers pushed back the American frontier and made contact with local Indians. Whenever unknown Indian tribes were discovered, most had their own distinctive tobacco customs. In the Pacific north-west, Indians 'are very fond of smoking tobacco and they inhale the smoke, which intoxicates them and makes them ill, but they keep on doing it'.[3]

They offered tobacco to a host of deities and for all sorts of reasons; as gifts for the spirits of the dead, to ask for, or to give thanks for safe travel, for peace, for war, for worship. Some Indians cultivated tobacco, others picked it wild. Some rolled it into cigars, others packed it into a pipe. It was also smoked for pleasure in clay pipes. Not surprisingly, tobacco was also an item of trade, barter and negotiation among the Indians. But the existing, pre-Columbian tobacco trade was as nought compared to what followed. Within a few years, tobacco, the old Indian crop, was in demand globally, sought and traded for by peoples around the world. In time, tobacco was to make 'more fortunes than all the silver of the Indies'.[4] Though the Europeans led the way, before long the whole world was quick to follow the road to tobacco addiction.

Tobacco quickly established itself as a major item of international maritime trade; valuable in itself and as barter for other goods. It had a use wherever trade was conducted. When the *Norman* left London in 1714, bound for Africa to collect 300 slaves, it carried in its cargo '300 pounds of tobacco; 10 gross of pipes ...' As the slave prison ships rode at anchor off the African coast before heading westwards towards the Americas it was crucial for the slave traders to keep their slaves as secure and as happy as possible – so they plied them with tobacco. James Penny, giving evidence about the slave trade to Parliament in 1789, confirmed that slaves on board the slave ships were 'supplied with Pipes and Tobacco; both Sexes sometimes will smoke ...' Tobacco had another use on board the slave ships. When slaves died (as they did in horrifying numbers) it was customary for the sailors to fumigate the holds: 'Scraped the rooms, then smoked the ship with tar, tobacco and brimstone for 2 hours, afterwards washed with vinegar.'

The curiosity went unremarked. By the time tobacco had become a major slave-grown crop in the Americas, the finished product was used, among other purposes, to pacify and to cleanse the quarters of new Africans bound for the slave colonies of the Americas.

Europeans in the Americas quickly took up the habit of the Indians, thereafter taking the custom – and its production – to the far corners of European trade and settlement around the world. Tobacco travelled wherever Europeans traded and settled. It invaded Asia along existing routes. In 1749 for example, a vessel sailing from Luzon in the Philippines for China carried eight chests of tobacco in its cargo. Tobacco took hold in India; from there it was transhipped to other Asian destinations. Indeed the tobacco plant – replete, thought Europeans, with mysterious virtues – was quickly transplanted around the world; to Spain in 1558 and quickly thereafter to France, England, Italy, the Balkans and Russia. A Manilla galleon took it to the Philippines in 1575. It appeared in Macao after 1600, Java in 1601 and in India and Ceylon about 1605–10. Ships trading from the Philippines took tobacco to China. Thanks to the expanding Atlantic slave trade, tobacco found a new home in Africa. The irony of course was that the first mass producers of tobacco were Africans – transplanted to the Chesapeake for the specific purpose of tobacco cultivation.

What made this global acceptance and transfer even more remarkable was the simple fact that there was, initially, no real producer-market behind tobacco.[5] Indian production in the Americas was simple, or culled from the wild. European settlers in the Americas came to appreciate that here was a crop which gave pleasure and might even yield commercial profit. It was a robust plant, easily adaptable and transferable to new regions.

Tobacco's arrival in alien communities often provoked fierce opposition from a range of educated and official opinion. Kings, ministers and clerics railed against the weed. Prohibitions of various kinds and effectiveness were hurled at tobacco and its consumers; in England in 1604, Japan 1607–9, the Mogul Empire 1617, Russia 1634, China and the Papal States in 1642. Such edicts did little to impede the inexorable spread of tobacco, which also made inroads into Africa – thanks largely to the expanding slave trade of the Atlantic system. It was however in its native region, in the Americas, that tobacco flourished most dramatically. And it was here, thanks to European conquest and settlement and, ultimately, to the labours of imported African slaves, that tobacco, an export crop, became one of the key elements in the transformation of the Atlantic economy.

Initially it was merely an item of curiosity, brought home from the early New World settlements in the Caribbean and the Chesapeake. Very quickly, and for reasons which are impossible to fathom – save possibly to suggest it was a matter of addiction – the initial curiosity was transformed into a massive and growing consumer demand. After 1618 settlers in Virginia began to specialise in tobacco, and from the 1620s that colony's fortunes were firmly rooted in it.

The Dutch were the first Europeans to develop a major appetite for tobacco – understandably, given their early forays into Atlantic trade and settlement. Amsterdam quickly established itself as the major European trading centre for tobacco,[6] and the Dutch addiction to it was frequently reflected in the work of Dutch artists of the seventeenth century.[7] This Dutch smoking habit spread into Germany and thence into Russia (helped there by Peter the Great's passion for tobacco). In England, however, tobacco had to overcome the animosity of James I, whose dislike of tobacco is perhaps one of his best-remembered legacies. Such personal foibles, even when monarchical, could do little to stem rising popular demand. Fed by the emergent power of the Virginian planters, serviced by an expansive maritime and commercial interest, tobacco became ever more important, not least to growing numbers of British investors who, like the Dutch before them, had major stakes in tobacco; in shipping, warehouses and distribution, in massive loans to Virginians, in local shops and taverns – even in the manufactures of cheap clay pipes.

From an early date, contemporaries recognised tobacco's addictive power. In 1616 a Scot denounced it as 'an weade so infective as all young and ydill personis ar in maner bewitchet theirwith'.[8] Though early proponents of tobacco stressed its medicinal virtues, it was soon apparent that the weed was narcotic. In 1597 a contemporary complained that smokers consumed it 'for wantonness ... and cannot forbear it, no, not in the middest of their dinner'. Chain-smoking was a recognisable vice by the early seventeenth century. One MP remarked in 1621 that ''Tis death to some to be barred tobacco'.[9]

Yet it was fashion which, initially at least, established tobacco as a distinguishing feature of elite social life in the early seventeenth century. Smoking became a modish habit, with gifts of tobacco and snuff routinely passed among the wealthy alongside other costly gifts.

Like so many other exotic commodities, tobacco entered European usage to a fanfare of praise for its medicinal benefits and health-giving virtues. Doctors, apothecaries and men of science announced its wonderful effects. It could ease venereal disease, soothe the troubled, help in 'the forgetting of all sorrows and miseries'.[10] One doctor thought tobacco important for all people engaged in heavy physical labour. Some claimed they would prefer to do without food than tobacco. Others claimed that in the form of snuff, tobacco was good for head colds and to bring on sneezes. Lord Herbert took tobacco 'against certain rheumes and catarrhs that trouble me'.

A host of advocates published medical defences of tobacco. It was, in various forms, good, apparently, for most human conditions. Good for the treatment of 'Cephaloea and Hemicrania, provided these Disorders arise from a cold Cause of Flatulence ... '. It was good for tetanus, 'and for Pains of the whole Body ... '. Toothache could be eased by rubbing the affected tooth with tobacco juice. Complaints of the breasts were curable by applications of tobacco. Perhaps most ironic was the claim that 'The smoak of Tobacco-Leaves received into the Mouth sometimes afford Relief to asthmatic Patients ... '. When applied hot to the stomach, tobacco was good for 'Rumbling of the Intestines, and Flatulence'. It was proclaimed for its beneficial effect on the spleen, the uterus, for chilblains, for arthritis, carbuncles, for wounds. It was, in short, a wondrous new drug with widespread, almost universal application. It could even allay hunger and thirst.[11]

There was, however, another side to the argument, and from the mid-seventeenth century new medical and social voices began to denounce tobacco. Worst of all were its social effects. It persuaded men to linger in the ale-house with their friends, 'the whole of the Day smoking Tobacco'. Money spent on tobacco might be better spent on life's necessities. Moreover there was growing evidence that tobacco was harmful, though some of the arguments now seem bizarre. Brains of smokers were, it was claimed, blackened by tobacco. More acceptable today was the complaint that tobacco was 'possessed of a highly-narcotic Quality' which stupefies the smoker. It dulls the smell, ruins the taste, spoils the appetite, makes men yawn a lot and gives them 'a hoarse and shrill Voice and a stinking Breath'.[12] However tobacco's aroma could quickly disguise a multitude of even more unpleasant odours, which characterised contemporary life. Any social gathering – even the most vaunted and wealthy – generated smells which contemporaries frequently complained about. The literate often denounced the stench of the common people (no accident that they became known as 'the great unwashed'); servants in prosperous houses, the bad breath and garlic of crowded public places (in the theatre for example), all could be masked by copious tobacco fumes. Unfortunately, smoking became so popular in the early seventeenth century, that smokers created their own unpleasant and anti-social smells. Tobacco, said Robert Burton, was 'commonly abused by most men, which take it as Tinkers do Ale, 'tis a plague, a mischief, a vicious purger of goods, lands, health'.[13] But above all else, what critics most disliked was the swift transformation of tobacco from exclusive to popular taste and the consequent ubiquity of tobacco smoke.

In the early days of smoking in Britain, prosperous young men made great display of their new fad by flaunting their tobacco in public places. When times were good, even craftsmen and the middling ranks of tradesmen displayed their well-being by smoking in taverns.[14] Initially, then, tobacco was a sign of prosperity and standing, but it quickly passed from the upper to middling reaches of English life, and by finding a home which was to be its main forum for the next two centuries – the tavern – tobacco had found a sure means of transition to a much broader, more popular consuming (male) public. By 1614, complained Barnaby Rich, 'there is not so base a groom that comes into an alehouse but he must have his pipe of tobacco'.[15]

The alehouse became the main retail outlet for tobacco – despite the proliferation of specialist tobacco shops. By the 1630s, taverns across the length and breadth of England sold tobacco. Though the bulk of the trade centred on London and the West Country (closest to the ports – London and Bristol – which served the tobacco colonies) tobacco was sold throughout the north of England and into the Scottish borders. Publicans were especially active in promoting tobacco, inviting customers to take a pipe along with their drink. It was reported from Durham that 'For the first salutation is, Sir will you taste a pipe of excellent and rare ... tobacco?'

English alehouses received their tobacco from itinerant dealers, generally working on behalf of bigger wholesalers. In the 1620s James Becke from Winchcombe, at the centre of a Gloucester-based tobacco growing industry, travelled throughout the Midlands, selling tobacco to alehouses and collecting money from previous sales. In 1637 John Homson sold 6–7 pounds of tobacco to an Oxford victualler. But the perfect habitat for tobacco was the alehouse and the coffee shop. Initially a means of impressing neighbours and friends (a man of the middling rank about to enjoy a pleasure fashioned by the wealthy), tobacco quickly passed into the world of working men. By the late 1620s, smoking in the alehouse was established as one of those 'rites of good fellowship'. Along with drinking, to which it was inextricably linked, smoking had become a key aspect of male sociability and companionship. And, like alcohol, it also had a narcotic effect; numbing life's miseries and blanking out dreary pains. Men unable to afford their own pipe could 'drink' from the communal pipe which was passed from man to man in the alehouse.[16]

By the early seventeenth century tobacco was cheap and accessible. In towns it could be bought from specialist shops. Barnaby Rich wrote that tobacco was available from 'apothecaries' shops, grocers' shops, chandlers' shops'.

The fact that tobacco was on apothecaries' shelves gives some clue to the early – and continuing – belief in the medicinal powers of tobacco.[17] People reached for tobacco for a host of ailments. Unnerved by the first signs of the plague in London in June 1665, Samuel Pepys's first reaction was to reach for the reassurance of tobacco.

> It put me into an ill conception of myself and my smell, so that I was forced to buy some roll tobacco to smell to and chaw – which took away the apprehension.[18]

It seemed to have a similar effect on animals. Two years later, when Pepys was being driven to Islington, one of the horses collapsed. The coachman, convinced the horse was about to die,

> blew some tobacco in his nose; upon which the horse sneezed, and by and by grows well and draws us the rest of the way as well as ever he did.

The coachman swore that his remedy was common among men who dealt with horses.[19] Gradually tobacco moved on from the apothecary shops and could be purchased in a host of shops throughout Britain.

This rise in tobacco consumption might appear at first glance to be largely a transformation in domestic mores. In fact (and like the consumption of tea) it was habit which depended on massive changes on the far side of the world. The story of tobacco was the story of the Chesapeake region of North America.

The initial precarious battle for early settlers in Virginia was simply to stay alive (a battle won in large measure thanks to the help of local Indians). They then embarked on various forms of cultivation. They tried to cultivate sugar, copying the successful Dutch example in more southerly colonies. Sugar in Virginia failed, but once they turned to tobacco, after 1618, the fledgling colony thrived.

There was land in abundance and it was settled initially using free, indentured and slave labour. Thanks to the remarkable river systems of the Chesapeake Bay, the tobacco planters of Virginia and Maryland were able to get their produce easily to the water's edge and thence to the Atlantic ships. In the 1620s, some 65 000 pounds of tobacco left the region for England. Ten years later the figure had risen to more than one million pounds each year. By the 1670s the Chesapeake planters exported more than 20 million pounds. As the volumes increased, as ever more land was brought into tobacco production, the growing band of Chesapeake planters needed more and more labour. Between 1630 and 1680 75 000 indentured Britons migrated to America, but those numbers still failed to satisfy the planters. They faced problems with their indentured labourers who, once cleared of their indenture, understandably wanted their own land. Planters for their part wanted labour that could be tied more effectively to the land, and with fewer restrictions. By 1700 the planters had turned to the solution long in existence in the sugar colonies to the south: African slave labour.

Slaves had been landed in Virginia in the early days of settlement but as late as 1660 there were perhaps a total of only 1700 in Maryland and Virginia. North American planters turned initially to the West Indies for slaves and, gradually, black labour began to replace white labour throughout the tobacco regions of the Chesapeake. In the eighty years between 1690 and 1770, some 100 000 slaves were imported, the bulk of them direct from Africa. But as the local black population thrived and increased (its natural increase in sharp contrast to the sluggish population growth of Jamaica – which had to rely on African importations for growth), the Chesapeake tobacco planters had less need to buy from Africa. They came to rely on their own slaves to propagate future generations of tobacco slaves.[20] The fruits of these slaves' labour filled the holds of the ships which headed into the Atlantic each autumn and spring (though the timing changed in the eighteenth century). In the ten years from the mid-1670s some 170 vessels plied the Chesapeake trade each year; four to five vessels arrived in the Bay each week. In wartime (almost as common as peace in the eighteenth century) convoys of tobacco ships, carefully shepherded across the Atlantic by the Royal Navy, laboured to bring this luxury crop to the smokers and snuff-takers in stately homes, alehouses and coffee shops throughout Britain.[21]

It is impossible to be precise about the dates, but by the mid-seventeenth century tobacco was consumed on a massive scale in Britain. In the course of the 1630s and 1640s the producers dropped their prices, to a quarter or less of the original selling price.[22] By the late 1630s the volume of tobacco landing in London – 1.8 million pounds – was sufficient for about a quarter of the population to smoke two pounds a year. Though a great deal was re-exported, smoking had made the breakthrough, to become a mass habit among all social classes.

Perhaps the best indication of mass consumption was the simple fact of taxation. Governments of the early seventeenth century, woefully short of income, seized any new opportunity of generating tax. Retailers of tobacco were licensed in 1633, and thereafter tobacco, like other tropical imports, subsidised the state via duties. Successive import duties more than doubled the initial cost. After a hefty increase in 1685, importers began to seek ways round the duties; bribing customs officials, falsifying weights, claiming good tobacco to be damaged, and creating a complex system of re-exports followed by smuggled re-entry.

As with tea, the import duties on tobacco had created an absurd situation. They had, from the government's position, become counter-productive, bringing the law, and relations between the people and government officials, into disrepute. They also created major cottage industries and communities devoted to smuggling. Taken together, smugglers and legitimate importers were able to satisfy the tobacco smoker to the extent of two pounds of tobacco per head throughout the first half of the eighteenth century.[23]

The oddest feature of the figures amassed by economic historians is that smoking seems to have peaked in the late seventeenth century. Indeed *per capita* consumption of tobacco in the nineteenth century did not reach the levels recorded in the 1620s. Beneath this welter of data, the simple truth seems to have been that smoking took off rapidly and universally in the early seventeenth century. It was, from first to last, the preserve of adult males, and once the market had become saturated, it was impossible to expand *per capita* sales. It was only the relatively recent advance of cigarettes and new marketing, aimed at females, which pushed tobacco consumption back to the levels it had reached, so quickly and unpredictably, in the early seventeenth century.[24]

In addition to the alehouse, the other late eighteenth century outlet for tobacco was the country shop, with its range of provisions, notably tropical produce – tea, sugar, tobacco – which people consumed in such large amounts. By the end of the eighteenth century even the most inaccessible of villages was likely to have a small shop where tobacco could be bought. For those without access to a shop, tobacco was available from pedlars and from market stalls.[25]

Tobacco was smoked in white clay pipes which were mass produced, cheap, and stocked by shopkeepers and innkeepers by the gross. (The clay which was first used in the development of pipes later became a key ingredient in the development of the new pottery ware which so transformed cooking, eating and domestic arrangements by the end of the eighteenth century). Pipes could be found everywhere. They littered contemporary life, cropping up in profusion in archaelogical digs, and regularly appear in contemporary paintings. Time and again, Dutch painters of the seventeenth and eighteenth centuries, in capturing scenes of everyday life in the Low Countries, provide graphic evidence of the ubiquity of clay pipes. It was a commonplace remark that: 'a Hollander without a pipe is a national impossibility ... If a Hollander should be bereft of his pipe of tobacco he could not blissfully enter heaven.'[26] The popularizing of pipe-smoking in Britain – the simple fact that everyone could partake in the alehouse – tainted the habit with the tone of the common usage. As more and more working men turned to pipes, their social superiors found other ways of ingesting tobacco; seeking the pleasures of tobacco without the taint of the common people. Even the names of some pipes – the 'alderman', later the 'churchwarden' – hint at superior status.

In catering for the nation's smokers, pipemaking became a new industry in itself. Pipemakers in Salisbury incorporated themselves into a craft guild as early as 1619. In time of course pipes became evermore varied and complex in design, manufacture and material, (the now-familiar 'briar' pipe did not make an impact in Britain until the 1850s). On the continent, pipes (and smoking) were more varied. Travelling in Germany in 1798–9 Coleridge remarked on the 'Men with pipes of all shapes and fancies ... cane, clay, porcelain, wood, tin, silver, and ivory ... many with silver chains and silver bole-covers'.

The local etiquette of smoking also surprised Coleridge. He was amazed to see a man dancing, waltzing, with a pipe in his mouth. In Hamburg he was no less taken aback to see men and women playing cards and drinking coffee and '*all* the Gentlemen *Smoking* at the same *Time*'.[27] The Germans clearly had not evolved the English habit of segregated smoking: working men enjoying a pipe in masculine retreats. By the time the Dutch pipe industry (centred on Gouda) declined, in the late eighteenth century, pipe smoking had become ubiquitous in Holland, even among certain sections of women.

In Britain by the late eighteenth century there was a marked and increased dislike of smoking, in fashionable society, for a number of reasons. The sheer messiness of filling, lighting and emptying a pipe, its noxious fumes, all transgressed the new-found emphasis on more genteel social conduct. The simple roughness of smoking caused offence among people who had developed a new attachment to 'sensibility'. Tobacco intruded an element of crudity into a social world which prided itself on refinement and sensitivity. Of course polite dislike of smoking was also related to the fact that smoking had become popular among working people, and was closely associated with drinking and plebeian merry-making. Tobacco was, then, one of the elements which distinguished polite, refined society from its plebeian and polar opposite.

While fashionable society turned against smoking, working men picked up their pipes whenever they could. When working men gathered for social or even political purposes, the instinct was to reach for the tobacco. Rules governing Manchester weavers in the 1750s stipulated that their meetings must be businesslike; they were not 'to regale themselves with Ale and Tobacco'. An organisation of cordwainers about the same time levied fines for 'calling for drink or tobacco without leave of the stewards'. Plebeian pleasures were invariably marked by drink – and tobacco. Even in rural Wales, local dancing was followed by 'a great jug of ale at their knees and a piece of tobacco for each'.[28]

Though fashionable society had turned its back on smoking, it did not abandon tobacco completely, turning instead to snuff. At first, the user simply made snuff by grating a leaf of tobacco. As the habit took hold, tobacco manufacturers began to produce and distribute their own brands. From the commercial viewpoint, snuff had the advantage that it could be easily adulterated with parts of the tobacco leaf unusable for the smoker. It was also made by a simple process and undertaken by poorly-paid workers. But with development of more sophisticated versions, offering a range of scents and flavours, there emerged a specialisation of production, though it always remained simple and inexpensive.

Snuff-taking lacked the obvious, anti-social results of smoking – the smoke which clouded the room, stained the teeth and filled the lungs of all nearby – but it had its own distinctive, unpleasant by-products. Charles II was described by one unsympathetic commentator as 'repulsive-looking with his snuff-plugged nose'. His Scottish agent, Lauderdale, was forever 'rifling the King's snuff-box'. Among the prosperous, there evolved a special etiquette and language of snuff-taking. Fashionable society swiftly became accustomed to men and women pushing snuff up their nose, sneezing out the contents in displays which later observers thought repulsive.[29]

At its height of fashion, snuff was carried in a snuff-box, the best of which were exquisite works of contemporary craftsmanship from across Europe and Asia. In royal circles, snuff-boxes reached remarkable levels of lavish extravagance. When Marie Antoinette married Louis XVI, among her various wedding presents she received fifty-two gold snuff-boxes. It was perhaps predictable that this habit – of snuff-taking and carrying snuff boxes – would in time pass down the social scale and become common throughout society. Snuff-boxes soon became ubiquitous. They lay on tables in coffee houses and taverns. Fashionable ladies carried small snuff-boxes with them as they promenaded. Servants picked up the habit.

> Betty the Chamber-maid, Molly the House-maid, and Mrs Cook, would never have thought of buying Snuff Boxes but to imitate their Mistress; and the Girl next door, just come from the country, seeing Mrs Molly (while washing the stone steps at the door) set down her mop to take a pinch of Snuff, thinks all London maids do likewise, and she to be sure must resemble them.[30]

When the founder of the Wills tobacco company set out from his Bristol headquarters to sell his wares in the West Country and Wales, he loaded up both with tobacco and snuff, knocking on the doors of shopkeepers and publicans. By 1790 he and his agents were selling tobacco and snuff in equal volumes.[31] By the late eighteenth century, visitors to Paris were struck by the degree to which fashionable usage had already permeated the plebeian substrata. In 1775 Mrs Thrale was impressed when she saw a stonemason set aside his fashionable coat – and snuff-box – to set to work on a piece of marble. On the eve of the Revolution inventories of the contents of humble homes show that a third of them contained snuffboxes. There, and in England, there was a remarkable expansion of what one historian has described as 'populuxe' items; 'inexpensive versions of aristocratic luxuries'[32] Cheap wooden snuff-boxes proliferated in Britain. In Scotland however snuff-taking was popular rather than exclusive from an early date. 'The popular southern ideas of a Scotchman and his snuff-box are inseparable'. There, snuff was pushed up the nose with a quill or ladle rather than sniffing it.[33]

Tobacco intruded itself into every corner of Britain but it is one of the great curiosities of the spread of tobacco (and tea) that it was effectively driven forward by the distinctive networks of smugglers. In seeking new, unorthodox routes into the country, smugglers adopted outlying and remote points of entry. They brought their goods ashore in remote coves, inaccessible stretches of beaches, places where local communities were especially parochial and isolated from other parts of the nation; spots where suspicion of outsiders could be relied on to rebuff the curiosity and prying eyes of government officials. This also had the effect that exotic produce was introduced direct into remote communities, by-passing the formal procedures of London and the other maritime entrepots.

Tobacco reached remote spots in rural Britain by other, more legal means. It spread outwards from the centres of fashionable life. The social habits of fashionable people were shaped in the centres of propertied life – London, the spa towns and that small group of provincial 'capitals' (York, Norwich, Exeter, Bristol and Newcastle), which were the natural social centres for local aristocrats and the wealthy. Moreover three of those cities were ports, with direct and (for the period) relatively swift access to London and the outside world. Within these centres of local influence, the new habits of superior people took hold, just as they did in the spas and London, before fanning out among poorer groups. This is what happened in the case of tobacco.

Geography also helped. The nature of mainland Britain and the system of its ports, with their links to the wider world, provided a network of entry points for imported goods. From the dockside, imported tropical items were easily moved into the neighbouring hinterland. There is however a temptation to think that the major ports controlled most of the flow of imported tropical goods. In fact, as with the slave trade, there were a myriad ports and seaside towns which were locked into the rapidly expanding Atlantic trade in the seventeenth and eighteenth centuries; exporting British manufacture, importing the produce of the Americas, transhipping goods to and from Europe. These 'outports' grew dramatically as urban centres, marked by a rising population and by the creation of new, efficient port facilities. Towns which are now by-passed by the main arteries of international maritime trade were integral to British economic well-being before the rise of modern industrialisation; Great Yarmouth, Whitehaven, Sunderland, Hull and many other smaller ports.[34] The leading outports jockeyed each other for pre-eminence, rising up or down the league tables of growth and importations from one decade to another. Scarborough, for example, imported a greater tonnage than Bristol in 1709. Later Liverpool outstripped Bristol.[35] All, in some way or other, were affected by smuggling (known, pointedly, as 'free-trading').

As the eighteenth century advanced, a small number of provincial ports began to dominate overseas trade. On the west coast, the battle for pre-eminence in the lucrative trade to the American colonies and Africa was fought out between Bristol and Liverpool. But Whitehaven emerged as a growing rival for the distribution of the tobacco trade.[36] When we examine the geography of those ports and their hinterlands we can appreciate how goods and their associated social habits could penetrate remoter parts of the nation. For a start, all those ports were served by an immediate hinterland; the goods and raw materials, foodstuffs and export commodities were hauled or shipped (by river, later canals) to the ports for onward shipment to Europe, the Baltic and the wider world. The woollens of the Cotswolds, the metals of Birmingham found their way to Bristol; the textiles of Lancashire passed through Liverpool, the foodstuffs of the Scottish lowlands were deposited in Glasgow – all of them *en route* to distant destinations. Whitehaven was unusual. It acted as the major entrepot for the tobacco trade, re-exporting goods to Ireland, Holland and other European ports. But Whitehaven itself lacked an economically vibrant hinterland to sustain its own export trade. As a result, from the mid-eighteenth century it was rapidly overtaken in the tobacco trade by the emergent city-port of Glasgow.[37]

The major ports in the tobacco trade concentrated, of course, on the legal trade. It was on their quaysides that tobacco was landed legally, bonded and duties paid. But the enterprising merchants of the new ports, many of them with their own distinctive 'rags to riches' life-stories, were alert to the shady opportunities afforded by so massive and so popular an import trade. It was common practice in Liverpool for example to claim for damages to tobacco in transit. The consequent ill-gained income enhanced profit levels, and made available still more money for further investment in port facilities. It was – like smuggling – a curious phenomenon; illegality assisting buoyant economic well-being. Furthermore it was actively supported by Liverpool's MPs in the early eighteenth century.[38]

Wherever tobacco was imported, there it was also sold and distributed, throughout the port's hinterland and beyond. By the mid-eighteenth century, the bulk of tobacco importation had moved north to Glasgow. Until the late seventeenth century the economy of Scotland was much inferior to its English neighbours, to say nothing of the more mature economies of mainland Europe. But in the early eighteenth century, Glasgow emerged quickly, to become a major international port with its own 'sophisticated financial and commercial system and a vigorous urban culture'. This was made possible, above all else, by tobacco. By mid-century almost a half of all Scottish imports consisted of tobacco. All but two per cent of that figure passed up the Clyde. This success sprang from the Treaty of Union of 1707 which permitted the Scots to trade direct with the colonies in North America. For some years past, Glasgow merchants had been trading with the tobacco planters via Whitehaven, forging crucial trading links and acquiring important commercial expertise. What followed was a remarkable success story which transformed Glasgow, created massive local fortunes and helped to transform the urban face of the city itself.[39] Many of the important features of the city today, buildings, street names and civic monuments, are the fruits of the tobacco prosperity of these years.

The rapid development of British ports, and the importance of the tobacco trade in many of them, provides one way of tracking the routes by which tobacco spread into Britain. At its simplest, the growth of the maritime trade to and from the tobacco colonies meant that few parts of Britain were very far away from tobacco supplies. In the major ports tobacco was stored and processed before it was moved onwards to other parts of Britain and the world and the merchants also prepared tobacco (and snuff) for local consumption. Shops and alehouses in the ports, local companies devoted to tobacco processing and local retailing, travelling salesmen and pedlars;

all ensured that tobacco took local root. And this was of course quite apart from the tens of thousands of men who sailed the Atlantic ships, or served in the military on the very edges of colonial settlement and who returned with the produce and habits of distant colonies and flaunted them before their British peers.

To cope with the demand for tropical staples, shops, often of the humblest kind, sprouted throughout Britain. And basic to those shops, especially the country shops, was tropical produce. If, by some freak, the local alehouse did not have tobacco, it could be bought from the nearest country shop – or from a pedlar at the local market. Tobacco thus became ubiquitous. It could be bought in most places by the mid-eighteenth century. But its consumption offered a distinctly male culture which was fashioned in the camaraderie of the alehouse. Women had access to tobacco mainly through snuff. But that too faded.

In the century and a half before 1800 pipe-smoking clearly had enormous personal and social consequences. Smoking blackened men's teeth, congested their lungs and increased the habit of spitting. Contemporaries were in no doubt of smoking's awful effects.

> This narcotic Quality of Tobacco, is the Reason why great Smoakers are, during the whole of their Lives, afflicted with a continual Spitting ... [40]

Doctors recognized that tobacco was the cause of many of their patients' complaints. Dr Alexander Johnson who practised in Jamaica, reported in 1787 that one of his Kingston patients, Mr Jon Vernon, used 'a Great deal of Snuff through the day, which causes him to spit up and expectorate'.[41] Spittoons and sawdust on the floor were essential requirements for any alehouse.

Tobacco seemed to offer few attractions for women. Some fashionable women smoked, and for a while snuff provided an alternative way of ingesting tobacco (George III's wife was known as 'Snuffy-Charlotte'). But women who smoked were regarded by contemporaries (and were frequently portrayed by artists) as low and degraded. In its Indian origins and in European cultural practice smoking was predominantly male. Once rooted in the alehouse, tobacco was certain to remain a male pleasure. As such it became part of contemporary masculinity; a defining characteristic of manliness. To smoke was to be a man; smoking for the first time became one of those rites of passage which marked off boyhood from manhood.

Smoking also helped to define femininity; smoking was unladylike. Women who smoked were not likely to be ladies. Of course tobacco was not alone in this, for there was a whole range of new social activities which served to draw an ever-sharper line between the world of men and women. They were artificial, socially devised, often commercially based (and therefore encouraged and kept in place by powerful economic pressures). But collectively they served to shape the broad distinctions of gender which were in place on the eve of the industrial revolution.

The most obvious distinguishing mark that tobacco left on men was perhaps its smell. Men who smoked, smelled of tobacco. The deposits of tobacco-smoke on clothing, in the mouth, in the hair, announced the arrival or return of menfolk. Novelists often referred to the distinguishing tobacco-smell of male company.[42] It was partly to avoid being similarly tainted that polite women quit the dinner table to leave their menfolk to light their tobacco.

In the first years of British smoking, pipes were offered to women. In the early seventeenth century, women keen to flaunt their husband's rising prosperity sometimes smoked as proof both of their spouse's well-being and their own social daring. Within a century however such displays of female smoking had descended, and were largely restricted, to the low life. Fashionable men were shocked if they discovered that their womenfolk had smoked.[43] Dutch painters were especially fond of portraying lewdness and dissipation in the company of female smokers. Women who mingled on terms of boozy familiarity with smokers, who became the participants in tavern life, were anything but ladies. Blowing smoke in a woman's face was a 'sexually insulting jest'.[44] Drunkenness, sexual licence and smoking – all went together in scenes of squalid disapproval. Here was a world into which no self-respecting woman, however poor or rich, wished to enter.

Women who enjoyed their tobacco were thought eccentric and unconventional. In 1720, one of the few people to own a carriage in Salford was 'Mrs D.', a 'respectable old lady ... of sociable disposition ...' Unable to 'conform to the new-fashioned beverage of tea and coffee; whenever, therefore, she made her afternoon's visit, her friends presented her with a tankard of ale and a pipe of tobacco.'[45]

Any woman of status who smoked was likely to catch the eye and be remembered, for the simple fact that it was unusual and eccentric; the sign of someone who defied prevailing customs and who stood out from other women of her station.

Women who persisted in smoking in the early eighteenth century were poor and generally old. Indeed it became a caricature of old age to portray it as a wrinkled old woman with a pipe in her mouth. The popular association between poverty, old age and tobacco was a favourite device of writers, from the late eighteenth century onwards, in characterising the destitution of old age as an old hag with her pipe and tobacco.[46] There may be a simpler explanation; that the old habits, of women smoking, persisted in more inaccessible corners of the kingdom and remained natural – traditional – among the old. Time and again, those who remarked on meeting women who smoked described their old age; such women were in effect survivors of a former age, smoking where younger women had renounced the habit and left it to their menfolk.

Pipe-smoking was of course a clumsy operation. The pipe needed cleaning; the smoker needed an extra implement to hold the tobacco. (Dutch painters made blatant use of the sexual innuendo of poking fingers into the apertures of tobacco pouches.) Smokers also needed access to a light. Tobacco had to be cut and crushed, fitted into the pipe, padded down regularly when lit; the embers and ashes knocked out – and the whole dirty process begun again. This simple routine alone – familiar and acceptable enough to men down the ages – was unlikely to appeal to respectable women who cared for their looks, their clothing and cleanliness, and for whom clean hands were, by the mid-eighteenth century, a sign of contemporary female beauty and style. For the poor, few of these qualities mattered.

To assemble a pipe of tobacco was cumbersome, sometimes difficult to undertake in the open, often unacceptable in the place of work. Taking a pinch of snuff was however simplicity itself. It was possible to enjoy a moment's pleasure, an instant pinch of snuff, at work without disturbing routines or even without being noticed. Flora Thompson remarked on labourers' wives finding pleasure in snuff ('I couldnt do wi'out my pinch of snuff. 'Tis meat an' drink to me.') late in the nineteenth century. This association between working women and tobacco served merely to confirm the distance between smoking and polite females. Wives of ordinary British sailors and soldiers, following the eddies of warfare around the world, were famous for their smoking habits. Here again was another aspect of plebeian life which confirmed the propertied in their dislike of tobacco for women.

Polite women not only did not smoke but, in time, began to agitate against their menfolk's commitment to tobacco. In part this is thought to have been a result of the years of warfare, between 1793 and 1815, when hundreds of thousands of men returned from years of military service in which drink and tobacco formed the most readily available solace of everyday life. One women claimed that the military 'are professions that spoil a man for domestic life'. The Navy was the worst: 'grog and tobacco soon destroy them'.[47] The main drive against male smoking, the determination to segregate smokers, came later, as part of that transformed Victorian etiquette. Smoking carriages on trains, smoking rooms in private homes, men retiring from the ladies to enjoy their tobacco and after-dinner drinks; all and more were aspects of Victorian propertied culture which assigned smoking to particular locations in public and private places.

Along with other tropical staples, tobacco even made its impact on British domestic architecture. Rooms specifically designated for smokers began to appear in grander English homes by the late seventeenth century. There were smoking rooms in a number of stately homes – Charborough in 1690, Cannons 1727, Kedleston 1767 – and though some men daringly smoked in other rooms, polite society did not approve. Such smoking was plebeian and popular – a habit which had slipped its aristocratic and propertied moorings to find its true level at the base of society. By the end of the eighteenth century, 'tobacco had been banished from polite society'. When it returned it did so – yet again – courtesy of royal patronage.

At a dinner in 1824 in honour of the Duke of Sussex, brother of George IV, Prince Puckler-Muskau introduced the

German habit of passing round after-dinner cigars to the men, 'which I never saw before in England', said the Prince. It was a habit confirmed by the influence of another German Royal, Prince Albert, after his marriage to Victoria in 1840.[48] Resistance to smoking lingered on, however. Wellington would only allow guests to smoke in the servants' hall. Sterner critics, learning that guests had smoked, refused to invite them back to their homes. The Bishop of Rochester went so far, in 1855, to confess that he would have refused ordination to a candidate, had he known the man had smoked in a bedroom in the Bishop's palace. Those, like Wellington, who allowed guests to smoke only in the servants' quarters made a telling comment on relations between the classes as much as on smoking. Gradually however smoking reasserted its respectability in landed homes – provided it was restricted to the designated room, a fact observed by the changing design of Victorian country homes which made special provision for the smoking room.

Menfolk retired to the smoking room – more and more fitted with a billiard table – where they discussed matters thought unfit for female ears. There they smoked (and drank) in a masculine culture which, in a private setting, was the mirror image of their social inferiors, doing much the same thing, but in the alehouse and tavern. In places, the smoking room – infamously a retreat for bachelors – was highly elaborate. In time men even dressed for the occasion, donning their ever more elaborate smoking jackets. The smoking room came to exercise a powerful hold over the men of propertied Britain. Those who chose not to join in its rituals and conventions, with its close links to London clubs, to field sports and to the wider, almost masonic world of propertied masculinity, were looked down on; men who did not 'play the game'.[49] Yet this revival of smoking in the landed home marked something of a revival for smoking in polite society. And it is significant that men now smoked cigars, not pipes.

Cigars were new to Britain, but in fact were the earliest form of tobacco smoked. Las Casas, defender of the Indians in New Spain, reported in the early days of contact that Indians smoked dried leaves rolled into a cigar-shaped form. It was this form of tobacco which took hold in Spain, helped by the development of the high quality Cuban tobacco industry. It was simply assumed that Cuba alone produced tobacco worthy of the best cigars; for centuries the island produced the only sought-after cigars. Travellers to Spain regularly returned with tales of the Spanish addiction to cigars. Northern Europeans were struck by the fact that Spaniards seemed to have a cigar permanently on their lips. King Ferdinand VII, restored to the Bourbon monarchy in 1814, was apt to bestow the very best of cigars as a sign of favour and friendship.[50]

Few doubted, then or since, that the most excellent cigar tobacco came from Cuba, grown, in the early nineteenth century, by a rapidly expanding number of small plantations, and produced by black labour – slave and free. From its profusion of tobacco estates, Cuba disgorged an amazing volume of high quality tobacco. Visitors there in the early nineteenth century were astonished by the amount of tobacco smoked by Cubans – of all classes, ages, colours and both sexes. Even lunatics in the local asylum were allowed cigars. Visitors had cigars thrust into their hands as soon as they arrived. But it was to the export market that most Cuban tobacco was directed; three times as much was exported in the 1850s as in the 1830s, and most of it went to satisfy the voracious European appetite for cigars. At the height of the industry, in the 1850s, Cuba exported 360 million, mainly to Europe and North America.[51]

The British interest in Spanish cigars was first acquired by the thousands of British troops engaged in the Peninsular War against Napoleon. They and subsequent visitors returned home convinced that Spanish males did little but smoke cigars.[52] Thanks to the profusion of Cuban supplies (with a consequent fall in prices) and to the changed trading agreement which allowed British consumers access to Cuban products, the cigar helped to revive smoking among men of the British landed classes. Yet the settlement and economic development of other tropical regions in the course of the nineteenth century proved conclusively that good tobacco could be grown elsewhere, in the Philippines and Borneo, for example.

The end result was that the cigar was responsible for reinstating smoking within the fashionable propertied home by the mid-nineteenth century. But it was carefully located, in the smoking room or men's 'den', away from female company and minimizing the amount of damage which tobacco smoke inevitably caused to household fixtures.[53]

Of course smoking remained firmly entrenched in places of public drinking. For that reason alone it attracted the ire of a number of teetotal activists who sought to bring an end to the evils of both drink and tobacco.[54] Thomas Cook, founder of the famous travel company which bears his name, was a vehement opponent of the 'filthy practice' of smoking and was apt to lecture anyone within earshot about the evils of tobacco. Yet it is surely significant that his teetotal son, John Mason Cook, became a smoker, 'with a special fondness for cigars'.[55] Here was a simple, personal example of the way cigars had, by the mid-nineteenth century, once more rendered smoking respectable among propertied males.

Who could possibly have imagined the history of tobacco, from those first encounters with Indian peoples, through to the early nineteenth century when smoking had become a global industry (and health hazard)? Of course it embraced a host of forms – from the most exclusive and costly of cigars through to cheap, adulterated tobacco for the pipes of poor men. It was, in the west at least, overwhelmingly a male pleasure; a habit which consciously excluded women and helped to sharpen the line between the contemporary social worlds of male and female. It was, by 1800, a democratic pleasure. It offered no real barriers of class or cost to exclude the humble. Yet that had not always been the case. Initially tobacco had been the exclusive preserve of the rich and the highly-placed. Two hundred years later, it was the pleasure of the common man. In the process it had served to immiserate not only the heavy smoker (plagued from one generation to another by deteriorating health), but it had (along with other produce) consigned untold millions of workers into slave systems which transformed the population of the Americas in order to sate the European appetite for tobacco.

# 6 The Aztec Drink: Chocolate

In that area of the Americas where the marauding Europeans first sought the elusive city of El Dorado, the city of gold, they found wonder and treasures beyond their dreams. After the wealth of Aztec Mexico City and the Peruvian riches of the Andes, nothing seemed too far-fetched; who could doubt that a city of gold really existed?[1] In the face of such treasures, that gold and silver plundered with bloody abandon from indigenous people, and goaded by persistent rumours of yet more riches waiting to be found elsewhere in the region, the Spaniards could be forgiven for ignoring or minimizing many of the more mundane discoveries. They were after all, in a new world where everything looked strange, even the flora and the fauna were unfamiliar. Yet some of the apparently inconsequential finds were to prove commercially valuable and crucial in transforming western taste. Who among the Spaniards, for example, could see the value of the humble, indigenous cocoa bean?[2] But even at the time, the Aztec people prized the cocoa bean and its derivative, the drink of chocolate.[3] Long before the Europeans disturbed the world of the Indian peoples, chocolate was enshrined in the ancient Toltec myth, which affirmed that Quetzalcoatl, the feathered serpent god, had planted the chocolate tree in the region of southern Mexico.[4] In time, this traditional Indian food was to take its place among the western world's most sought-after commodities, as Europeans transplanted the Indian bean around the globe, converting great swathes of the world to its production and manufacture.

When the Aztec kingdom demanded tribute from subject regions, it accepted both chocolate and beans for the royal coffers. Among the lists of donations received we know of '20 chests of ground chocolate', '80 loads of red chocolate' and '200 loads of chocolate'.[5] Chocolate was a favoured beverage among the governing elite of the Aztec empire, though it was unrecognizable to modern tastes. Early descriptions tell how

Mexican chocolate was 'a compound of roasted ground cacao beans mixed with red pepper (chilli), a cinnamon-like spice (very likely allspice), achiote (a red seed used as a colouring agent), and sometimes vanilla.'[6] It was whipped into a froth until almost solid; it was then easy to drink or eat. The Aztecs consumed it cold, though drinking it required a special knack.

> opening the mouth wide, in order to facilitate deglutition that the foam may dissolve gradually and descend imperceptibly, as it were into the stomach.

It was thought to be nutritious enough to sustain a man on a long day's march.[7] Few liked it more than Moctezuma [Montezuma]. Laced with vanilla and spices, served in golden goblets and spoons, 50 jars were prepared for his daily consumption, 2000 for the royal household.[8]

The cocoa bean was an important means of exchange. A 'tolerable good slave' could be bought for 100 beans. It was also a durable food which, thought Peter Martyr, formed 'Blessed Money', because it 'exempts its possessor from avarice, since it cannot be long hoarded, or hidden underground.'[9] It was grown in various parts of Central and South America and a thriving interregional trade developed in the cocoa bean. The taste for chocolate was widespread, first among the native peoples of Central America and later among those Spanish settlers in the region who adopted it, mainly as a drink but also in certain cooked dishes (some of which are cooked to this day). At first however the Europeans disliked chocolate, 'more suited to pigs than men' in the words of one observer.[10] All that began to change, thanks in the main to sugar. Chocolate drinks laced with sugar (thanks to the emergent slave-based sugar cane economy of the Americas) quickly became fashionable among settlers in New Spain by the 1590s. Chocolate-drinking became a polite social ritual among Spanish settlers. In Chiapas in the south of Mexico priests complained when their sermon and mass were interrupted by servants delivering chocolate drinks to their mistresses in the congregation.[11]

It was a curious fact that the indigenous Mexican cocoa plants soon mirrored the fate of the native peoples around them. Like the Indian peoples of the region, the cocoa bushes fell victim to the advance of European settlement; they began to die out and Mexico came to depend on cocoa imported from other regions. Cocoa from Cuayaquil (Ecuador) for example was shipped into Mexico and Central America for much of the seventeenth century.[12] Guatemalan cocoa, imported into New Spain, was made into bars of chocolate, which in turn was grated and mixed with water, to produce a chocolate drink. From there, the chocolate was exported to Seville – and thence to other parts of Europe.[13] By then, chocolate had undergone that strange transformation from being the exotic drink of native peoples to a luxury taste of the conquerors. And it was natural enough that the habit would spread even further afield. Spanish settlers, returning home from New Spain, inevitably influenced Spain itself with many of the customs they had acquired on the other side of the Atlantic. At first, not everyone in Spain liked chocolate. In 1604 Joseph Acosta described it thus;

> The chief use of this cocoa is in a drinke which they call Chocolate, whereof they make account, foolishly and without reason; for it is loathsome to such as are not acquainted with it, having a skumme or frothe that is very unpleasant to taste... Yet it is a drinke very much esteemed among the Indians, whereof they feast noble men as they pass through their country.[14]

Like other staples, cocoa was soon transplanted into other suitable growing regions of the world on the back of European exploration, trade and settlement. From its native region, between the Amazon and the Orinoco, cocoa was planted as far north as Mexico City, later to Trinidad in the Caribbean and thence to neighbouring Venezuela. The Spaniards tried to maintain their control over the supplies of chocolate but once Spanish imperial power began to wane, their economic grip over their American possessions began to slip. As Spanish imperial power declined, cocoa-growing quickly spread to other South American regions – notably in Ecuador, Colombia, Peru, Bolivia and the Guianas. What prompted this agricultural proliferation was of course demand – the knowledge that there was a market in Europe for exotic produce. Imaginative and inventive agriculture could yield untold material bounty. Subsequently Europeans took the cocoa plant to a host of tropical colonies, part of the remarkable agricultural experimentation which was one of the generally unnoticed features of European imperialism.

Cocoa spread around the world. The Spaniards took it to the Philippines in about 1670 and possibly to the Celebes. The Dutch took it to Indonesia and also planted it in São Tome off West Africa. By the early nineteenth century, cocoa production had spread into Brazil (which exported about 3000 tons by 1851). But it was the Gold Coast which eventually came to dominate world production by the end of the century. First planted there as late as 1890, the first cocoa yield, the following year, weighed a mere 80 pounds. Twenty years later the Gold Coast exported 120 million pounds.[15]

Long before then however, the fashionable status of chocolate-drinking in the Americas was in decline. As Spanish America evolved into ever more sophisticated societies the urban elites in the region sought to enhance their status by aping the fashions of their peers in Europe. Visitors measured the rise of local sophistication and gentility by the development of European customs. Drinking chocolate was the habit of less refined locals, and the habit gave way to more cosmopolitan style. The middle classes of Bogota for example were deemed to be on the rise when they abandoned chocolate, first for coffee and then for tea, in the early nineteenth century.[16] And the pattern was repeated throughout the region.

Chocolate made a familiar entry into Europe, taking hold initially as the exotic fad of the rich and as a taste acquired initially by Europeans in the New World. But chocolate in its Mexican format (i.e. bitter, with spices and chillies) remained deeply unattractive to European palates. The first exports to Spain 'consisted of beans mixed with sugar and spices'. Later beans were shipped in their natural state.[17] Recent research has shown however that much of the 'cacco' trade to Spain was in chocolate form, not as beans or nuts. The chocolate was packed into crates exported to Europe. In the words of one author in 1672,

> I am persuaded that there is no better Chocolate to be had in England, than that which Mariners and Sea-Men bring; which is made up in the Country where cacao naturally grows.[18]

Thus the fad of the New World spread among elites of the Old – but thanks to the addition of cane sugar. Like tea and coffee, chocolate has a naturally bitter taste but once sugar was added, all of them became acceptable, indeed attractive, to Europeans.[19] Thereafter, and thanks to the efforts of African slaves, Europeans turned to those sweetened drinks on a scale, and with an increasing attachment, which astonished contemporary observers. Hot, sweet chocolate, quite unlike its original Mexican format soon took hold in Spain, before spreading rapidly to other parts of Europe, promoted by the fashionable example of aristocracy, the educated and by peripatetic clerics. A book of 1631 described how chocolate was now 'much used in Spain, Italy and Flanders'.[20] In the next 20 years, chocolate was to be found in courtly circles across western Europe. By mid-century it was on sale in London.

Though cocoa exports from the Americas were, at first, a Spanish monopoly, the spread of cocoa production to other regions of the Americas made it easier for other European powers to evade the restrictions of fading Spanish power. This was of course but a small aspect of the commercial and imperial contest played out between the major maritime European powers. In this case, once the taste for chocolate developed outside Spain and became a fad throughout western Europe, the Spanish colonies alone could not satisfy demand. It was in the interests of other European nations, notably the Dutch and the English, to encourage the cultivation and export of tropical goods in their own colonial settlements. And as consumer demand for tropical staples grew throughout Europe, the suppliers in the colonies could scarcely keep up with demand. Cocoa production spread from one colony to another. From the Dutch island of Curaçao for instance, the Dutch took cocoa to Venezuela and thence to Amsterdam. By the 1630s the trade in cocoa was securely in Dutch hands and Seville gave way to Amsterdam as the market for cacao. Once England seized Jamaica from Spain in 1655, production slipped out of Spanish hands. Even so, Spain maintained a thriving chocolate trade. In the 1650s, perhaps half a million pounds of cocoa was imported into Spain. Four times that amount was shipped in the 1660s. By then, the Dutch shipped more than one million pounds of cocoa.[21] Not surprisingly, the English, flushed with their newly acquired Caribbean possessions, hurried to join in.

Though the origins of this new social habit were clearly colonial, it had its immediate local inspiration in the quicksilver changes and upheavals in European metropolitan fashion. Fads and social emulation were the key forces which drove one imported produce after another into wider social usage. So it was with chocolate. European royalty was an instrumental force. When in 1660 Maria Theresa, the Infanta of Spain, married Louis XIV of France, she brought to the French Court a passion for chocolate. It was said that she had two great loves: her husband-king, and chocolate. Prompted by the monarchy, French aristocrats also turned to chocolate. Gossip at the French Court had it that the Marquise de Coetlogon 'drank so much chocolate when she was expecting last year that she was brought to bed of a little boy as black as the devil, who died'. A more likely explanation was the fact that her morning chocolate was delivered to her bedroom each morning by an African slave.[22] (At much the same time, the Portuguese Queen of England was enthusiastically promoting her own favourite drink, tea, at the English Court.)

Like the early seeds transplanted to other parts of the world, these cultural habits of society's elites were formative. In courtly circles, fashion was *the* crucial determinant of status and approval. In a world where power lay in proximity to or distance from royalty, it was important to follow royal examples (or at least not to be seen to deviate too far from them). In both these cases – chocolate in France and tea in England – the taste for the fruits of empire quickly established a new European base and took root, thanks initially to royal patronage. But they quickly spread to other groups. In Amsterdam, the mid-century market for cocoa, the drink took hold among men of the mercantile class. There, and later in London, the new drinks (coffee and chocolate) found a prospering home in the places of drink which began to proliferate close to the place of mercantile work.

In England chocolate closely followed the route of other staples. From the first it was sold alongside coffee in the coffee houses which emerged in London from the 1660s. But chocolate was, and continued to be, more costly than coffee and remained the drink of more prosperous people until dramatic changes in cultivation and production in the nineteenth century made it genuinely cheap to produce and widely popular.

Long before the English began to debate its benefits, there had been a lively debate about chocolate among the Spanish. Its alleged medicinal benefits and its aphrodisiac qualities were paraded as part of that broader social and medical discourse about new tropical commodities. As it increased in popularity, chocolate was promoted by contemporary men of science. In their turn, commercial advocates of chocolate proclaimed its beneficial virtues. Thus did fashion, novelty and science combine to promote this alien substance among prosperous European elites.

Like other tropical foodstuffs, chocolate was often denounced as a costly and unnecessary frivolity. As early as 1673 it was dismissed in the *Harleian Miscellany* as a luxury which diverted consumption from domestic products. To some it was an unwelcome 'inflamer of the passions', to others it had that host of beneficial qualities so commonly claimed in new-found exotic produce. Contemporary science and medicine began to analyse chocolate (as they did most new staples) for signs of medical virtues – or dangers, and on those criteria it was promoted or denounced. It was promoted, among other things, for its 'wonderful faculty of quenching thirst, allaying hectic heats, of nourishing and fattening the body'.[23] Of course it may well be true that hot, sweet chocolate provided an instant and refreshing infusion of energy and invigoration; a bodily sense of relaxed good feeling which could easily be interpreted as good health.

Whatever the cause, chocolate began to take its place in British life. On sale in coffee-houses, (in some cases, in 'chocolate-houses') chocolate was first advertised in London in 1657:

> in Bishopgate St, in Queen's Head Alley, at a Frenchman's house, is an excellent West India drink called Chocolate to be sold... [24]

Already well-established in other European cities, chocolate first made its name in England as a West Indian product. This was perfectly understandable – but again only in the context of empire. These were the years when the British were acquiring their own Caribbean empire. In 1655 the British had taken Jamaica (quickly to establish itself as the prime Caribbean possession) from the Spaniards, enabling the island's cocoa groves ('walks'), established by the Spaniards to feed the growing British demand for chocolate. It proved a short-lived boon, for a blight in 1670–1 killed off most of Jamaica's cocoa.[25] By 1684 the island had only 32 cocoa plantations (compared with 246 sugar plantations). A new generation of Jamaican settlers turned to sugar on a massive scale, and the rise of Jamaican sugar served to push aside local efforts at cocoa production. Whereas the early planters in the island had believed that the cocoa tree was among 'the most profitable trees in the world', sugar profits persuaded planters to switch production.[26] Nonetheless, more and more chocolate found its way to London, its acceptability promoted by the very same sugar that flowed from the new plantations. The cost dropped, mainly because of adulteration by retailers, who mixed it with grain.

On 24 November 1664, Pepys drank it, apparently for the first time: 'To a Coffee-house, to drink jacolatte, very good.' In fact a range of exotic drinks was available to customers of coffee and chocolate houses. Evelyn noted in his diary in 1682: 'They also drank of a sorbet and jacolatt.' People who wanted to buy chocolate to make up into drinks at home could also buy the ingredients at these shops.

Like all tropical imports, however, chocolate proved an irresistible target for governments keen to expand their excise income. As early as 1660 excise duties were imposed on the volume of chocolate consumed or sold. Later duties were imposed on imported cocoa beans and as chocolate consumption increased, new Acts of Parliament levied fresh tariffs. Licenses ordered the words 'Dealer in Cocoa-nuts, Chocolates etc' to be emblazoned above a merchant's door. Chocolate on which duties had been paid was formally stamped. In a move that would have troubled modern chocolaholics, anyone in possession of more than 6lb of chocolate or cocoa was deemed to be a dealer.[27]

Bought in solid slabs or cakes, chocolate was broken down into smaller pieces for melting, blending and whisking into a drink. And from its initial toe-hold in the coffee-houses, it gradually gained acceptance in prosperous homes. By the early eighteenth century consumption of drinking chocolate had grown to the extent that 'chocolate mills' – special whisks for mixing the crude chocolate with other ingredients – became a feature of fashionable kitchens. In 1703 for instance the *London Gazette* advertised for sale 'Lackered Tea-Tables, Chocolate Mills'. Fifty years later, chocolate mills were commonplace. Those domestic cookery books aimed at the properous housewife, keen to manage an up-to-date kitchen, and able to offer the best of fashionable cuisine, simply assumed that all good kitchens would possess a chocolate mill.

Throughout these early years of chocolate consumption, the British took chocolate as a drink. It was however an awkward drink to concoct. Quite apart from the complexity of preparation, chocolate had its unattractive qualities. Drinking chocolate was made from crushed cocoa beans, which contained 50 per cent fat (cocoa butter). To counteract the fat, flour was normally whisked into the drink to make it more palatable. Other recipes involved leaving the drink to stand before skimming off as much of the fat as possible. In her important household manual, *The Experienced English Housekeeper*, Elizabeth Raffold described how to prepare chocolate.

> Scrape four ounces of chocolate, and pour a quart of boiling water upon it, mill it with a chocolate-mill, and sweeten it to your taste, give it a boil and let it stand all night, then mill it again very well, boil it two minutes, then mill it till it will leave the froth upon the top of your cups.[28]

Clearly, here was a costly and a time-consuming drink which required space, equipment, time and patience. And who could afford such time and costly complications for a mere drink? But whatever the preparation, the final drink always contained a substantial quantity of heavy, fatty substance which many people did not enjoy. The technique of being able to separate the buttermilk from the crushed beans was not devised until the early nineteenth century, by C. J. van Houten in Holland. Thereafter drinking chocolate was more readily processed by manufacturers, and drinking chocolate more easily prepared by the consumer. With a new kind of drinking chocolate widely and cheaply available, its popularity grew by leaps and bounds.

The early history of chocolate in England differed from other tropical drinks. Though it took its place alongside tea and coffee in the coffee-houses of late seventeenth-century

London, chocolate failed to make the impact of the other two drinks. Initially at least, men who, like Pepys, became regular visitors to the capital's coffee-houses, sampled all the new drinks on offer before settling on their favourite beverage. In the 1660s all three drinks were equally available. Within a generation however coffee had won the day and became the pre-eminent social drink in public – alcohol apart, of course. Indeed the coffee-houses themselves provide a clue. Men's drinking clubs were 'coffee-houses', not 'tea' or 'chocolate' houses. Tea and chocolate were soon relegated to the social dominance of coffee. Instead, the other two drinks took an entirely different social trajectory. Tea became the drink which was offered within the home, developing its own elaborate rituals and etiquette of preparation and consumption, with its often costly equipment, which itself became an essential display in all fashionable drawing rooms – and even, eventually, in the humblest of kitchens.[29] It was a drink which, because of its primarily domestic location, became the focus for a distinctively female sociability. Clearly, tea was not a uniquely female drink. But in the domestic routines which evolved around it, especially in fashionable homes, tea-drinking became an aspect of contemporary femininity, paralleling the public role of men gathering in their favourite coffee-house. In all this, chocolate took strictly third place, until the technical advances of the nineteenth century and the resulting emergence of cheap drinking chocolate – later eating chocolate.

We know that some people acquired chocolate from friends and relatives who had settled in the West Indian islands, and sent back local produce as gifts.[30] But compared to other drinks, the volumes of chocolate imported into Britain were very small. As late as 1837, when Victoria came to the throne, the British imported less than 5000 tons of cocoa for domestic consumption. Curiously, more than half of that amount was consumed by the Royal Navy. The revolution wrought in the nineteenth century, with new systems of growing cocoa but, more importantly in processing it, made chocolate a genuinely popular drink – and food. By the time Victoria died, the import figures had increased to 20 000 tons. By 1915 it stood at 50 000 tons.[31]

Perhaps *the* most curious fact in the history of chocolate consumption in Britain (and in large parts of the world) was the transformation effected by a small band of English Quakers, notably Fry, Cadbury and Rowntree. Their efforts, which helped to transform the taste of the British people was part of that remarkable impact which Quakers had on business and industry, on both sides of the Atlantic, from the mid-eighteenth century onwards. Their initial involvement with chocolate seemed accidental. Joseph Fry, the first of the great Quaker chocolate manufacturers, was successful in a host of businesses: in china, soap and chemicals and in devising a new typeface. But he is best remembered for his chocolates. Trained as an apothecary before settling in Bristol, Fry, in common with other apothecaries, recommended the use of chocolate for medicinal purposes. This was but one example of that broader use of new tropical staples encouraged by doctors and apothecaries in the seventeenth and eighteenth centuries. Fry experimented with chocolate, offering the public 'The best sorts of chocolates, made and sold wholesale and retail by Jospeh Fry, Apothecary, in Small Street Bristol'.[32]

Here was a more profitable business than being an apothecary. Fry however was not the first chocolate man in Bristol. Walter Churchman had been in the Bristol chocolate business since 1728, and in 1731 had been granted a royal patent for a new water-driven machine: 'invented for the expeditious, fine, and clean making of Chocolate to greater perfection than any other method in use.' The business was continued by his son following Churchman's death, but in 1761 it was offered for sale in the local newspaper: 'Mr Churchman's Chocolate Mills and works there, which, being a Secret cannot be exposed to view.'[33]

The business, and patent, were bought by Fry, and his chocolate business began to prosper. Eventually he moved into a small factory to process the beans. Alert to whatever new system emerged (in those years of early technical and mechanical change), Fry introduced a Boulton and Watt steam engine to chocolate processing in 1795.[34] It was no accident that at much the same time, technical and mechanical innovations were being introduced in chocolate processing in North America, in France and Germany. Initially, Fry sold 'Churchman's Chocolate', trading on his predecessor's name and reputation, but in time he was to establish a name for himself which far surpassed any other in the contemporary British chocolate industry.

Fry's pre-eminence as a chocolate manufacturer flowed from two main factors. Firstly, he was interested in innovation and experimentation (a direct offshoot of his work as an apothecary). Secondly, he was a Quaker, a member of a sect steeped in a particular business ethic and which provided a major network of trading and business contacts, all of whom helped each other. Fry was but one of many successful Quakers who, collectively, made such an impact on the business culture of the late eighteenth century. Fry was also helped by living and working in Bristol, which in the early 1700s had become the major British port for that burgeoning trade to and from Africa and the Americas. It was a city with excellent communications to a deep hinterland, embracing a region from Birmingham to the West Country, and which serviced that city's export trades to the rest of the world and, of course, provided a rich market for Bristol's imports and products. Bristol ships often returned from trips to the Americas with cocoa and chocolate in their holds.[35] No less crucial perhaps for Fry was the proximity of Bath.

There the nation's fashionable and rich sought health and pleasure through the latest medical and social regime, taking the waters, but enjoying when they could that myriad array of local diversions. The commercial links between Bath and Bristol were close, and trading companies, notably those selling tea, fought over the lucrative trade of both communities.[36] It was only the briefest of journeys from the warehouses of dockside Bristol, teeming with goods from the wider world, to the shops and salons of Bath. Merchants and traders found in Bath the most receptive of commercial prospects: wealthy people eager to buy their wares and fashions, if persuaded that their goods were *à la mode* or healthy. Chocolate had a tradition (in England at least) of both. It had emerged in the late seventeenth century as a product to be found on the shelves of both apothecary and grocer. A hundred years later, it was an item in those homes which provided guests with entertainment and dinner and which prided themselves in offering all the latest culinary delights.

More than that, although Bath had a large and growing residential population (whose social tone had noticeably declined in the course of the century) it was perhaps more famous for its transient population of visitors. Those people returned home at the end of the season to London and the provinces, taking with them the most recent fad and social habit acquired in Bath. In this way the exclusive habits of the better-off were disseminated throughout England – and even further afield.

Understandably, chocolate remained primarily the drink of the better-off. Yet for all the efforts to modernize chocolate-processing (to invest money and ideas in the manufacture of the produce) it failed to make the impact of the other two major drinks until the mid-nineteenth century. Complexity, costly preparation and unattractive qualities (as a drink) served to disadvantage chocolate. By the time technical change produced a cheap and easily managed product (mass-manufactured and marketed to an urban population), tea and coffee were deeply and securely entrenched among the British people's social habits.

Processing tea was simplicity itself; brewing it was even easier. Coffee demanded a little more time and effort, but even then, the effort was as nothing compared to the complexity of chocolate preparation. It was then hardly surprising that chocolate failed to 'take-off' until the 1830s in any way comparable to tea or coffee, although it was in place – a familiar, common foodstuff on shelves in homes and shops across Britain, and with a niche in social usage. Thanks to pioneering Quaker enterprise all that changed and chocolate consumption became part of the British way of life in the course of the nineteenth century. The British confirmed their reputation as lovers of sweet things by consuming rich chocolates by the ton. It was, by then, hard to imagine the Aztec-Mexican origins of this drink and luxury food. Along with a myriad other tropical imports, chocolate had become thoroughly British.

# 7 Feeding the People: the Potato

The 1790s were the decade of crisis for British society. To compound the reverses of war against revolutionary France and the corrosive inroads of democratic ideals at home, the rapidly expanding population of Britain was blighted by hunger. In 1795 especially, the British people starved. Hunger riots were common, public disturbances widespread and the fabric of social order (always delicately poised) was sorely tested.[1] Yet, for all that, it could undoubtedly have been worse – and would have been – without the help of the humble potato. Then, and later, this simple foodstuff proved itself to be the salvation of millions.

It is difficult now to think of this simple crop as utterly exotic. But in origin it was as foreign and strange as any. Here was the basic food of Indian peoples of the Andes *altiplano.* They and other peoples of the west coast and the mountains of South America belonged to planting cultures. In such stark and inhospitable regions it was the potato that enabled the population to survive. Easily grown and simply kept, the potato could even be stored at cool, high altitudes. It could also be moved around without much difficulty. These remarkable virtues, displayed for centuries in the Andes, were hidden from outside eyes but were later to be tried and tested in Europe.[2]

The potato seemed unappealing at first. Grubbed from poor soil, at high altitudes, it seemed more appropriate to poor Indian peoples than to their conquerors. Yet, within a very short time, the Spanish came to appreciate its worth. It was, wrote a Spaniard to 1536 'a gift very acceptable to the Indians, and a dainty dish even for the Spaniards'. In the course of the sixteenth century more and more commentators in Spanish America stressed its virtues – as a cheap, easily produced crop for local labour and, suitably cooked, as a delicacy for more refined Spanish palates.[3] It was inevitable that this hardy and adaptable foodstuff would come to the aid of Spaniards foraging for supplies in the region. Sometime after

1536, Spanish ships on the Pacific coast of Peru and Chile began to feed their crews on local potatoes. Its benefits were quickly appreciated, and gradually it spread to other regions of Spanish America; a hardy stand-by for sailors and settlers uncertain of imported or local food supplies. Others visiting the region were bound to encounter the vegetable. The first English comments on the potato came from John Hawkins during one of his infamous early slave-trading voyages into the Americas in 1564–5. In the Caribbean his crew tasted the potato for the first time: 'the most delicate roots that may be eaten, and do far exceed our parsnips or carrots'.[4]

The potato's European reputation as a reliable food was thus first established among European sailors with experience of the Americas. Drake for example received gifts of potatoes on different voyages and was quick to recognize its nutritional value, both at sea and on land.[5] The potato was ideal in the early days of settlement and exploration. Spanish and British settlers – and their African slaves – in their initial pioneering days had first of all to ensure survival, and the potato was a natural ally. An early guide to life in frontier Barbados urged all prospective planters to turn their slaves and workers in the first days 'to felling, cleaning, and planting a *Potato peece of 4 acres*'.[6] In time other transplanted crops took their place alongside the potato in the slave colonies of the Americas,[7] but from the first days of settlement through to the end of slavery (and beyond) the potato proved to be a dietary mainstay. Planters annually turned over their slaves to work in the potato patch. On 2 July 1777 Alexander Johnson had his Jamaican slaves 'digging in the potatoes'.[8] When, in 1834, slaves were freed in the British colonies, the Abolition Act specifically decreed the potato to be one of the foodstuffs which slave-holders should provide for their freed slaves.[9]

From these European outposts in the Americas – among sailors, settlers, planters and imported Africans – the potato became part of the 'Columbian exchange', when it crossed the Atlantic and was adopted in parts of Spain by 1569. Its spread to other parts of Europe was slow and fitful. By the 1580s the potato had appeared in parts of western Ireland. Its exact arrival there is uncertain. It may have come ashore from ships of the Armada which were wrecked and plundered on the west coast. It may have been imported by men with experience of the New World or with contacts with Spain. But it also seems likely that Spanish fisherman, working the waters of the western Atlantic, deliberately planted potatoes in Ireland for food they could turn to on the nearest land.[10] Whatever the truth of these confusing speculations, it is clear enough that the American potato was to be found in Europe by the end of the sixteenth century. But no one could have imagined, from these tentative origins, the extraordinary role it would play in the subsequent history of Britain.

As potato cultivation spread steadily in Ireland, it became clear enough that the crop offered great advantages, replicating its virtues already revealed in the Americas; it was simple, cheap and easily grown. In short it was an ideal foodstuff for the common people. Potatoes, said one observer in 1688, 'may be propagated with advantage to poor people, a little ground yielding a very great quantity'.[11]

There was however a sinister aspect to the spread of the potato throughout Ireland. The potato's success was in part a consequence of the rapacious English conquest of the island. Thousands of peasants, driven from their lands by English and Scottish settlers were forced to search for land and food. The potato offered them salvation, for it was a crop which was naturally suited to a wet unyielding terrain and to the Irish climate. It could be cultivated on marginal lands. It also encouraged that other essential ingredient of Irish peasant life: pig-breeding, for pigs, like people, were readily fed on potatoes.[12] Dispossessed by their conquerors, trapped by the environment, the Irish seemed fortunate to have the potato. But their luck was to run out in the 1840s and they were to pay a terrible price for turning to that alien South American crop.

Long before the Great Famine of 1846, the Irish peasantry – with their pigs and potatoes – were an image of wretchedness. They were in the grips of landlords who exacted harsh and uncompromising demands, obliging even their humblest of tenants to pay excessive rents and tithes: '... the Lord is a poor Tyrant and the Peasant a poorer Slave.' The peasantry toiled to extract a bare subsistence from the soil, yet they also had to pay an exploitative tithe, to support an alien church and an alien landlord class. The tithes in England were bad enough; in Ireland, they were oppression itself.[13] Visitors to that troubled land were shocked (in a world less easily shocked than our own) by the bitter relations between tenant and landlord. In those years of the great slave empires in the Americas, visitors to Ireland did not feel the comparison between Irish peasantry and black slavery too far-fetched.

One visitor after another wrote in horrified disbelief at the distressed condition of the Irish people. Everywhere the story seemed the same: filthy hovels (more like English pig-sties), shoeless, ragged families, and armies of wretched people living 'in filth and nastiness upon buttermilk and potatoes ...'[14] Periodically, when nature blighted the crops, this communal wretchedness teetered on the edge of something even worse. It was as if the Irish were serving a numbing apprenticeship for the disaster to come.

By the time Arthur Young toured Ireland in 1776–9, the potato was ubiquitous. Though historians now dispute many of his overall impressions,[15] it is clear enough that wherever Young travelled he was struck by the meagre food of the local peasantry. The potato seemed to be the first, the last and the only source of sustenance for the poor. From one place to another, Young's comments took the form of a refrain on the potato.

> *Their food is potatoes and milk ...*
> *Their food principally potatoes and oatmeal ...*
> *their diet is milk, potatoes and oat bread ...*
> *Their food, potatoes and milk for nine months of the year ...*
> *Their food in summer potatoes and milk, but in spring they have only potatoes and water ...*[16]

Irish poverty was patchy rather than universal. But those who saw it at its worst recited a grim litany of deprivation the like of which were virtually unknown in mainland England – and the more shocking for that. Dearth, a meagre diet and wretched conditions seemed to go hand-in-hand with a rising population.[17] It was, in the words of one writer in 1766, an 'ill-fated country' ruled by the potato. Yet despite these problems, the vegetable clearly had enormous potential. It could be planted, grown and harvested easily, on modest land, with little capital or skill. It was in fact a reliable mainstay of a labouring population edging, so it seemed in Ireland in the course of the eighteenth century, towards starvation, as the expanding population seemed to outstrip the ability to produce adequate foodstuffs. Where once the potato had seemed fit (in the eyes of Englishmen) only for cattle and pigs, its potential for humans began to win over the dubious critic. Even Arthur Young changed his mind returning from his visit to Ireland to urge English farmers to use the potato to feed 'the labouring poor'.

The exploitative, hostile conditions between Irish peasants and their landlords had served to convert Ireland into that monoculture which became both a caricature and a potential disaster for the Irish people. The full consequences of this dependence on the potato still lay many years ahead. In the short term however, Ireland had offered a test-bed for the changing food systems which were to revolutionize much of Europe in later years of population growth.

At the end of the seventeenth century, a number of English agricultural commentators had urged the adoption of the potato as an animal feed. A century later the crop had more than proved itself as an important element in the diet of working people in a region which was rapidly emerging as the pace-maker of industrial change. England was late – and slow – to accept the potato. In part this was because the English were largely unaccustomed to cultivating root crops. Even experienced farmers and gardeners had to seek advice when first confronted by potato cultivation. In the course of the seventeenth century, this new root appeared in a number of gardens of experimental horticulturalists. It was also grown, as a luxury, in the vegetable gardens of the well-to-do. Even so, it seems clear that throughout the first half of the seventeenth century, potatoes were unusual in England; more an item of curiosity than of basic diet.[18] When they appeared, in account books and menus in prosperous homes, potatoes were costly and eye-catching. This began to change in the late 1600s.

Throughout these early years the potato – like so many other exotic goods – tended to be available only to the wealthy. Hard as it may seem to imagine now, the potato was rare, and therefore exotic and costly. In the 1620s potatoes cost a shilling per pound. By the end of the seventeenth century the cost had dropped to one or two pence. In the words of one writer, 'The Virginian Potado is become *plebeian* in Shropshire.' And not just in Shropshire. Contemporaries noticed that the vegetable had begun to appear in gardens throughout Britain. It was, wrote Edward Philips in 1678, 'now common in English gardens, whose Root is of great vertue, to comfort and strengthen the body'.[19] By the end of the century this recently exotic crop was being sold by hawkers on the streets of London.

In common with other exotic foods, the potato was a topic of confused discussion among social commentators and men of science. The latter sought to locate its qualities – or dangers – before bestowing a seal of approval. Not surprisingly the potato had more than its fair share of medical opponents, though much of that disapproval focused on the association between poverty and the potato. In Switzerland, claimed a local physician, the scrofulous common people were those who seemed to live on potatoes.

> I am persuaded, myself, that the scrofulous troubles which prevail in our Cantons are entirely the result of this harmful dietary and the absence of exercise.[20]

They also asked; was the potato an aphrodisiac (a myth which soon faded among its disappointed upper-class consumers)? What were its medicinal powers; did it bring strength – or merely flatulence – to the commonfolk? In the first edition of the *Encyclopaedia,* it was simply dismissed:

> One blames, and with reason, the potato for its windiness; but what is a question of windiness to the virile organs of the peasant and the worker.

The questions, and explanations, were as varied for the potato as they were for most other new foodstuffs. One author told his readers (in what must surely rank as one of the oddest of romantic suggestions) that potatoes 'are flatulent, and therefore some use them for exciting Venus'. A number of observers claimed that the potato was good for 'procuring bodily lust'. Another felt that that it 'incites to Venus'. In time, Ireland seemed to yield plentiful evidence of the potato's lusty qualities. Where commentators saw poor Irish families, overburdened by gaggles of children, there they saw the aphrodisiac power of the potato at work. What else could explain such fecundity in the midst of undeniable destitution?

> It is favourable to population; for it has been observed, that in the western parts of Ireland where it is almost the only diet of the labouring poor, it is no unusual thing to see six, seven, eight, ten and sometimes more children, the issue of one couple, starting almost naked out of a miserable cabin ...

Time and again, commentators, notably in the seventeenth century, returned to the potato's aphrodisiac qualities; good for lust, it could restore potency in men, counter infertility in women.[21]

Whatever the reality – whatever benefits and disadvantages bestowed by the potato – it spawned a mythology which proved remarkably durable in a number of European societies. The growing familiarity with the potato can be gauged, in England, by a simple test. The word itself – 'potato' – crept into the vernacular and the image of the potato was used with increasing frequency by English writers from the sixteenth century onwards. And like other imported foodstuffs, the social trajectory of the potato was downwards; it began life at the top of society, but was later transmuted from the costly and the rare to commonplace. The process was familiar, the potato travelling from the rich man's garden before ending up in the poor man's plot.

One consequence of the growing interest in gardens, displayed by wealthy Elizabethans (under European influence) was the introduction of vegetable gardens attached to landed homes. Thereafter, vegetables (which had so far played a minor role in the English diet) became more commonplace in that of propertied English people, its fame promoted by a range of prevailing claims and myths. It is surely significant that most of the early English references we have to potatoes are about their royal or noble origins. Household accounts, the shopping lists of the rich and famous, recipes from wealthy homes – these and similar sources provide clear enough evidence of the original high status of the potato in England. It was beyond the reach and the pockets of the common people for much of the seventeenth century.

The wealthy came to appreciate the value of the potato, not so much for themselves but for the poor. John Evelyn, for example, did not like its taste, but recognized its social utility and potential. It was of 'excellent use for relief of poor, yea and one's own household when there are many servants, in a dear year'. It was appreciated that the potato could offer people insurance against lean times. The English began in effect to discover what the Indian peoples of the Andes had known for centuries: that here was a crop which could be stored, in the ground, and used as a last resort in times of hunger.[22] But too great a reliance on the potato as a single crop was to bring disasters of its own.

The poor (initially at least) remained suspicious of the new crop. In times of dearth, when the potato was offered to hungry people who were unaccustomed to it, they resisted. They tended not to like the unknown, preferring foodstuffs which were tried and tested. Slowly however this resistance was worn down, as ever more people accepted the cheap and easily-managed virtues of the potato.

In England, the potato began a familiar transition. As it found its way into more and more vegetable gardens, it spread 'from the gardens of the great houses to those of the smaller but yet substantial homes of the larger farmers and the professional classes'. It was a crop which also received a degree of scientific support from men in the Royal Society, keen to find cheap, manageable foodstuffs for an expanding population; a national safeguard against the threat of famine.[23] Men familiar with the potato's rapid spread in Ireland experimented with it in England – but progress remained uneven.

It was no accident that when the potato came into widespread cultivation and consumption, it did so in the part of England which, for obvious geographic and cultural reasons, had strong ties with Ireland. Lancashire was the first area to take to the potato on a significant scale and become the main producer in England. The crop had been introduced in the middle of the seventeenth century and had established itself in the south-western mosslands of the country by 1680. There was even a specialist potato market in Wigan. By the mid-eighteenth century potatoes were being exported, through Liverpool to Dublin, and as far as Gibraltar. But this production was to be even more important closer to home, for by the late 1700s the abundance of potatoes in Lancashire was to prove vital, feeding the expanding population in an era of change, in the local textile industries, with markets in

Oldham, Rochdale and Manchester. Lancashire was held up as an example of what the potato could achieve.[24] In large part, it flourished because of Lancashire's suitable physical environment, with its mossy soils and damp climate. Much of the crop was grown on smallholdings and the potato acted as a supplement to other foods, augmenting the diet but not dominating it (as happened in Ireland). It took its place alongside cereal foods, the oatmeal breads which formed the basis of plebeian diet in the region. It was to be one of the oddities of the story of the potato in mainland Britain that it thrived, and then challenged other foods in areas where local people were committed to cereal or barley crops. Yet here was a transformation. Whereas at the end of the seventeenth century, agricultural commentators had advocated experiments with the potato as an animal feed, a century later it had become an important part of the diet of working people in those areas of mainland Britain which were emerging as key industrial regions. By 1800 the potato was an integral part of the diet of a new industrial work force.[25] By then the potato had also begun to thrive in other, more distant parts of the country. The crop made major inroads into Devon and Cornwall, later into Somerset and Gloucestershire. In Herefordshire it was reported to be 'gaining ground every year: near towns in particular'. In the south of England, potatoes were grown only in gardens and were still produced mainly for feeding pigs. But potato cultivation inside the capital was, understanding, still rare, with the exception of the few gardening enthusiasts.[26] London's supplies of potatoes came courtesy of the Irish who worked smallholdings in Essex. The crop had also made inroads into the markets and diets of other urban areas – in Bristol and Oxford for instance. Though the spread of the potato was slow and uneven during the first half of the eighteenth century a distinct pattern was emerging across the country. The local gentry and landed classes were among the first to turn to potatoes, grown in their own plots and gardens (worked by their hired gardeners of course) while poorer people tended, initially, to ignore vegetable.

One factor which helped the spread of this food to new regions was the network of English markets. In the course of the eighteenth century, new goods – manufactured, imported and foodstuffs – crept into communities which might appear at first glance to lack an effective shopping system. As ever more people found themselves living in an urban habitat, the local markets provided access to foodstuffs which were grown in their hinterland. Potatoes began to appear on market stalls, from the plots of nearby smallholders, and into the homes of town dwellers.[27]

For working people, the process of urbanization created new difficulties with food. The nature of urban life – its physical restrictions and limitations – meant that more and more people were simply unable to grow their own foodstuffs. A growing army of working people were forced to acquire their basic foodstuffs by buying it in the open market place. It was, of course, a complex, uneven process; a rising population, (a growing proportion of them town dwellers), the irresistible march of the constructed, urban habitat, and the gradual erosion of common lands, all served to distance people from food production. For those able to cling to their traditional plots, the potato represented cheap and simple food cultivation. But such people formed a contracting minority, and even in the countryside, between 50 and 60 per cent of the rural poor had to buy their food. In towns of course, the figure was nearer to 100 per cent. However we juggle the data, it is clear enough that, by the beginning of the nineteenth century between 65 and 70 per cent of the English people depended on *purchased* food for their sustenance.[28] Stated crudely, there was an increasingly large proportion of the population dependent on market forces for their food. If the market turned nasty, if food became scarce and/or costly, a very large section of the English people would be in jeopardy. This is precisely what happened in the 1790s.

Despite our concern here with one particular food, there was an extraordinary variety of foodstuffs grown across England, each dictating its own peculiar eating habits and fads among local people. Any innovation – and it is hard to think of the potato as an innovation – was understandably resisted. The lower orders, though often urged by their betters to plant and to eat potatoes, remained reluctant – a sign of the strength of attachment to other traditional foodstuffs. When Arthur Young travelled through the country in the 1760s, he found potatoes in abundance only when he travelled in the north, and even there the picture was uneven. On later journeys, however, he realized that they had spread, though not always as fast or as far as he would have liked (anxious as he was to promote the potato as the working man's mainstay).[29] Agricultural improvers often faced resistance when urging people to turn to the potato. When Thomas Coke tried to persuade his tenants in Norfolk to follow his lead and grow the potato, their response was frosty: 'perhaps it wouldn't poison the pig.'[30]

Food, then as now, touched on people's deepest persistent values and customs, and represented of course much more than mere nutrition or the satisfying of hunger. Food and eating were part of an entrenched local culture; elements of those daily, annual or agricultural rituals that shaped people's lives and expressed a host of values and beliefs. Popular or widespread attachment to particular foodstuffs and dishes could not easily be disturbed or replaced by the simple exhortation of visitors or local pioneers. In the cases studied so far, the lower orders came to adopt the culinary habits of their betters, accepting foods and drinks imported from the far ends of the world. They were initially reluctant, however, to accept the potato, not least because they had existing, alternative foods of long standing. Sugar, coffee, chocolate or tea on the other hand did not compete with or threaten to replace existing foods. The new staples were not in competition with existing necessities or luxuries. The potato on the other hand had to overcome the inertia of tradition; it had to break down the attachment, going back generations, to other foods. Indeed it is symptomatic that what really nudged growing numbers of people towards the potato was simple need, sometimes desperation. When times were hard, when traditional foodstuffs were in short supply – or non-existent – when hunger stared people in the face, this vegetable seemed a realistic and affordable alternative. Though it was clear, objectively, that an increasingly urban people, in a society with uncertain food supplies (especially in the years of major warfare between 1793 and 1815) could be fed more easily and cheaply by the potato than by any other crop, the problem remained; how to persuade people to change their habits.

Among that army of commentators (itself expanding by the late eighteenth century), which gazed anxiously at the changing face of Britain, the inexorable rise of population was the most worrying change of all. How was this population to be fed? The major political and military upheavals of the last quarter of the century (the wars first against revolutionary America and then revolutionary France), gave the problem added urgency. There seemed, quite simply, too many mouths to feed on existing systems of cultivation and distribution. This was moreover a time of heightened (after 1789, sometimes hysterical) political debate. The common people had acquired a new democratic vocabulary, fashioned in America and France, and had gained political self-confidence (at least in the towns and cities). They seemed no longer willing to listen to the dictates of their betters, or merely to accept the status quo. A rising population, the spectre of encroaching hunger, the example of France after 1789, all this and more singed the comfort of the propertied classes. It was precisely from within this context that Malthus and others wrestled with the problem of the poor, with their food supplies and with the dismal prospects for the future. The prognosis looked simple but grim. In the words of Adam Smith: *'No society can surely be flourishing and happy of which the far greater part of its members are poor and miserable.'*[31]

In the 1790s, especially in 1795 and 1797, this process reached levels of despair not seen in living memory, as tens of thousands teetered on the edge of starvation. It was in these years that the common people, the 'wretched faces', found themselves hectored by clerics, politicians and landowners who urged them to turn to the potato for their salvation and diet.[32] Like the military conflict itself, this battle for the hearts and minds of the British people was a close-run thing. In the worst crisis years, relief agencies were all but overwhelmed by hungry people.[33] The potato came to their rescue.

Potato cultivation spread across Britain in the last years of the eighteenth century, driven forward by a series of overlapping forces – by poverty, population increase, by the force of example and by the contagion of increased availability. A great deal of the potato crop went to feed cattle. But it had also settled in ever more gardens and plots. Some people remained convinced that the potato would never take hold locally; that the poor were too committed to their traditional breads. But such attitudes *did* change, under the pressure of dire events and the persistent threat of mass starvation. The price of bread corn rose markedly in the 1770s and 1780s, precisely the years when the potato became more acceptable outside its traditionally popular regions of England. Thereafter, in the war years until 1815, the potato became the basic source of sustenance among large numbers of the poor.[34]

1795 was the crisis year; the year when few could ignore the precariousness of the nation's food supplies. It was obvious in different ways. The poor felt the problem in the rumbles from their hungry bellies; the government and propertied orders saw the crisis in the political strains and social unrest which rippled across the face of the nation. Hunger became a major political problem, worse possibly than at any time since the years of Elizabeth I. The poor law system was clearly inadequate (resulting eventually in the new Speenhamland system). The harvests of 1794 and 1795 were disasters which prompted a concerted drive to persuade people to move into potato cultivation. Men of property, but especially the clergy, set out to woo the poor consumer with the attractions of the potato. Events conspired to help them; their promptings, the stark absence of much-favoured breads, and the obvious benefits of potatoes, all seemed to wear down popular resistance. More and more people turned to the potato as the mainstay of their diet. In the words of *The Times* in September 1795: 'From the apprehension of a second year of scarcity, potatoes have been everywhere planted and their produce has been generally great.' Historians of British agriculture have been struck by a simple fact: after 1795 family budgets among the rural poor invariably included the cost of potatoes. Before that date, it had been unusual.[35]

In those terrible years of the mid-1790s, it was hard to distinguish the greatest threat to the status quo; the ascendant triumph of French arms, the strength of domestic British radicalism – or the simple corrosion of hunger among the common people. It was a hunger which ate into the nation's soul, fuelling political resentment and even transmitting the infection of despair into the heart of Britain's defences – the Royal Navy (in the naval mutinies of 1797). The century stumbled to a close through a series of desperate years; Irish rebellion, naval mutinies, bubbling domestic discontent. But above all else the pangs of collective hunger gnawed at the fabric of

British life. Had more people starved, the British system might not have survived. The French *ancien regime* had collapsed in the midst of widespread hunger. The British could easily have gone the same way. That it managed to struggle into the next century was in no small measure because the people's hunger was partly assuaged by the potato. Not for the last time, this peculiar gift of the Indian peoples of a remote part of South America had proved the salvation of other poor people on the far side of the world.

It is a striking fact that so many commodities of the wider world had infiltrated domestic British life by the end of the eighteenth century. Millions of people of all social ranks had come to depend on key foodstuffs and ingestibles for their nourishment and pleasures. Indeed they came to regard them as normal, so much a part of the unquestioned fabric of local life that their exotic origins had been lost in the mists of time. Who even *thought* of the potato, or of tobacco, as crops acquired from the Indian peoples of the America? Yet in the tortuous transmission of exotic crops into the fabric of European life, it is all too easy to view the process as the mere accidental by-product of trade and overseas exploration. It was, on the contrary, no mere exchange; no haphazard cross-over of peoples and goods between regions and cultures bumping into each other. At the heart of this transfer lay a harsh and ruthless exercise of power and ascendancy. Clearly, the acquisition of the potato was not in itself an act of that violence. But it flowed inexorably from the European conquest of the regions and the people of the Americas. In return for European domination, the Americas yielded materials which invaders, initially at least, scarcely imagined as important. Most were mere curiosities; costly luxuries destined to tickle the fancy of European elites. But within a century those distant products became the essentials of millions. None was more spectacular in its consequences than the potato which, on the eve of industrialization in Britain had become the necessary sustenance of armies of British working people. But if we need proof of the rapacious relationship which underpinned the Columbian exchange we need to look at another food which, like all the others discussed so far, established itself as a basic ingredient in British diet by the late eighteenth century. It is also a food whose history provides one of the most telling and instructive insights into the relationship between Europe (in this case Britain) and the wider world in the years after Columbus. Let us turn then to the story of sugar.

# 8 The African Gift: Sugar

The British are notorious for their sweet tooth. But this was not always so. In its early years in Britain, cane sugar was rare and costly. Throughout the Middle Ages sugar came to England from the Mediterranean and North Africa, bought by the weight or in loaves. Used to liven the dishes of the wealthy, it appeared in the household accounts of monarchs, aristocrats and higher clergy, and of those people keen to please others by offering them the height of contemporary culinary fancy. Sugar was used as an ingredient ('Sugar and spice and all things nice') and to heighten or diguise the taste of other foods. It had become a basic ingredient in the kitchens of the rich by the fifteenth century, its final form often appearing on their tables at the more elaborate meals which highlighted their ceremonies and festivals. Mixed with other ingredients, notably almonds to create marzipan, sugar could be shaped into the most elaborate (and durable) of fanciful shapes, a fashion which had crept into Europe from North Africa. Men prospering in business and trade, and keen to stake a claim to superior social rank, adopted culinary displays as a way of announcing their status; they invariably used sugar. People who were anxious to illustrate their standing often expressed their ambitions through complicated dishes made from sugar. One such, in Oxford in 1503, 'exhibited the eight towers of the university'.[1]

By the sixteenth century, in the wake of European colonization, the Atlantic islands of Madeira and the Canaries began to replace the Mediterranean as the main centres of sugar production. As supplies increased, more and more people in Britain used sugar. They were still, however, people of the prosperous classes, many of whom lacked ancestry and social standing but who were anxious to impress outsiders that their wealth gave them access to the social habits of monarchs and aristocrats. Lavish displays of costly food and drink were crowned by sugary displays – all as much for prestige as for consumption.

Sugar remained costly however; a pricey imported luxury, affordable only by a minority with spare cash. By the sixteenth century, when the first sugars from the Americas began to reach England (initially via Europe) one pound of sugar (at one shilling) was the equivalent of a labourer's wages for two days.[2] As sugar imports from the Americas grew in the course of the seventeenth century, prices fell and sugar slowly began to enter the social lives of humbler people. As it did so, those who previously flaunted their displays of sweetness in order to broadcast their position, turned to other commodities as evidence of their status. Here was a pattern which was to be repeated time and again over the succeeding centuries, as material well-being incorporated ever more people, driving the luxuries of the elites into the homes of the humble. Superior people consequently sought their pleasures and their displays of affluence elsewhere.

Along with other exotic goods, sugar arrived in England with a reputation as a medicine. A host of earlier societies had placed great store by sugar's curative and restorative qualities and it had a well-established niche in the influentiual traditions of Arabic medicine. Sugar was an important ingredient in a host of pharmacological preparations; used on its own, or in mixtures with other items, it was to be found on apothecaries' shelves throughout Europe in the early modern period. As sugar became more readily and cheaply available in the sixteenth century, its medicinal use increased. A number of contemporary medical authorities found in sugar (alone or in combination with other ingredients) an amazing range of wonderful cures and restorations: 'it mitigateth and openeth obstructions, It purgeth fleagme, helpeth the reines, and comforteth the belly.' Of course similar claims were made for a host of other items shortly after they made their first appearance in England. Tea, coffee, tobacco (even drinking seawater) all were alleged by their medical proponents to bestow the most miraculous of cures. Tropical staples then acquired their initial reputation and following in Europe as attractive additives to the apothecary's shelves.

Medical opinion about their value soon divided, however. To some, the increased use of sugar posed serious medical problems: it

> rotteth the teeth, making them look blacke, and withall, causeth many times a loathsome stinking-breath. And there-

fore let young people especially, beware how they meddle to much with it.[3]

This attack, published in 1663, came at a time of rising sugar prosperity, thanks to the slave islands in the Caribbean. Such views were not likely to endear themselves to an increasingly powerful West India lobby of merchants, shippers, manufacturers and planters, whose expanding wealth was based on sugar. The heart of the debate may have been medical – what benefits or problems were caused by sugar? – but behind the debate there lurked powerful vested interests keen to promote sugar, and to advance the belief that it was not merely enjoyable in itself, and as an ingredient with other foods and drinks, but also that it was healthy.

The most vigorous of sugar's medical advocates claimed that it was good for almost every part of the body; for the very young, for the very old, for the sick and for the healthy. It cured and prevented illnesses, it refreshed the weary, invigorated the weak. There were, said one writer in 1708, more than 300 medicines which contained sugar. And this was quite apart from its use in preservatives, pastries, cordials, cooked foods and puddings, all made possible by 'this noble juice'.[4] By that time, of course, the early eighteenth century, the price of sugar had plummeted, and this once-exclusive foodstuff which, not long before, had been an elaborate and costly item found only in the homes of the rich, had entered most people's homes. Sugar was now popular and ubiquitous – thanks to armies of Africans toiling in the cane fields of the West Indies.

Over the course of the seventeenth century, the cost of sugar fell by a half. In the fifty years to 1750 it dropped by another third. Though never really cheap, sugar had become universal by the early eighteenth century. Indeed as early as 1660 the English consumed some two pounds of sugar each year – mainly as a sweetener with other foods and drinks – and by the end of the century *per capita* consumption had risen to more than five pounds. A century later, on the eve of the French wars in the 1790s, the English ingested more than 20 pounds of sugar each year. The most explosive growth in English sugar consumption – more than 40 per cent in a decade – coincided with the emergence of tea drinking.[5]

The British liked their sugar refined. To cater for their tastes businessmen in ports throughout the country constructed refineries to process the crude sugar which arrived at the dockside in large hogsheads of unrefined sugar. Most of England's 50 refineries in the 1650s were located in London. A century later there were 80 in the capital, 20 in Bristol and likewise refining houses at 'Chester, Liverpool, Lancaster, Whitehaven, Newcastle, Kingston-upon-Hull, and Southampton, and a number in Scotland'.[6]

Sugar refineries were notorious fire hazards; one refiner shifted his business to Liverpool after London's Great Fire of 1666. The high premiums levied by insurance companies persuaded a group of refiners to form their own insurance company in 1782 – the origin of the modern Phoenix Assurance company. By the end of the century, there were some 150 refiners in Britain, of whom about a hundred were still located in London.[7] From those refineries sugar quickly spread to the whole nation. Sugar was everywhere. It was on sale in country shops and on the stalls of travelling pedlars. It was used in cooking and baking, in drinks and in medicines. Indeed it has been calculated that 10 per cent of all the money spent by the British on food was invested in sugar (or its derivative, treacle) and tea. Time and again, critics bemoaned the addiction of the British – especially working people – to sugar. Like tea – to which it was obviously and closely related – sugar seemed an extravagance; an imported luxury copied from the habits of social superiors.

When Sir Frederick Eden surveyed the habits of the English poor in the 1790s (a decade marked by rising destitution and, in many areas plain starvation) he was irritated to find sugar on the table of poor families wherever he turned. His family of six in southern England, living on £46 a year, bought two pounds of sugar each week. It was much the same in the north, where he studied a family of five who spent 10 per cent of their very low income on tea, treacle and sugar.[8]

Sugar had comprehensively penetrated the British diet by the late 18th century. The new cookbooks published for the discerning female managers of prosperous homes (and of course the books themselves were indicative both of rising prosperity and of a growing social attachment to a more sophisticated cuisine and entertainment) described a myriad uses for sugar. For the rich, there was that array of elaborate concoctions which had for centuries adorned their tables at lavish meals and feasts. For the rising middle classes – keen to join the circle of culinary pleasures – there was a host of fancy cakes and desserts. For the poor, left with the scraps of society's offerings, there was simpler fare; but that too was laced with sugar or treacle. 'Hasty pudding' contained treacles; so too did porridge. It was however for their desserts that the English reserved their most lavish additions of sugar:

> Hot puddings, cold puddings, steamed puddings, baked puddings, pies, tarts, creams, moulds, charlottes and bettys, trifles and fools, syllabubs and tansys, junkets and ices, milk puddings, suet puddings...[9]

Authors of eighteenth century cookbooks simply added the phrase 'sweeten to your taste' to their list of ingredients.[10] They knew that sweetness was not at issue; merely the degree of sweetness required by the cook and consumer. This list of items to be sweetened goes on and on and will be familiar to most British readers because it speaks to modern, not simply historical, experience. By 1800 the British consumption of sugar had grown by 2500 per cent in the space of the past 150 years.[11]

The amount of sugar arriving in Britain was very small in the early 1600s. All was changed by the rapid development of the slave colonies of the West Indies. The transfer of cane cultivation from the Mediterranean came in steps, first to the newly colonized Atlantic Islands and thence to those small islands off the African coast – notably São Tomé and Principe Jose. From there it was but a hop to the African coast itself. Sugar from the Atlantic islands was being marketed in Europe even before the establishment of the first tentative settlements in the Americas, in the wake of Columbus. And much of that sugar was cultivated by Africans.

When Columbus made his second voyage to the Americas in 1493, he carried with him sugar cane from the Canaries. By 1516 the first cane sugar was grown in the New World, in Santo Domingo, and shipped back to Spain. It was cultivated and processed by enslaved Africans, in a reprise of the labouring systems which had developed in the Canaries and the islands off Africa. It was a sure sign of the commercial importance and promise of the crop that wherever Europeans settled in the Americas they tried to grow sugar. With the prospect of good sugar prices in Europe, settlers everywhere tried to tap the land by turning labour over to sugar cultivation. By the late sixteenth century, led by the Portuguese, later the Dutch on their sugar settlements in Brazil, some of the bigger plantations employed 200–500 slaves. Understandably, the British were eager to follow suit when, from the 1620s, they too began to settle their own New World colonies. For many settlers, however, sugar proved a great disappointment (in Virginia for instance) but other regions succeeded beyond the wildest dreams of settlers and their London backers. And nowhere succeeded quite so spectacularly as Barbados.

The British turned to the Dutch, both for investment capital and for experience (in Brazil) of growing sugar. Though a range of crops were tried in Barbados in the early days, it was sugar that provided the bonanza settlers dreamed of. Within a generation of the British settlement, there were more than 300 plantations on the island; by 1690 there were almost 900. The island's high ground was dominated by hundreds of windmills, used for crushing the sugar cane. Here was a beautiful and fruitful wilderness which disgorged prosperity for the hard-working and the lucky. The original smallholdings began to give way to bigger plantations, as planters learned about economies of scale and the fortunate found themselves able to buy out struggling neighbours. The island was soon dominated and controlled by a core of senior planters, some with massive holdings, who flaunted their wealth in the island and Britain. They were living proof of the bounty that flowed from the sugar colonies. But the people who made all this possible, who created plantocratic wealth and satisfied British demand for sugar – the African slaves – got very little for their efforts.

There were some 20 000 slaves in Barbados in 1660, a figure which doubled in the next ten years. And though Barbados eventually developed a relatively stable local slave population, new Africans continued to arrive – normally in abject physical condition and all having suffered the horrors and traumas of the Atlantic crossing. Not surprisingly, many of the newly-arrived Africans were sick on arrival. Of the 180 000 landed in Barbados between 1700 and 1760, 50 000 died within the first three years. It seemed even worse in Jamaica, settled 25 years after Barbados in 1655. With perhaps 9000 slaves in 1670, Jamaica's black population increased dramatically in the rapid drive to sugar cultivation. Jamaican planters hurried to copy their Barbadian predecessors (and used their experience) by converting as much land as appropriate to sugar. The more land they brought into cultivation, the more slaves they needed. The more sugar they produced to satisfy apparently limitless British tastes, the more Africans the plantations devoured. By 1790 there were some 190 000 slaves in Jamaica. The main reason for the growth of the slave populations of the British Caribbean islands was sugar, though more and more of them were drawn into other work, in a range of diversified tasks and labours. But behind all this, behind the drive to sugar cultivation, was demand and taste 5000 miles away, in Europe.

The West Indian slaves were the human pawns in a remarkable economic system perfected by the British. Theoretically based (at least initially) – on a highly protected British market in which outsiders had little place, where British goods and produce enjoyed privileged access and movement, the 'mercantilist system' was never adequate to deliver enough Africans to the planters. Planters wanted – needed – more slaves than the formal system could deliver and in time the trade in humanity developed into a more open system. As it did so, ports the length and breadth of Britain hurried to benefit by dispatching local ships to trade in Africans. The British thus became the key transporters of human cargoes across the Atlantic in the course of the eighteenth century. The structures of life on the plantations and, above all else, the harshness and privations of life as a sugar slave had disastrous effects on the slaves' well-being and on their ability to reproduce. Planters therefore needed to turn to Africa for replenishment of their labourers. Thus, from the first days of sugar development in the Caribbean through to the parliamentary ending of the slave trade in 1807, Africa provided labour, in vast numbers, far beyond the ability of Europe, for instance, to provide free labour to toil in the sugar fields. Few could imagine sugar cultivation without slave labour.

In the seventeenth century, more than a quarter of a million Africans were imported into the British islands. Much of that trade had been conducted by the pioneering Dutch slave traders. By 1730 however, the British had become the dominant force in the Atlantic slave trade. Each year in the eighteenth century, the British shipped some 45 000 slaves across the Atlantic. Between 1690 and 1760 they transported about 1 200 000 Africans. In the next 50 years they carried 1 613 000. In the broad history of the Atlantic slave trade, the British carried some three million Africans into the New World. And all for what? The sole purpose of that African presence in the Americas was to produce crops to satisfy the tastes and needs of the western world.

The pioneering lead in sugar production fashioned by Barbados was overtaken by Jamaica in the eighteenth century. On the eve of the American Revolution, the 775 plantations on that island were worked by more than 200 000 slaves – Africans and their locally born descendants – (three times the number in Barbados). Jamaica's sugar revenue was worth £1.6 million a year and the island was far and away Britain's most valuable colony in the Americas. Indeed the planters became a byword for wealth and for the vulgar displays of their opulence in Britain and in the Caribbean. Returning to Britain with the fruits of their slaves' labour, they bought their way into land, property and political power, strutting the social stage, in London and the fashionable watering-holes, often to the amused distaste of 'old money'.

Sugar did more than revolutionize the tastes of the British people. It put into place a major economic and strategic system which lasted for more than two centuries and saw the lines of British trade and production directed along routes and towards destinations which were to dominate British global interests long after. The British involvement in West Africa and the Caribbean persisted long after slavery had ended, part of that continuing legacy of empire which proved more difficult to unravel than to create.

On top of that, sugar was the engine for the transformation of British overseas trade in a much wider sense. The old trading routes to and from Europe were now complemented as Britain placed itself at the centre of a remarkable global trading system, importing goods from around the world for its own consumption but also – and crucially – for re-export to other parts of the world. Europeans consumed sugar and tobacco transhipped via Britain; slaves were purchased on the

African coast in return for Asian textiles and cowrie shells from the Maldive Islands. What generated so much of this economic change was the simple cheapness of the goods which spilled forth from the cornucopia that was the plantation colonies of the Americas. The peoples of Europe were first of all seduced into buying the exotic products of the tropical colonies; soon they were addicted and could not imagine life without them. As they bought more and more tropical produce, the stimulus to British – and to global – economic activity was enormous. Stated crudely, a major consumer revolution was taking place. And it lay at the centre of what was part cause and part effect of the British rise to power as a world trader and as an international military force. It was, after all, the Royal Navy that guarded the shipping routes in the Atlantic. Indeed much of the military activity which swirled around the Atlantic in the eighteenth century was directly linked to considerations of British economic interests and the strategic issues of overseas possessions.

Even before the West Indian slaves produced any crops for export, they had to change the face of the world to which they had been brought. Unlike tea – the production of which remained hidden behind that veil of exclusionist Chinese secrecy in Canton – the produce of the Americas was closely controlled, cultivated, processed and shipped by Europeans (and the African slaves). At first however, the Europeans saw nothing in the Americas but a wilderness that promised much but had to be tamed, cleared and brought into organized cultivation (quite apart from the persistent threat posed by the native peoples of the region). The slaves shaped the fields, built the roads, constructed the dwellings, the walls; indeed most of the man-made artefacts of the tropical colonies were, in some way or other, the work of the slaves. And of course it was their efforts that conjured forth the harvests from the land, and that filled the ships which plied the Atlantic shipping lanes.

From the first, sugar was perhaps the harshest of crops. All the indices of slaves' social experience were at their worst in the sugar settlements; work itself, mortality, sickness, infant mortality, all and more were worse in the sugar colonies than in most other forms of slave work in the Americas. And 70 per cent of *all* slaves shipped into the Americas were destined, initally at least, for work in the cane fields. Field work, in large gangs, was harsh, and the discipline administered by the whites and their agents even harsher. Nor did life's tribulations end when the acres of sugar cane had been cleared and removed from the fields, for it was then transported to the factory for processing; a hot, noisome and exhausting business. At the peak times of the sugar harvest, (between January and June) field slaves were driven from the fields to work in the neighbouring factories. Long before a European proletariat had been tamed for factory work, African slaves had been similarly disciplined for work in the West Indian sugar factories. Quite simply, sugar was, from first to last, a terrible taskmaster. And all this was in addition to whatever slings and arrows local whites might capriciously hurl at their slave gangs.

The sugar cane was crushed, the juice boiled, evaporated and refined in a series of movements through the sugar factory. Transferred to copper 'coolers', the sugar finally granulated and was then poured into large earthenware 'potts'. The raw sugar, still fairly crude and very wet, was loaded into large 1800 pound hogsheads, which were allowed to drain for a few weeks before the laborious task of transporting them to the coast. The sugar in the hogsheads was crude brown muscavado (which travelled better than other grades of sugar), but it was only partly refined. When the cargo was unloaded in Britain, the sugar needed further refinement – hence the proliferation of refineries in British ports. From there it was passed to the myriad shops and retail outlets which formed the network for consumer goods by the mid-eighteenth century.

Simply getting those vast casks of sugar to the ships involved demanding and strenuous efforts by the slaves. Plantations closest to water were the best placed to discharge their sugar (and its by-product rum). For inland plantations (and some of the most fruitful were developed in inland valleys), separated from coastal landings by difficult mountains, the tasks of transporting sugar meant a reliance on teams of oxen and horses, and suitably trained (and trustworthy) slaves specializing in transport and beasts. Long before the hogsheads were stored in the ships' holds, the sugar had passed through a number of hands, from factory to ox-wain to small boat.

Sugar was, then, a most cumbersome and difficult staple to cultivate, produce and transport. It required labour which was itself shipped across the Atlantic (after having been kidnapped and herded together in Africa), labour which was alien, which did not (at first) speak the Europeans' languages, was unaccustomed to the stinging perculiarities of sugar's labouring system; it was labour which died in horrifying numbers, which rebelled and resisted as a matter of course. The result of the slaves' efforts – the hogsheads of sugar loaded into the ships' holds – were utterly reliant on British shipping, itself vital both for imported goods and foodstuffs, and for the export of the sugar and rum. By the end of the seventeenth century 200 ships called at Barbados each year; about 100 at Jamaica.[12] Between 1696 and 1700, 615 ships landed in Barbados from Britain.[13] And hundreds of ships cleared from British ports bound for the first leg of that trade, to West Africa, to secure the African slaves needed in the sugar fields of the West Indies. In the 1730s, 378 ships left Bristol for Africa; between 1764 and 1769, 449 left Liverpool with the same purpose.[14]

Whatever difficulties were faced by planters and traders in producing sugar – problems with the natural environment, with labour, with transport, problems created by military and civil unrest (to say nothing of the natural difficulties posed by the crop and the produce) – the sugar lobby was not easily deterred or deflected from their lucrative task of bringing sugar to the British consumer. Above all else, the sugar lobby was an amazingly persistent and durable group, surviving warfare, slave rebellion, devastating hurricanes and fearful levels of slave mortality. Their sole ambition was to grow rich on the success of sugar. And as a result, ever more sugar descended on British ports from the mid-seventeenth century onwards. The few thousand tons of the early 1650s had become more than 23 000 tons in 1700. A century later the figure had increased tenfold, and stood at some 245 000 tons.[15] Thereafter, when a wider world turned to ever-cheaper sugar (more and more of it grown by non-slave labour, much of it, later, extracted from sugar beet, not sugar cane) the consumption of sugar reached astronomical levels. By 1830 world production reached 572 000 tons; 30 years later it stood at one and a third million tons.[16] By then, the former slaves of the British West Indies had become a free black peasantry, struggling to come to terms with their new-found liberty in a harsh economic and social climate. Yet it was their efforts, and those of their forbears, which had been so important in changing the face of the modern world in a host of ways which few of them could have recognized. At its simplest, they had converted the world to a desire for sweetness. As the slave colonies of the British Caribbean had become black (an image, visitors were apt to say, of Africa itself) so did the British become utterly addicted to the sweet produce of slave labours. But so too were they wedded to the produce grown by unknown armies of Chinese labourers on the other side of the world.

Sugar was consumed in any number of ways, but if any single factor goes to explain the rise and persistently high levels of British sugar consumption it must surely be their habit of drinking sweet tea. It was that mix of tea and sugar which so annoyed prosperous commentators when they gazed with incomprehension at the eating habits of the mid-eighteenth century British poor. Writing of Nottinghamshire, Charles Deering said:

> ...being the other day at a Grocers, I could not forbear looking earnestly and with some Degree of Indignation at a ragged and greasy Creature, who came into the Shop with two Children following her in as dismal a Plight as the Mother, asking for a Pennyworth of Tea and a Half pennyworth of Sugar, which when she was served with, she told the Shop-Keeper: Mr N. I do not know how it is with me, but I can assure you that I would not desire to live, if I was to be debarred from drinking every Day a little Tea.[17]

And, presumably, a little sugar to taste.

Yet it was surely a curious fact that tea, in its native Chinese habitat, was not taken with sugar. And wherever the association between tea and sugar was established (in India for example under the Raj and following the creation of the Indian tea industry in the 1840s) it stemmed directly from British influence. The simple question remains unanswered; why had the Chinese enjoyed their tea for centuries without the addition of tea, but the British, by the early eighteenth century, could not imagine one without the other? Cost alone will not explain the matter. It is perfectly true that the cost of both sugar and tea fell dramatically, at much the same time. But why put the two together, in a custom which was new and quite out of keeping with the traditional methods of drinking tea?

It is clear enough (from Dutch sources) that people were adding sugar to their tea in the 1670s and 1680s. Thirty years later it was common there and in Britain, and in another twenty years sweet tea was to be found in all social classes in Britain. It seems then that it was in the years 1685–1700 that the habit spread quickly and universally in Britain. And these were the very years when the recently established sugar economy of Jamaica began to disgorge its produce to the British consumer. Between 1700 and 1730, the slave population of the island probably doubled (to 80 000). In 1700 Jamaica produced only half as much sugar as Barbados; by 1730 it equalled its Caribbean rival in sugar production. A generation later, Jamaica not only produced four times as much sugar as Barbados, but actually more than a half of the total output of all the British islands. The 4500 tons of Jamaican sugar produced in 1700 had grown to 13 000 tons in 1730.[18] These were precisely the years when tea and sugar came together in what, subsequently, commentators have taken to be the traditional British way of drinking tea. But, like all traditions, this had a specific origin, and was rooted in the particulars of British overseas expansion and settlement.

The decades of massive sugar importations paralleled changes in the use of sugar. The earlier lavish displays of sugar-based foodstuffs – the ornate sculptures and figures to adorn the tables of the rich – became less fashionable. As sugar became more popular, so it declined as a recognizable and distinguishing feature of the life of the wealthy. What social cachet was there to be had from flaunting a substance now within the economic reach of everyone and which, increasingly, found its way into millions of cups of tea? The wealthy continued to use sugar of course, just as millions of their poorer contemporaries used it. Henceforth sugar in the homes of the rich became just another ingredient kept by servants in pantries and kitchens, to be added to whatever dish or drink seemed appropriate, rather than offered as a display of status and wealth. The lady of the house used it when she entertained her lady friends to afternoon tea. By the early eighteenth century, tea-drinking had become common to all sorts and conditions. But the rituals involved were clearly different from social group to another. Though upper- and working-class people all drank tea with sugar, the social rituals of tea-drinking were sharply demarcated by the distinquishing rituals of different social classes.

The well-to-do evolved elaborate and stylish tea-drinking ceremonies. Tea was taken in the home, at specific times, using costly equipment – and all to its own highly ritualized etiquette. Tea of course had its medical applications, but these had become much less important by the late seventeenth century. The major impetus towards polite tea-drinking was its fashionableness. As early as 1694 Congreve's *The Double Dealer* noted that women were 'at the end of the gallery, retired to their tea and scandal, according to ancient custom, after dinner.'[19]

The lady of the house left the dinner table to prepare the tea, a habit which seems to have launched the pattern of ladies retiring to enjoy their own company over tea (or coffee), leaving the menfolk alone. As the eighteenth century advanced, tea became part of that encroaching *chinoiserie,* which included porcelains, silk carpets and Chinese wallpaper; only the wealthy could afford such items. Tea for breakfast, and afternoon tea became part of the daily ritual of propertied life by the early part of the century.

There are any number of contemporary paintings which capture these tea-drinking rituals. The furnishings, the surroundings, the tableware; all and more speak to the world of prosperous social habits. It was a routine of domestic life which was quickly translated to the well-to-do in the American colonies. There too tea was drunk with sugar. It was a drink to which guests were invited in the afternoon, offering an occasion for card-playing, for courtship and for social chit-chat, (and did so into the nineteenth and twentieth centuries). On both sides of the Atlantic, fashionable tea-drinking rituals continued long after tea itself had become the drink of the common people. But wherever artists captured eighteenth century tea-drinking rituals, there among the display of cups, saucers and teapots, was to be found the sugar bowl. The standard tea-set of the early 1700s, whether in porcelain or metal, contained a matching sugar bowl. Another indispensable item on the tea table was a pair of sugar tongs. The portrait of a 'Tea Party in the Time of George I' (now kept in the Colonial Williamsburg collection) displays all the tableware needed for tea – including the silver tongs. Along with teaspoons, such tongs provide clear enough evidence of the connection between sugar and tea. But, again, the habits were cheapened by time and widening usage. By the mid-eighteenth century, sugar tongs were available in cheap wooden form.[20] The alliance of sugar and tea was, then, as common in respectable society as it was among the poor. The woman and her dirty children, offending our observer in Nottinghamshire by their grubby presence, insisted on both tea and sugar. So too did the grandest of ladies, dispensing tea to her fashionable friends in the most expensive of porcelain or silver teaware.

At precisely the same time that Chinese tea began to arrive in ever greater volume, slave-grown sugar arrived in Britain in increasing abundance. It was no accident that, thereafter, the increasingly powerful West India lobby, those men at the heart of the slave colonies and their supply system, actively *encouraged* tea consumption. They knew that the more tea the British drank, the more sugar they would need. Unlike the Chinese, the British could not drink their tea without the sweet additive. The end result of this simple combination was not only the development of this distinctive British taste – thereafter exported round the world wherever the British lived, settled or explored – but the securing of crucial trading routes to the Caribbean and to China. Only those who criticized the apparent luxury of the poor for consuming foodstuffs imported over such vast distances pondered about the curiosity. The rest – the millions of British tea-drinkers – simply got on with their tea-drinking pleasures.

It was an unexplained oddity that the British addiction to tea is unlikely to have developed without the availability of sugar. And cheap, ubiquitous sugar was unthinkable without African slaves. Chinese labourers and African slaves came together to create, and then satisfy, one of the most widespread and durable pleasurable needs of the British people.

# 9 The Cause of All Distress: Plantations

The British appetite for those staples which were disgorged by returning ships in ever greater profusion did more than simply transform the tastes of the western world. In cultivating those crops, vast regions of the world were brought under careful, regulated cultivation. The wilderness was won over and converted to the fruitful and profitable production of crops, many of them not even indigenous to the region. From Java to Jamaica, Virginia to Assam, from Fiji to Malaya, Brazil to Congo, tropical regions were utterly transformed by the drive towards managed tropical agriculture. In time, of course, those regions – and many more – yielded an amazingly diverse bounty to outside investors. But of all the agricultural systems they tried, it was the plantation, above all others, which left an indelible mark on huge expanses of the world. By the seventeenth century wherever Europeans settled they turned to the plantation as a means of settlement and economic development. Of course it did not always succeed. But when they found the right locations, and the ideal combination of circumstances – as they did with increasing regularity – here was a system (of land settlement, labour-management and political control) which in a short space of time began to yield material returns like no other. It profited European settlers, traders and sailors, and it enriched their backers at home; in the banks, merchant houses – and governing circles – in Lisbon, Amsterdam, London and Bordeaux.

The British initially developed the plantation system for the more effective colonization of Ireland. It was to give the invading English and Scots a form of land-ownership and political control which would subdue the native peoples and win over the land to the benefit of the settlers and their mother country. The planting of Ireland was, in the words of Roy Foster 'to provide laboratory conditions for the chemistry of the civilizing process.'[1] Carefully planned outside Ireland, this alien solution to the Irish problem – how best to subdue, civilize and exploit local peoples, and to intrude into their midst an alien settler class – was to sow the seeds of discontent for the next three centuries. It was a special case. But historians of the plantation have generally overlooked Ireland. Yet here was an early example of what could be achieved by alien, restless people, keen to shift from their homelands, and searching for ways of imposing themselves in distant parts of the world. Ireland no less than Barbados or Virginia was to bear the scars of plantation settlement long after the original purpose had been forgotten.

When the English embarked on their early settlements in the Americas, many of the pioneers were aware of what had already been tried in Ireland. Raleigh was only the most famous of a host of English adventurers and settlers who approached the Americas with memories of Ireland. What they needed in the New World was a beach-head; secure, garrison-like settlements which would provide safety against native peoples (and other Europeans), permit the development of the local land and provide a trading link to the metropolis. Once secure, such bases became a mix of the Irish plantation settlements and the trading outposts established by Europeans in Asia.[2] Despite some early failures, the plantation proved an ideal system; a perfect means of conquering the land, overawing local peoples and creating wealth. But it needed more hands than could be provided by the pioneering settlers. Labour was to be the key to the success or failure of many plantations. And the problems of labour were to become paramount when settlers turned to new crops.

The plantation had been a well-established feature of economic organization long before Europeans looked to the Americas. Western Europe's first effective encounters with the plantation had been in the era of the crusades. An eye-witness account of the first crusade told how

> in these fields... were certain ripe plants which the common folk called 'honey cane' and which were very much like reeds... In our hunger we chewed them all day because of the taste of honey.[3]

Sugar cane from the plantations of the eastern Mediterranean found its way to Europe, establishing, as we have seen, that taste which was to remain an elite fad until the cheapening of cane sugar in the seventeenth century. Sugar was produced on plantations in Tyre and Tripoli (Lebanon), Cyprus and Sicily – and those plantations were worked by slaves drawn from throughout the Mediterranean region. The sugar plantations of the Mediterranean were small however, but as sugar production moved on from the Mediterranean and into the Atlantic islands of Madeira, the Canaries and Cape Verde, the size of plantations increased. Finally, as European maritime expansion and exploration moved ever further south, the islands in the Gulf of Guinea provided an ideal spot for plantation sugar production.

Each step forward on this progress towards firmer European colonization of the wider world brought greater sophistication in the plantation production of sugar. Even before the move across the Atlantic, the sugar industry had changed. Production became more sophisticated, it was backed by complex international finance, and it generated growing prosperity for European traders and backers. But all this was as nought compared to what was to follow. Perhaps more important still, the economic *potential* of a plantation system became increasingly attractive to those interested in overseas colonization and economic development. There were plenty of backers, governmental supporters and entrepreneurs keen to invest in whatever developments seemed viable in those distant experiments over the horizon.

After a number of unsuccessful attempts, in 1517 the Spanish successfully planted sugar in Santo Domingo. Later they undertook smaller developments on other islands they had conquered in the region. But their interest and energies were sooned lured elsewhere, namely to Mexico and Peru, where the wealth of the New World revealed itself in the most fabulous displays of precious metals. Plantations thrived elsewhere, however, notably in Portuguese Brazil, where from the 1540s sugar cultivation took hold, doubling in the first 20 years and again over the next two decades.[4] By 1600 more than 16 000 tons of sugar was produced by Brazilian plantations. No one could now doubt that here was a commodity – and a region – which, with careful plantation management, could sweep all before it. In Brazil, the plantation had proved its value. With technology from the Atlantic islands, labour from the locality, finance from Antwerp, Portuguese settlers had shaped rudimentary plantations. But from early days, they faced the problem of labour.

The Indian peoples in Brazil (and, as we have seen, throughout the hemisphere) died off on contact with Europeans. Following the example of their mentors and predecessors, settlers in Brazil turned to Africa for a regular – and apparently inexhaustible – supply of labour. In the form of slave labour, it had the added advantage of being permanent (if it survived, of course). Slave owners did not have to worry about the end of their labourers' contracts. Better still (for the planters) the slaves bequeathed their bondage to their offspring. In the words of one commentator on slavery, 'The Negro slaves are never out of their *Bondage*, and the Children they get, are likewise perpetual *slaves*.'[5]

The example of Brazil – where the plantations were transformed by African labour – was very quickly followed by other Europeans as they settled into their own colonial outposts, especially on that arc of islands in the Caribbean.

The importance of the plantation in the settlement of the British American colonies can be gauged from the fact that a Committee of the Privy Council was created in 1660 to oversee the process; later it was superseded by an even more important Council: the 'Council of Trade and Plantations'. The British launched their first tropical plantations in Barbados where the pioneering smallholders soon began to give way to bigger plantations. By 1650 there were about 300 of them, most on the leeward shore, affording a spectacular reminder to arriving vessels of the source of the island's prosperity. Two decades later there were 900. From the right spots, it was even possible to see 400 windmills (used for crushing the cane). Less visible in such vistas – but crucial for all that – were the armies of slaves, mainly Africans, whose sweat made everything possible. From one island to another, a similar story repeated itself; of pioneering smallholders (soldiers, adventurers, migrants from other colonies – a remarkable mix of peoples and cultures) quickly giving way to ever-larger plantations. And the reason was sugar.

Within a generation of settlement, maps of the sugar islands showed the terrain dotted with plantations. The vistas of the islands were slowly changing. As more and more land was brought into cultivation, the savage beauty of the islands took on a entirely different face. With the bush cut back, burned and reconstituted, where once there had been luxuriant primeval foliage, there was now the more orderly arrangements of man-made systems; of fields and tracks, of buildings and walls – and acres of sugar cane. But what made everything possible were the slaves, imported in vast and growing numbers from the ships arriving from the African coast; disgorged – the human cargoes of that pestilential trade – they were destined for a lifetime's labour in an alien habitat. The planters and their agents waited for the Africans with an impatience born of pressing economic necessity. 'And these they Buy on Ship-board, as men Buy Horses in a Fayr.'[6]

Maps provide one way into the story. An early map of British Jamaica named 146 plantations; 13 years later they had increased to 690.[7] Their origins were simple. A mere handful of slaves, indentured whites and their generally poor owners clawed at the land, rendering it fruitful and providing themselves with a decent habitat. Their first task was to create shelter for themselves; thereafter to plant food. As Jamaica boomed, its early smallholdings giving way to larger plantations based on sugar, the centre of economic and political gravity shifted from Barbados to Jamaica. Contemporaries felt confident that 'in a short time without doubt it will become the most potent and richest *Plantation* in the *West Indies*'.[8]

The islands were plantations; their basic social atom was the plantation; their governing and social elite consisted of plantation owners – and the great bulk of the population (imported African slaves) toiled on the plantations. Of course beneath these facts lay a much more complex social and economic mosaic. But the plantation had, by the late seventeenth century, established itself as the crucial element in the settlement and development of the tropical New World. Though the British now led the way, thanks to the sugar revolution, a similar tale could be repeated elsewhere in the tropical Americas. What dazzled outsiders – and what lured settlers from Europe (despite the appalling risks of death and disease) were the stories of remarkable material success. Land, in those 'Gardens of the Indies', coupled to servile African labour would yield a bounty beyond the wildest of expectations. Of course it required good luck as much as hard work (mainly by the Africans). But few doubted that the plantations were a cornucopia; the instrument from which flowed wealth in an abundance rarely known before.

At first the plantations were crude; a clearing of land on which black and white lived out a basic and barely sufficient pioneering existence. But with sophistication came the sugar. And with sugar came profits and the ability to transform the plantations. They began to take on the shape that remains in the mind's eye. In some cases we can capture that image because the same plantations survive to this day. The fields, the factories, the roads, the slave villages and huts; the specifics varied but the broad outlines were familiar to all visitors to the islands. In the most spectacular cases, the planters were able to retreat from the confusion of plantocratic work into those wonderful homes, built on commanding positions, on hilltops, on the bend of the river, close enough to keep an eye on the slaves but far enough away from slave noises and smells.

From that motley band of settling whites there emerged that new social group – the plantocracy – which became a caricatured byword for colonial wealth (though only the minority rose to such heights). They were the equivalent of the Indian nabobs; people of immense wealth and standing whose prosperity was fashioned on the far edges of colonial life (notwithstanding the fact that many were crude and lacked the cultural attributes of the European groups to which they aspired). They stood for the fabulous riches of empire. As time passed, the more successful planters, who came to dominate their islands' economies, were able to build bigger and bigger plantation-holdings. By the mid-eighteenth century, half of Jamaica's planters owned more than 500 acres. In 1774 the medium-sized Jamaican plantation, worked by 200 slaves, was 600 acres. By the 1770s, the average slave-holding in the British islands stood at 240 – with the inevitable problems of labour discipline and social control attendant on large slave-holdings. Here then was that unique mix which was to prove so important: American land, African labour and European investment and management. Each ingredient was vital. But the most dramatic – so extraordinary and far-reaching in its consequence on both sides of the Atlantic – were the slaves. The ships from Africa disembarked armies of slaves; by 1772 about 1.5 million had been deposited in the British islands alone.

In colonial North America it was different. There, slaves formed a much smaller proportion of the overall population. Rarely did they outnumber the whites but here, once again, the plantation proved the crucible for the American slave experience. North American plantations were smaller than their West Indian counterparts; on the eve of American Independence, the large majority of Virginian slaves were owned in small groups of five or fewer, though successful planters tended to develop ever bigger slave and tobacco holdings. Of course we remember the wealthier planters, those able to construct those beautiful houses which today stand as elegant reminders to plantocratic wealth and power. It was a curious mix; houses which were sophisticated reminders of Europe on the very edge of colonial and African dangers.[9]

Nowhere in North America resembled the Caribbean more than South Carolina. There, with the development of the rice plantations between 1690 and 1720, slaves came to outnumber whites. In 1740 there were some 40 000 Africans in the region and it was they who, again, broke the savage back of the hostile local environment, converting the unpleasant and dangerous coastal swamplands into those extensive rice plantations whose produce flowed back to Europe. Everywhere we look – whatever the local crop produced by the slaves – the broad outlines were the same; toiling masses of black slaves living, by and large, in rural poverty, cheek by jowl with prospering planters who were able to retire to their fashionable great houses, to local urban communities or even to retreat with their profits and newly-created status, back 'home' to Europe.

There were enormous differences between these plantations in the Americas. Some were massive, toiled over by armies of Africans and supervised by an elite of prospering whites. Others were tiny; places where black and white worked closely together, sharing the same tasks of tobacco and coffee cultivation, processing and packaging. On sugar and rice plantations, work – at the height of the season, at the arduous times of planting and harvesting – was tough in the extreme. Other crops – grown in gentler environments and at a less exacting pace – were less damaging to the labour force (a fact confirmed by the demographic data from the different regions). But in all cases, it was the plantations' labour forces that created the wealth and life-styles of their owners, the planters, and shaped the European taste for those distant fruits of empire.

Each tropical crop had its own cycle of loading, dispatch and shipping; from the waterside of the Americas to the dock-sides of Britain. But, as demand grew and as produce increased year by year, the British gave a warm welcome to the fruits of empire. Coffee for the London coffee-houses from the Blue Mountains of Jamaica, rice (20 million pounds in 1720) from the steamy lowlands of South Carolina (destined to be both starch and nourishment), tobacco from the vast reaches of the Chesapeake destined for pipes and snuff boxes, from the highest to the lowest. And, of course, that sweet additive for a host of other drinks and dishes – the sugar from the slave plantations on most Caribbean islands.

Who could doubt, as they enjoyed these varied products, at home or in the convivial environment of the tavern or coffee-house, that the plantation was a quite remarkable institution. It had transformed, firstly, Ireland; later, huge swathes of the Americas. It was the instrument which had brought the wilderness to heel, had cowed and disciplined millions of Africans and, as if all that were not enough, had been the source of apparently limitless wealth to Europeans on both sides of the Atlantic. It was scarcely surprising that Europeans would turn to the idea of the plantation wherever they traded or settled as a means of securing the best returns (for themselves) from tropical regions. Not only that, but the experience of the Americas had shown that plantations could be successfully worked to the profit of all (save the labourers) even in the absence of suitable local labour. Experience in the Americas had confirmed that labour could be recruited (bought, bartered or contracted) in one part of the globe, shipped to a distant region and there licked into profitable shape by the plantation system. Thanks to superior European technology, firepower and ever-increasing economic strength, labour in the colonial fringes was no longer a problem. Surplus labour could be conjured forth from one quarter of the world to enhance plantation development in another. It was a bizarre twist of events.

What made the plantations doubly attractive was the wealth they produced for that lucky elite who occupied the great house. The material well-being, the homes, the exiled splendours of planters from across the Americas, were frequently remarked on in London and Britain's fashionable watering-holes. Those who saw the planters on their home patch could not but admire their domestic wealth, especially the grander homes in North America. Caribbean planters on the other hand sometimes got it wrong. Bryan Edwards for examples noticed the contrast

> between the general plenty and magnificence of their tables (at least in Jamaica) and the meanness of their homes and apartments; it being no uncommon thing to find, at the country inhabitations of the planters, a splendid sideboard loaded with plate, and the choicest of wines, a table covered with the finest damask, and a dinner of perhaps sixteen or twenty covers; and all this in a hovel not superior to an English barn.[10]

Many of these West Indian planters were clearly magnates of remarkable standing able to command the best that money could buy. Looking back, we can see that much of their status was mere pretence; many of them were indebted to agents, shippers and bankers, often on the other side of the Atlantic. But appearances counted. And few appeared grander than the most notable of planters.

It seemed then that the plantation was vindicated at every turn. There was of course a debit side to what most Europeans viewed as a success story. But the price for plantocratic success was generally paid by humble people who were out of sight and out of mind; those legions of servile labourers, plucked from their homelands in their millions, subjected to the unimaginable horrors of the Atlantic crossing and then consigned to a lifetime's bondage. The damage which the plantation system inflicted on Africa was incalculable. So too was the damage done to the peoples of the Americas (though that process had been set in train by the disease-bearing Europeans before the introduction of the plantation). As plantations and other European settlements absorbed ever more land, native peoples moved on, drifting away from that fatal contact which brought them little but suffering; disease, drunkenness, dislocation and death. They secured a few material items in return of course – and access to the white man's God – but how could these be weighed in the balance against the collapse of their own cultures, and the destruction of their own cosmologies? They lost their lands – so often the very basis for their beliefs and customs – in that inexorable European drive to engulf the best (later the entirety) of the Americas. Clearly, there was more at work here than the mere plantation. But we need to remind ourselves that the plantation was the effective springboard for the subsequent invasion of the Americas. From the Plymouth plantation, south to Virginia and South Carolina; from the Caribbean settlements to Brazil, the plantations enabled Europeans to launch their invasive settlement of the Americas.

The plantation's prime purpose and justification lay, however, in its ability to conjure forth tropical staples. In the process, they brought into being a quite remarkable – and global – trading and economic complex. Though the plantation was integral to that economic system, in time changes in other sectors would have massive consequences for the plantations themselves. What would happen, for instance, if the supply of labour dried up? With the exception of North America (where the slave population began to reproduce itself from an early date) most plantation societies in the Americas relied for the increase of their labour force not on natural growth, but on the slave trade; on the continuing importations of new African slaves. Indeed the plantations, and planters, became such prominent issues in metropolitan life because they and their spokesmen were active in promoting the slave trade. The plantations needed the Atlantic slave trade and powerful lobbyists were active throughout the seventeenth and eighteenth centuries in the major metropolitan centres promoting it.

By the late eighteenth century no one doubted, when they discussed plantations, that they meant *slave* plantations. The one could not exist without the other. Yet time was to show that the plantation was wonderfully malleable and could quickly adapt to a world of free labour (although in the process imposing on the labour force stringent conditions that corroded their freedom). In the last decade of the eighteenth century however the slave planters' world began to fall apart. The seismic changes unleashed by the American, but more especially the French Revolution, destabilized the slave plantations. The plantation found itself under fierce attack from a growing band of abolitionists, who singled out the plantation as the cause and occasion of the misery of the slaves; the magnet which lured millions of Africans to their wretched fate. These attacks were inspired by a changing sensibility. It was increasingly difficult (in philosophy, if not in economics) to justify slavery in a world persuaded of the idea of the rights of man. In a political debate which hinged on the ideals of 'Liberty, Equality, Fraternity', plantation slavery stood out as the worst example of the old order's shortcomings. If any single institution from the old regime deserved to be removed it was surely slavery. The problem however was that western consumers wanted – and consumed in growing profusion – the fruits of slave labours. Perhaps they should be persuaded to deny themselves their pleasures on behalf of the slaves?

Wedgwood manufactured an abolitionist cameo emblazoned with the motif 'Am I not a Man and a Brother?'.[11] Here was England's greatest contemporary entrepreneur appealing to the humane senses of people with spare cash for political luxuries. Indeed it was a sign of the political power of the consumer that abolitionists launched their 'anti-saccharite' campaign, designed to persuade people not to buy sugar. Their theory was simple. If fashionable society could be persuaded to forgo the sugar they consumed with their drink and food, the abolitionist campaign would edge forward. A fall in sugar consumption would hurt the planters and persuade them to treat their slaves better. And if they could treat their slaves better, those same slaves would enjoy a better quality of life, would consequently be able to reproduce more readily, and hence there would be no further need for the supplies of fresh Africans crossing the Atlantic. It was an analysis which was altogether too simple, but it had a distinct plausibility to an audience unfamilair with all but the broad outlines of the plantation complex. The abolitionist debate focused on the plantation, but once again the plantation was to prove itself remarkably flexible in the teeth of opposition. Although North America had learned to manage with its existing stock of slaves, the Caribbean slave plantations continued to need their regular infusions of Africans. After 1807, when the British ended the slave trade, the plantations had to revise their strategies. Thereafter, as the Royal Navy was ordered to impose the abolitionist policy, the West Indian planters were starved of new Africans. As the older generations of Africans died out, a new phenonenon emerged; a slave population born and raised in the islands, knowing only the plantations and their island hinterland. The plantations began to change, not least because planters had to adjust to the changing slave population; the old problems of disciplining and socializing Africans faded, to be replaced by other taxing problems. Yet plantations remained recognizably the same. They looked the same, they produced the same staples and the basic division (white owners and black servile labour force) remained the same. Whatever else had changed, plantations proved themselves resilient institutions.

When the British freed their slaves (between 1834 and 1838), large numbers quit the plantations. Freedom meant more than simply being paid a pittance to work for their former owners. In some places, especially on smaller islands where there was little or no spare land, the freed slaves had no real alternative but to continue to work on the plantations. In time however, the planters began to demand a new source of labour. They had heard that 'coolies' (indentured Indians) had been successful in Mauritius, and persuaded the Colonial Office to approve a similar scheme of importing some to the West Indies. By 1841, 7000 had settled in the Caribbean to do the work vacated by ex-slaves. Despite fierce opposition in Britain (led by the abolitionists) the scheme took off. It continued until 1919, by which time more than half a million Indians had been transported (in conditions which reminded unhappy observers of the old slave trade). Guiana attracted 250 000, Trinidad 134 000, and Jamaica 33 000.[12]

Few of the Indians returned home at the end of the five-year indenture, most merging with ex-slaves as poor peasants or plantation labourers. But they had been imported specifically to work on the plantations, and though the West Indian sugar industry went into steep decline, especially from the 1840s because of more open competition in the world sugar markets (and the availability of cheaper, non-cane sugars), their presence was, yet again, further evidence of the power and resilience of the plantations. It was an ironic twist that the former slave colonies of the West Indies now faced commercial opposition from new plantation societies. But, in a changed climate which was hostile to slavery, these new developments were based on plantations without slaves. India – not Africa – provided an ideal recruiting ground for cheap labour, which, though free, was heavily restricted – and (of course) poorly paid. In Mauritius and Réunion new plantations thrived, helped by the proximity of India and the co-operation of the British Indian authorities. Those experiments proved that plantations could succeed without African slaves. Having said that, Europeans continued to turn to Africa for many of their labouring needs in the West Indies, and both France and Britain developed 'voluntary' schemes to persuade Africans to migrate to distant labour, but only about 30 000 agreed to join.[13]

Plantations needed much bigger – and more reliable – supplies than this. And as proof of the continuing vitality of the plantation we need to recall that an *illegal* Atlantic slave trade continued long after the British abolition of 1807. Despite the Royal Navy, Europeans, Americans and Brazilians took great commercial risks to ship Africans (mainly from Central Africa) to the plantations of Cuba and Brazil. Between 1820 and 1870 the Royal Navy seized 1600 ships and 150 000 slaves from 'illegal' Atlantic slave traders.[14] There were plenty of people willing to risk everything to trade in African slaves for the simple reason that plantations continued to provide the western world with its much-sought-after staples.

Demand for the exotic produce of plantations was driven forward by the extraordinary rise in European wealth. The first half of the nineteenth century saw Europeans, led by the British, enriched by the rapid development of industrial change. Though many people were, in the short term, immiserated by industrialization, in time material well-being passed to most people, and on a scale few could have imagined. Ever more people were able to buy more and more items (clothing, furnishings, luxuries – and foodstuffs). Not surprisingly they bought tropical staples – which by the early nineteenth century were firmly established favourites among western tastes – in remarkable volumes. While the British *per capita* consumption of sugar in 1700 was four pounds, a century later it stood at eighteen pounds. By the mid-nineteenth century it had doubled.[15] Of course sugar was not sought for its own sake, but for its additive value to a range of other foods and drinks. And many of these other commodities also spilled forth from tropical plantations. Indeed plantations began to proliferate throughout the tropical and sub-tropical world, producing well-tested commodities, and offering new goods for the consumers of the western world. Staples began to appear in parts of the world far removed from their place of origin, or far from the regions where the plantations had brought them to such lucrative fruition. The United States was a case in point. It seemed almost inevitable that when American settlers began to spread into the west in the early nineteenth century, they would take the idea of the plantation with them. Perfected in the Old South for the production of tobacco and rice, the plantation spread throughout the lower Mississippi Valley in the early nineteenth century. But now the plantation produced cotton – much of it destined primarily for the Lancashire textile industry; the city of Manchester's coat of arms shows a ship bringing cotton from America. At the beginning of the century, the fledgling US produced about 22 million kilos of cotton. Sixty years later they produced an astounding 726 million kilos. Only India – at 204 million kilos – came anywhere near this figure. The American cotton plantation had swept aside all other competitors.[16]

Sugar too began to appear in completely new settings (though the story of sugar had long been a history of successive migrations). The expertise of New World sugar planters was put to the task of developing new sugar industries around the world. On the Indian Ocean islands (Réunion and Mauritius), in the South African province of Natal, in the South Pacific islands of Fiji, new sugar plantations blossomed. And all turned to India for their cheap, indentured labour forces. In time, the imported Indian population would find itself at odds with the indigenous local peoples, with consequent social and political difficulties which continue to the present day. Plantations popped up wherever the habitat seemed suitable, though the labour force often differed from one region to another. In Hawaii, labour was drawn from China and Japan; in Queensland, workers were recruited (often fraudulently) from the Pacific islands. Plantations were happy to take their labour supplies from any suitable region, provided it was pliable, cheap and less-than-free.[17] When sugar cultivation began in the valleys of coastal Peru it seemed natural to turn to China for the labour. Where Africa had once provided an endless supply of enslaved labour, nineteenth-century tropical growth relied on the masses of India and China for willing, low-paid, pliant workers. Yet sugar was only one example of the rapid global spread of the plantation in the 1800s. To those men keen to tap the tropics for cheap labour and lucrative produce, the plantation provided the ideal tool. The seventeenth and eighteenth centuries had proved – through sugar (and tobacco) – the usefulness of the plantation. The following two centuries were to see the diversification of the plantation into a host of tropical enterprises.[18]

Western prosperity demanded and then devoured tropical produce in profusion. And as transportation improved, as medicine enabled Europeans to settle in previously inhospitable environments, and as technology advanced, plantations began to appear in completely new locations. Europeans developed advanced experimentation stations, planted local botanical gardens in the tropics and at home (Kew Gardens being perhaps the most famous), enabling them to make remarkable progress in the development, mutation and transplanting of tropical seeds, plants and roots. As Europeans settled new regions of the world they were able, once again, to transplant alien produce which quickly adapted to the new environment (even better, often, than the white settlers themselves). Staples which had been basic to western consumption for two centuries were uprooted from their traditional habitat and now found themselves transplanted thousands of miles from their native region.

Plantations in Asia came late, thanks mainly to improvements in transportation and the voracious late-nineteenth-century demand for new products – notably oils and rubber. They benefited from the old experiences of plantation management and, as before, often required alien labour: Tamils to Ceylon, Biharis to Assam, Chinese to Sumatra. Most of these plantations were developed close to the sea or access to the sea. Some scholars have been at pains to stress how different these 'new' plantations were. Closer scrutiny suggests how much they owed to their American predecessors.[19]

Tea was perhaps the most spectacular example of the new plantations. The old China trade was immensely inconvenient. Not only was the produce brought from the furthest reaches of the globe, but its cultivation remained in Chinese hands and beyond European control. Tea imports to Britain grew enormously, thanks to the removal of the East India Company monopoly in 1834 and the perfection of the fast 'clippers' after 1843. By mid-century, there were spectacular races to bring back the first China tea of the season. After a voyage of 99 days, ships docked in London within minutes of each other.[20] Such contests were doomed, however, by the opening of the Suez Canal (1869), though more directly by the growth of the Indian tea industry.

Europeans liked total control over their tropical produce, from planting to the final sale to the customer. They managed that, with tea, when production was shifted to India and Ceylon (Sri Lanka). Indigenous tea had been discovered in Assam, but it was the transplanting of tea to the hill plantations of Assam and Ceylon that shifted the focus of European (primarily British) tea-interests from China to India. In the process the patterns of trade, economic development – and consumption – changed quite dramatically. Put at its simplest, in the late eighteenth century the British were a nation of China tea-drinkers; by the late nineteenth century they were Indian tea-drinkers. And this was made possible, to a marked degree, by the rapid growth of major tea plantations, owned and managed by major British companies. Those plantations came to dominate local society much as the old sugar plantations had dominated life in the Caribbean islands. In Ceylon, plantation tea provided two-thirds of export revenue and dominated more than three-quarters of cultivable land.[21]

The figures speak for themselves. The first Assam tea was sold in London in 1839. Two years later the Calcutta auction rooms offered 60 000 pounds for sale. By 1865 Indian tea formed only 3 per cent of the tea drunk in Britain; in 1887 it was 50 per cent. Tea from Ceylon took off after 1876 when blight destroyed the local coffee industry and the local planters converted their plantations to tea. The result was the swift decline in British consumption of tea from China. In 1880 the British bought 114 million pounds of China tea (compared to about 44 million pounds of Indian). By 1900 the positions had been dramatically reversed, and the British drank 138 million pounds of Indian tea (and 92 million from Ceylon), compared to a mere 13 million pounds from China.[22]

And all the new teas came from plantations. Even in India, the planters sometimes found cause to look elsewhere for labour. They had enormous help in clearing land for plantations, in the form of local elephants. But they also turned to China for 'coolies'.[23] Plantations would turn to any part of the world for appropriate help. Management too was alien (i.e. European).

A similar plantation story unfolds wherever we look. Coffee, for example, had long since escaped its native region (Yemen) to find a more fertile and lucrative home in the hills of the West Indies. Now it thrived – on plantations – even further afield. The Dutch coffee industry boomed in Java. So too did sugar. They, and a few other crops, were ruthlessly imposed on an unsympathetic peasantry and a resistant land-tenure – via a plantation system. By the end of the nineteenth century, Java was described as a 'mammoth plantation state', with harmful effects on the well-being and cultural habits of local peoples.[24] Coffee's most dramatic transformation however took place in Brazil. Long after other Europeans had dispensed with slavery in their New World possessions, the Brazilians (and Cubans) continued to seek Africans to work their plantations. Sugar thrived in new regions of Brazil from the mid-nineteenth century but it was coffee that transformed the economy. In São Paulo, Rio de Janeiro and Minas Gerais the new coffee plantations turned, once again, to Africa. Dodging the abolitionist patrols (mainly of the Royal Navy), slave ships delivered 37 000 slaves a year between 1811 and 1850 to the booming coffee plantations. Moreover, even when the Atlantic slave trade was effectively cut off (by the late 1850s) Brazil's coffee plantations lured slaves from other regions of Brazil. Upwards of 6000 slaves a year were moved from older slave areas of the country to the thriving coffee regions, until the abolition of Brazilian slavery in 1888. On the backs of these slaves, the Brazilian coffee plantations moved with the expanding frontier. Once more, the slave plantations had proved an ideal weapon for bringing a savage frontier into profitable cultivation. And from those plantations coffee flowed in profusion to the consumers in Europe and North America.

This nineteenth-century Brazilian revival of plantation slavery was shared by Cuba. There the local sugar industry was highly mechanized by the mid-nineteenth century (unusual for an industry notorious for its technological backwardness).

The boom in local sugar drew slaves onto the new plantations. But the real revitalization in Cuban plantation slavery was in tobacco and in coffee. Tobacco tended to be grown on a multitude of small farms (their average was 30 acres) worked by a handful of slaves. By the 1850s there were some 9000 tobacco farms. Coffee however was a plantation crop, though the plantations were relatively small (300 acres) with about 30 slaves. This compared to the large Cuban sugar plantations, worked by gangs of upwards of 300 slaves. Cuba was a highly regionalized economy: sugar in the west, tobacco in the east.[25] Yet it was an irony that, as the western world turned against plantation slavery on ethical and economic grounds, the economies of nineteenth-century Brazil (coffee) and Cuba (sugar) thrived on the fruits of plantation slavery. Both were brought to an end in the 1880s: Cuba in 1886 and Brazil in 1888. Both succumbed to that potent mix of internal economic and political tensions, pressures from the metropolis and increasing opposition from powerful western interests which were, at once, abolitionist and capitalist. This, 'the last gasp of a system that had already begun to disintegrate a century earlier',[26] was not, of course, the end of the plantation. It merely confirmed that plantations did not need (indeed would not be permitted) enslaved labour from Africa (or from anywhere else for that matter). There were, after all, many other pools of labour readily available for plantation work, locally (Java, India, Ceylon) or from a distance (Fiji, Natal, Kenya).

Through all these changes in plantation history, the second half of the nineteenth century confirmed the value and utility of the plantation in the continuing process of colonial consolidation and metropolitan profit. Plantations continued to devour tracts of the tropical world, often at great cost to local land-tenure systems, and often damaging existing social and power relationships. A worldwide plantation system emerged which survives to the present day. Indeed the produce of plantations are so common – from the tyres on our cars to the coffee on our tables – that we simply lose sight of their plantation origins. Simply to list some of the commodities is to provide a menu of the modern western consumer. Sugar (the Caribbean), tea (India, Kenya, Sri Lanka), coffee (Central and South America, Java and the West Indies), soap (West and Central African palm oil), chocolate and cocoa (West Africa), bananas (South and Central America), tropical fruits (Hawaii, Africa and the Americas), rubber (Malaysia), coconuts, cloves and spices (East Africa and Arabia). The list could go much further.

Africa, once the prime source of plantation labour, now found itself exposed to another form of exploitation: the development of local plantations. As the nineteenth century advanced, large swathes of the continent found themselves drawn into plantation production, with the consequent damage to local landowning and social relations. Plantation slavery was common throughout the Soko Caliphate (Nigeria) throughout the nineteenth century. In Angola, the introduction of coffee plantations (and smaller sugar plantations on the coast) saw local labour locked into a system which was slavery in all but name. Plantations thrived in Madagascar and, for the production of cloves, grain and coconut, in East Africa – all worked by slaves. To the idealists in the Colonial Office, and to investors everywhere, the capitalist plantation promised a future of profitable investments, a pliant labour force, a market for British goods and a safe source of tropical ones. But the effects on Africa were corrosive.[27]

Plantations have, then, been a constant in the history of western economic involvement with the colonial, tropical peripheries, from the early days of exploration and settlement through to the recent years of transnational conglomerates which buy and sell chunks of the world's economy like a superior game of Monopoly. The plantation has stood the test of time. But like many other units of economic activity (factories, workshops, farms) the plantation is very deceptive. For a start, it is a remarkably varied institution. At the apogee of slavery, a sugar plantation was quite different from plantations producing coffee, cotton or tobacco. Life for a sugar slave, living in a local slave community and numbered in the hundreds, was qualitatively different from life on a small tobacco plantation, where black and white lived and worked close together. The nature of the crop and the environment in which it thrived dictated the nature of the slaves' working and, to a degree, social life. And so it proved in freedom as in slavery.

Plantations have had a poor scholarly press. In part this stems from their history. They were, after all, shaped by and instrumental in some of the most grotesque and inhuman exchanges between Europeans and colonial peoples. No other single institution was so instrumental in – as responsible for – the uprooting, relocation and thorough exploitation of so many subject peoples.[28] For the best part of four centuries, 'the plantation was synonymous with the exploitation of human labour'.[29] Even so bold a statement as this fails to recognize the unique nature, persistence and ramifications of that exploitation. After all, many other institutions have proved adept at exploitation. But few quite so perfected and honed that exploitation to the degree of the plantation.

Having said that, it would be wrong and unjust not to recognize that plantations have changed. One of the most persistent features of plantation history has been foreign ownership or control. Alien ownership and management has been seen as a brake on the economic and social well-being of the local labour force and, more recently, on the advancement of the local state freed from its colonial control. But too often the plantations of the post-1945 world have been viewed through historical lenses. In fact, newly independent states have sought to place plantation life and economy on a more modern footing. Governments in tropical societies actively intervene in the affairs of modern plantations: fixing wages, sharing equity, demanding local management and sharing profits. Of course such intervention has sometimes brought as much damage as social benefit.[30] Nonetheless, the experience of recent plantation history is often different from the history of the preceding three centuries.

The explanation of this change is simple enough. Until the end of World War II, the dominant theme in the experience of most plantation societies was the inextricable, though confused, entanglement with colonialism. Plantations were, in the main, an obvious (and generally malignant) bastion of colonial interests; outposts on the very edge of 'civilized' life which secured the economic and social interests of alien groups in the teeth of local people's opposition. For the best part of three centuries it was difficult to see what benefits accrued to local people from the plantations sustained by their efforts. Their own material returns were scant or non-existent (how much did slaves receive for their labours?). And when plantation workers were able to secure meagre benefits, it was generally by dint of their own efforts and little thanks to the plantation itself. West Indian higglers, Indian shopkeepers in Trinidad or Malaya, Chinese traders and merchants in Hawaii or the Caribbean – all and more owed their success to their own energies and enterprise, not to the plantations.

So much has changed since 1945 that it is often difficult to recall the plantation world of colonial society. Colonial independence ushered in new ways of viewing and managing plantations. Throughout, efforts have been directed towards enhancing commercial efficiency to the mutual benefit of workers, management and local government. Of course the toilers in the field – the cane-cutters, female tea-pickers and tropical fruit-pickers – remain poorly paid. But that, unhappily, remains the lot of rural workers across the developing world. At this point, the critique of plantation life comes full circle.

Plantations have had an unpleasant habit of coercing labour. Long after slavery and indentured labour had passed into extinction, plantations used new coercive methods of recruiting labour. Wages were often so low, and conditions so poor, that only compulsion would work. Colonial governments and agents imposed head and hut taxes to drive Africans into Lever's palm-oil plantations. The French, Portuguese and Belgians employed a variety of means to secure 'voluntary' plantation labour as late as the 1930s; but it was servile, indentured labour, excused by some as a necessary tool in the first phase of 'modernization'.[31] It was scarcely surprising that plantations – and even the broader economy they stood for – were prime targets for critics of colonialism. In recent years, scholars looking at the wreckage of colonialism have felt little less critical when gazing at modern plantations.

Plantations, of all kinds, have then never lacked critics. Political and scholarly critics are readily available to beat the modern-day plantation with a variety of analytical sticks. Moreover the style of plantation life (expatriate management enjoying the best of material pleasures, cheek by jowl with ranks of ill-paid peasant labourers) serves to lay bare the plantation back to the blows of its opponents. Plantations often look, at first glance, much like their historical (generally colonial) predecessor. And for those who dislike plantation history, it is tempting to gain intellectual revenge for the sins of the fathers by attacking the modern plantation. In truth, the plantation can never escape its miserable history. Moreover the plantation continues to exercise great sway over a number of societies and economies – in Queensland, in Zaire, in India, Sri Lanka, Malaya, Indonesia, East, West and Central Africa, Indo-China, the West Indies, Central and South America and the Pacific.[32] However modernized and reformed, so many plantations stick out as unhappy reminders of a world long cast aside; the plantations represent and speak of the world when the Europeans ruled vast tracts of it as the Lords of Human Kind.[33] Try as they may, proponents of modern plantations[34] cannot slip away from the historical memories and burdens bequeathed by the plantations' past.

All this seems far removed from those first plantations; of the English and Scots seeking to conquer and rule the turbulent Irish, of Europeans tentatively securing a place for themselves in the Americas, later in South East Asia. Those early plantations – crude in the extreme, in effect little more than outposts of empire – were to prove successful beyond enyone's imagination. Many failed of course, overwhelmed by an unforgiving habitat which was quick to retrieve ground lost to the settlers. Many too succumbed to the attacks of disease, of native peoples – and to fratricidal disputes among the Europeans. But, in time, the plantations more than proved their worth. They beat back the wilderness, drove out, destroyed or frightened away native peoples, discovered ways of creating agricultural bounty and of stimulating, then satisfying, metropolitan taste for their produce. Plantations devised new ways of disciplining labour. Never before had so many labouring people been marshalled so thoroughly, to such material effect, by small bands of owners and managers. Much later, with the onset of industrialization, European capitalists learned new techniques for the disciplining and control of industrial labour.[35] But the planters had already been down that road – with very great success. To a degree, it was a question of force and of violence (tools not generally at the disposal of industrial capitalists). Those first (enslaved) generations of plantation workers passed their working lives to a rhythm drummed out by capricious whippings and beatings.

It was however the structure and organization of the plantation which gave the best economic results. The pattern of local agricultural cycles shaped the distinctive management of labour; gang work, task work, switching workers from one job to another (first in the fields, then in the factory). Plantations maximized labour as best they could. Employing children and the old, men and women, the plantation paid little regard to conventional, contemporary wisdom about age or gender, choosing instead to bend their pliant labour force to the most pressing current needs. It is simple, in retrospect, to spot the flaws in this plantation system and easy to suggest where inefficiencies lay. But no system before it had yielded such success to owners, managers and backers.

Despite the broad range of types of plantations, they had recognizable features in common. They were first and foremost alien institutions, imposed in distant regions by alien settlers and their backers. They produced crops (themselves often alien to the locale), generally using exotic labour, and all for the satisfaction of distant metropolitan tastes – and profits. They were in effect beach-heads for the profitable exploitation of regions of the world which were distant from European powers but integral to European prosperity and well-being. Plantations also enabled Europeans to expand their physical control over regions of the world which might otherwise have proved impossible to dominate. They bestowed power, wealth and dominance. But they were most influential – albeit invisibly distant – in flooding Europe with exotic staples.

The plantation was, to repeat, a cornucopia; a fount of material plenty which poured out prosperity to its proponents and unexpected pleasures to millions of Europeans. That it also brought pain and misery on a previously unparalleled scale was a stark but undeniable fact. But who so much as thought of that uncomfortable fact as they enjoyed their fruits of empire, in the distant metropolis? The monetary price paid by British consumers was small enough to enable people of all sorts and conditions to partake of tropical staples. The price paid by the producers – the slaves and other servile peoples – was painful beyond recall.

# 10 Shops and Shopping

London was, of course, the centre of fashion. There, from the late seventeenth century onwards, could be seen the most lavish, obvious signs of material consumption. In and around the Court and among men and women of substance, grown fat on the proceeds of commercial and mercantile expansion, the latest whim, the latest styles, the most recent peacock-like displays were to be found. From London, the same people transplanted their social habits across the face of the nation; to their rural summer-time retreats, to the fashionable spas (later to the seaside resorts) and to the nation's provincial capitals. From those local centres, so far removed from the capital, the latest fads quickly fanned out among the prosperous in the provincial neighbourhood. Some thought that fashion seemed to take an eternity to reach into the deepest recesses of provincial Britain. But there could be no doubting where it all came from; its source of inspiration and its provenance was the capital.

London in the mid-eighteenth century was, as it had been since time out of mind, the epicentre of public fashion and consumption. Now however the emphasis on fashion and style had reached new, often absurd, levels of extravagance (a fact brilliantly recorded by the caricaturists of the age). Nor were these displays simply restricted to the fashionable 'season', that round of private and semi-private gatherings from which the public was excluded. When not flaunting their prosperous vanities among their peers at private or social gatherings, contemporary 'society' paraded to and inside that array of fashionable shops which lined the London thoroughfares, and which so dazzled visitors from the provinces and abroad.

The capital's best shops were quite spectacular, more lavish and eye-catching than anything to be found elsewhere in Europe. Not even Paris came close to capturing the excitement of London's fashionable shops. Men and women from across London and its outlying villages were drawn to the shops in droves.[1] The shops were, at once, suppliers of necessities, a centre of the latest designs, and a stage on which the prosperous could swagger while scrutinizing the goods on offer at a leisurely pace. Contemporaries often visited those shops simply to look – and to be seen. But they were seen not only by their peers. As they arrived and departed, they were watched (mocked, envied and often insulted) by their poorer fellow citizens. Humbler folk had to give way, to step aside, were held back, as their superiors swept up to the shop door. The lady whose carriage stopped outside a toy shop, in Hogarth's *Stand Coachman, or the Haughty Lady well fitted* (1750), obstructed the pavement; the passing poor simply climbed into and through her waiting carriage to proceed on their way.

> 'Tis hoped the fair Ladies from thence beware,
> How they stop a Free Passage with such Haughty Air.[2]

Carriages created a traffic jam outside the more fashionable shops. Inside, fawning shopkeepers (though the term is perhaps too humble for many of the owners and managers of the grander establishments) took great trouble to pander to their prosperous customers (even when they were simply idling away the day) and to keep out undesirables. Some of course could only gaze. Shopkeepers were interested in those who could afford to enter the shop and buy; or in those whose presence would add glitter and reputation to their name. With this in mind, they devised remarkable stratagems to lure them through the door.

Success depended on the shopkeepers themselves, and to cater to polite clientele, the shopkeeper was expected to be a man of refinement. 'He ought to speak fluently, though not elegantly, to entertain the ladies: and to be the master of a handsome bow and cringe: should be able to hand a lady to and from her coach politely ...' Endlessly patient, he was (ideally) never ruffled by customer demands, 'even if asked to unfold more than a hundred pieces of stuff'.[3] When Wedgwood pondered how best to press his new wares on the fashionable public he discussed the idea of expanding his London showrooms. His Grosvenor Square rooms were soon overcrowded. He considered opening up in Pall Mall, but that was too close to the 'common folk'. What he wanted was ample space where he could carefully arrange his wares, display his pattern books, and flatter and pamper to his fashionable customers: 'it will be in our interest to amuse, & divert, & please, and astonish, nay, & even to ravish the Ladies'.[4]

In London's shops, the 'commercial shop window of England' was to be found all the produce of the known world, shaped, packaged, threaded, shelved and displayed in the latest height of fashion. It offered an endless (and endlessly changing) seduction; visually attractive, tempting – irresistible to many. 'Let us,' said Johnson to Goldsmith, 'take a walk from Charing Cross to Whitechapel through I suppose the greatest series of shops in the world.' The foreign visitor was dazzled by the sheer abundance of the shopping splendours: 'they sometimes extend without interruption for an English mile.'[5] To Robert Southey, London's shops would keep him entertained for the rest of his life.

> Something extraordinary or beautiful is for ever to be seen in them. ... There is a perpetual exhibition of whatever is curious in nature or art, exquisite in workmanship, or singular in costume; and the display is perpetually varying as the ingenuity of trade and the absurdity of fashion are ever producing something new.[6]

It was surely symptomatic that Boswell first encountered Johnson in a London shop (a bookshop).

For those unable to sample the latest London fashions, traders began to open up premises in the provinces. Wedgwood for example opened showrooms in Liverpool, Bath, Dublin and the Potteries. Even without such facilities, provincial shopkeepers went to great trouble to keep abreast of London's fashions, making their way to London for ideas, products and inspiration, and transporting them back to their less exalted environment. Mr Towsey, a milliner and haberdasher in Chester, informed his customers that he 'is just returned from London, with a new and fashionable assortment'.[7]

Though fashionable Londoners were apt to scoff at the backwardness of provincial life – to poke fun at its slowness in following London's lead – in fact the capital's fads were quickly adopted, especially (and not surprisingly) in provincial capitals and in the spas. Shopkeepers keen to keep their customers abreast of styles, and the propertied classes themselves, wandering in that dreamy way from the London season to the watering-holes and their provincial homes, were the very instruments which ensured that the spores of fashions would spread across the country. Thus, the fads of metropolitan life –

including the adoption of tropical staples – quickly fanned out across the face of provincial England.

By the late eighteenth century a core of London's better shops had consolidated into a discernible district, forming a physical and recognizable network for the fashionable shopper. Oxford Street alone had 153 shops, for 'the whim-whams and fribble-frabble of fashion'.[8] The shops were designed to catch the eye, with bow windows to give maximum display space to their contents, with lavish displays of lighting (in a generally gloomy world) and carefully arranged displays within and in the windows. The bow windows of shops were so prominent – so bulged out over the footpath- that they were sometimes viewed as a public nuisance, and local authorities ordered them reduced.[9]

The creation of such elaborate shops was a costly enterprise. As early as the 1720s prominent shopkeepers were investing considerable sums in making their shops attractive to customers: 'Never was such Painting and Gilding, such Sashings and Looking-Glasses, among the Shopkeepers as there is now'.[10] It was no mere aesthetic exercise. The whole purpose was to lure people to the window, and then through the door. In 1786, Sophie von la Roche wrote,

> Behind the great glass windows absolutely everything one can think of is neatly displayed, in such abundance of choice as almost to make one greedy. Now large slipper and shoe shops for everything from adult down to dolls, can be seen; now fashion-articles or silver or brass shops, books, guns, glasses, the confectioner's goodies, the pewterer's wares, fans etc ...

Oxford Street seemed especially dazzling, its shops brilliantly lit by oil lamps, one colourful display replaced by another, from watchmaking to silverware, from confectionery to fruit. Foreigners were taken aback by the range, and the extravagance of London's shops. It was said a Russian visitor like 'a continuous fair'.[11] Those same visitors were in no doubt that this dazzling commercial display was a direct result of England's remarkable trade with the world at large. Indeed when they looked at the riverside, and scanned the London skyline, the explanation was laid out before them, in the lines of masts and rigging of the ships which were the maritime servants of the nation's remarkable commercial expansion. From their holds there spilled forth, almost daily, the produce of the world itself. Not surprisingly, London's myriad shops presented the prosperous consumer with almost any material object they could desire, from Britain and beyond.

Traditionally, shops had been the outlet for goods made in or close to the shop itself. By the mid-eighteenth century, all that had changed. London's attractive shops were in the new mode; modern shops which sold goods made elsewhere.[12] Now, the finest of British manufactures, or the staples and fruits of far-flung empire and global trade, all and more demanded attention in the shop windows of the capital. Little wonder that crowds of poor bystanders and rows of fashionable carriages jostled for space on the streets and pavements outside.

What made such shops so eye-catching and attractive was their relative newness. The British bought their goods, foodstuffs, clothing and luxuries in a quite different way from their forebears. Markets and market places had, for centuries, been the central institution for the buying and selling of goods, a role which continued despite the proliferation of shops in towns and villages throughout the eighteenth century. Market towns – more than 700 of them – served the main material needs of the British people. Almost everything was available from market stalls, but because markets were held on fixed days (once or twice a week) they were less than ideal for many people, particularly labouring people and those living some miles away from the market itself. Though most people lived within a 10-mile radius of the nearest market, in parts of the country people had to trek up to 20 miles to get there.

Working people rarely had trouble finding somewhere to buy their goods. Food was generally available from the local alehouse (landlords normally extended credit to poorer customers) and most villages had the basic food shops or outlets (the butcher and baker). Failing that, the travelling pedlar sold wares of the most varied kind, door-to-door, in the more remote communities.[13] It was these door-to-door pedlars who took the cheapest of goods – items broken down to their smallest volume, foodstuffs on the point of decay – to poor people in town and country.[14] But remote communities and small villages were also served by other networks. Shopkeepers in the towns worked a wider hinterland, their shops serving customers who lived miles away and to whom they delivered goods and foodstuffs by post and by coach services. As the eighteenth century advanced and as material well-being spread, however unevenly, to more and more people (until arrested by the war years of the 1790s) the old marketing system began to creak. What had been adequate since time out of mind was now looking increasingly redundant.

It was to provide for the changing and expanding population of England, that shops (however simple or crude ) began to increase, creeping into the remotest of places. But they were shops quite unlike their dazzling London counterparts. More and more of the items once sold only on market stalls began to find their way into local shops. Shops in their turn began to follow the changing population. As towns grew in size, and as new communities developed on the edges of old towns, the central location of many traditional markets were inconvenient for large numbers of people. Droves of people now found themselves having to *travel* to the central market. In many towns, the day was fast disappearing when the market had been at most peoples' doorstep. And as demand for goods and foodstuffs increased, ever more traders simply moved out of the market, setting up their stalls instead close to the new communities, operating from nearby rooms, taverns, houses and sheds. They were in effect opening new shops.

Bigger markets and fairs attracted traders from across the local region. Some men travelled from London, dangling their metropolitan goods before the gaze of an impressed provincial clientele. Thomas Minshull told the people of Chester in 1751 that he was coming north with an array 'of the best and newest fashions' (which included, interestingly 'sugar dishes').[15] But for all its virtues, selling goods at a fair or market could not compete with the attractions of a more leisurely, more critical browse through items in a shop. The more prosperous markets were hardly a substitute for that fashionable social *ambiance* which proved so attractive in London shops.

On a humbler scale than London's, fashionable shops began to spring up across the face of urban Britain. The bigger provincial towns developed into recognizable shopping centres by the late century, (a fact registered in the new but short-lived shop tax in 1785). This proliferation of shops not merely catered for the necessities of life, but also offered an array of non-essentials and luxuries – the same luxuries – notably sugar and tea – which so many contemporaries railed against when they saw them in the hands of the poor. But the sheer increase in the number of shops masked the range, for they varied enormously one from another. At the top end were the capital's luxury shops, providing the most costly and exotic of goods and the latest up-to-date metropolitan fashions; at the bottom, the shops (no more than a simple, sparsely filled room, with little on the shelves), catering for working people. But even in the meanest of shops the produce of distant colonies was available.

Prosperous provincials, growing in numbers and self-confidence, and ever keen to drape themselves in the styles fashioned by their metropolitan betters, were serviced by an expansive luxury trade throughout urban Britain. The shops which provided their furnishing, fittings and clothing occupied prime city-centre sites. As in London, these shopkeepers sought to improve the appearance and facilities of their shops; extending them, lighting them and generally copying the innovators in London. They bought their stock from London, eagerly acquiring the latest items or raw materials, and made them up into the fashions already paraded in the capital. Shopkeepers advertised their goods in local newspapers and on handbills, always claiming that their wares were good value, – the *latest* thing. Furnishings in Chester were proclaimed as 'of the most approved patterns'; toys proclaimed as 'intirely new, from London'. Booksellers promised to order books twice weekly – from their London suppliers.[16] London's fashionable tail was vigorously wagging the provincial dog.

The increase in shops is now clear enough but until recently historians had assumed that the rise of a heavily urbanized working class in the early nineteenth century was dependent for their supplies on markets and travelling hawkers. We now know that, following the pattern of the previous century, shops quickly followed working people into their new communities. Shops were established wherever the population settled. New working-class communities, on the edges of expanding towns, were serviced by their local corner shops. Often as poor as their customers and lacking any of the attractions of their city-centre counterparts, these local corner shops nonetheless offered working-class communities what they needed and wanted. They were general shops – which stocked life's basic ingredients. And among those ingredients, invariably, were the tropical produce so beloved of all British people.[17] Long before the obvious onset of industrialization, the fixed local shop was a feature of British urban experience, for rich and poor alike. Indeed it has been calculated that there were more shops per head of the population in the 1750s than in the 1950s.[18]

Among the profusion of shops in late eighteenth century Britain those selling tea stood out. Though it is tempting to be dazzled, like contemporaries, by the more spectacular versions, the typical shop selling tea was much less impressive. They were in fact mean and basic. Surviving accounts show their stock to have been pathetically meagre, the range restricted, the volume of goods small and the turnover limited. But, for small and large shopkeepers alike, profits were rooted in tropical staples – especially tea and sugar. One lady, Mrs Taylor of Edinburgh, ran a very small shop but in the course of one year she bought 244 pounds of tea and 15.25 hundredweight of sugar; those two simple items made up almost three-quarters of her annual purchases. She sold a ratio of 7 pounds of sugar for every pound of tea (though the generally-accepted ratio was 6–1). Since most working-class customers bought their tea and sugar by the ounce, Mrs Taylor needed many transactions to shift her stock.[19] Curiously, despite the low income of most of her customers, they did not buy the cheaper teas. The truth was, the British tea-drinker had developed a sophisticated palate and bought the best of teas when possible. The creation of a large, poor urban proletariat however drove ever more people towards the cheap and often adulterated teas by the early nineteenth century.[20]

One reason behind the proliferation of shops in the eighteenth century was cost; it was very cheap to set up shop in the first place. With perhaps less than £10 (which might be expected to yield an income of £50), anyone could set up in business. Such shops were particularly attractive to women (to widows with their mite), and to superior – literate – working men, keen to find alternative work or to supplement existing wages. It was they who opened shops which were so small that they rarely entered local trade directories. These were the shops, open seven days a week, most frequented (perhaps three or four times per week) by the local working poor. The typical shopper was female; the wife or daughter of the household, though men were more frequent shoppers than we might expect. They shopped to buy life's necessities – bread, flour, cheese and candles – along with tea and sugar. Those two commodities were generally bought at the same time.[21] The one needed the other.

Such shops were found in the remotest corners of Britain, far away from the main routes of commerce and passing trade. In the tiny village of Penmorfa, on the hills above Tremadoc in Caernarvonshire the local shop was owned by 'Roberts'. The nearest towns were 15 and 20 miles away and Roberts carried a wide range of goods. His groceries were few and sparse and they moved slowly, but they were available for people who made the long hard trek over the hills. Roberts had regular customers for tea and sugar. Mrs Anwyl was a particularly avid tea-drinker, closely rivalled by Owen Thomas Candllyn and Jane late Wern.[22]

Roberts's surviving accounts show that all those who bought tea were women. Here in the depths of Wales tea-drinking was, above all, a woman's drink. Not only that, but we know, from the notes which Roberts kept in his accounts, that many of the purchases of tea – and above all sugar – were secret; women clearly asked him not to tell husbands that they were buying such luxuries. Here, in what was clearly an isolated backwater, as remote as could be from the new shopping culture, exotic goods had made an impact, albeit furtively. Even the women of rural Wales had discovered the delights of tropical luxuries. British people had access to exotic produce no matter how remote their locality. Writing from Land's End as early as 1662 a Dutch visitor noted:

> everyone, men, women, young and old, [were] puffing tobacco, which is here so common that the young children get it in the morning instead of breakfast, and almost prefer it to bread.

He was also struck by parsons smoking pipes as as they rode on horseback through remote Cornwall.[23]

It was of course in towns and cities that shops were most numerous. In London (where the great expansion in shops occurred earlier than in the rest of the country) there were almost 24 000 shops, and possibly many more in 1797. No neighbourhood, however poor, was without its shops, tucked away in courts and alley-ways. Of course the very great bulk of such shops were far removed from their gaudy, luxurious contemporaries. Their owners were poor, earned little, had meagre stocks and frequently complained of the precariousness of the life of a shopkeeper. The story is the same wherever we look. In the northern capital of York, the great majority of shopkeepers were of low income, paid low taxes and made small profits. The city's largest tea dealer, William Tuke, had an income of only £300 a year. Yet, *in toto*, almost half of the revenue which passed through the nation's shops passed over the counters of small shops.[24]

Although individually, the shopkeepers did not make much money, collectively they formed the backbone of the retail trades in Britain. To call the British a nation of shopkeepers was not so much a Napoleonic insult as a simple description which touched on the very nature of the British people by the late eighteenth century.

Contemporaries were struck by the growth of shops, even in the late 1600s, and most strikingly in smaller, village communities. Though debate continues about the timing and numbers involved, few now doubt that more and more shops were established in the course of the eighteenth century. Furthermore – and more central for our interests – they were increasingly selling new imported goods, notably sugar, tea and tobacco, alongside local foodstuffs and clothing.[25]

Shops grew most easily in market towns with their existing trading networks and their own culture of local marketing and consumption. Smaller shops bought their goods from local suppliers and manufacturers (often buying on credit). We can tell when they concentrated on selling to low income groups because they simply broke down their goods for sale into the smallest of units; an ounce of tea or tobacco, a few ounces of sugar. Poorer customers in their turn, like the shopkeepers, often bought these handfuls of goods on credit.

The rash of shops which covered the face of Britain by the early and mid-eighteenth century have yielded inventories which have provided historians with some remarkable details. The most valuable items in their stocks were textiles and clothing; the most important innovation was the stock of groceries. And among those groceries, the most lucrative were those which came from abroad. The most powerful incentive to the establishment of small shops was the demand for tropical staples, above all tobacco, tea and sugar. In buying these goods, in small amounts, low income groups became frequent shoppers, returning regularly to replenish their supplies. Thus, they became in effect frequent customers – visitors who entered the shop and might be tempted to buy other items. It was an obvious step for shopkeepers to capitalize on these patterns by stocking other goods which might tempt the consumer. Understandably the new breed of shopkeepers began to put more traditional wares on their shelves: the soap, candles and foodstuffs which were the stock-in-trade of market stall holders.[26]

The newly acquired tastes of the British people for tropical staples were enormously attractive to shopkeepers, not least because they had a fast turnover. They also yielded a good profit margin. 'It was the selling of goods that people had to buy constantly that made shop retailing attractive.'[27] The addiction of the British people to the fruits of empire had helped bring into being an institution which quickly became an integral feature of British experience; the small local shop to be found in the smallest and remotest of communities.

The shopkeepers of Britain had a curious press. Though, in an oft-repeated phrase, they were 'the wheel whereon the inland trade turns', many contemporaries disliked the power they seemed to exercise, particularly over low-income groups. This seemed especially shocking when so much of their trade was in providing 'luxuries' from the far ends of the world. Yet they were, after a fashion, merely providing what their customers demanded. Moreover, in the form of the extensive credit which they offered to rich and poor they acted as banks. This was doubly important among those lower income groups for whom cash was unpredictable and sparse. It was the shopkeepers, especially the smaller ones (themselves no higher in status or income than many of their customers) who enabled the poor to enjoy goods previously held to be the preserve of the rich. Shopkeepers, in the words of Adam Smith, were responsible for 'breaking and dividing... rude and manufactured produce into such small parcels as suited the occasional demands of those who want them'. Working men and women could only buy goods on a daily basis; they could not set food aside for other than immediate use. Again, Adam Smith had his finger on the pulse. It was the shopkeepers who enabled the workman 'to purchase his subsistence from day to day, or even from hour to hour, as he wants it.'[28]

As we have already seen, shops at their most lavish involved their owners in considerable investment; it was a presentational sprat to catch a consuming mackerel. Most shops were not like that, however, relying instead on local customers and on the accidents of geography and circumstance to drive local, low-income customers to their door. Once inside the shop, poorer customers did not feel out of place, because the shop was almost certain to be austere, ill-equipped and with little on the shelves save the barest of necessities. We know it was often the case when shopkeepers died that they left behind extremely small volumes of stock. They, like their customers, could not afford to order goods in any volume. Poor shopkeepers, poor customers; both were dependent on the other. Yet is was an odd fact that they were related by transactions for exotic fruits of empire. And it was this social curiosity that so irritated one propertied commentator after another.

In provincial towns, as in London, there was a hierarchy of shops. If the largest number of people took their flimsy trade to poor, local shops, local elites turned to more substantial premises which mirrored, on a humbler scale, the splendours of shopping in London. The ties to London were often direct, for major provincial shops placed specific orders with the better London houses. Provincial shopkeepers' advertisements, which made up the bulk of local newspapers (and brought in the bulk of their income) offered goods to local 'gentlemen and tradesmen', all ordered and delivered by post. Such advertisements, along with that proliferating world of trade cards, gave extensive local coverage to shopkeepers' work – their address, their goods, their competitiveness – and their ability to compete with or conjure forth goods from London itself. Those people who felt themselves to be even more superior often ignored their local shops entirely, preferring instead to deal direct, from their provincial retreats, with London shopkeepers. Major tea companies, Twinings for instance,[29] supplied their provincial clients with orders on request, ranging from large consignments (95 pounds of tea in one order in the 1790s ) through to small parcels made up for particular local customers. One order, for Lord Duncan Alex Ross in Scotland, and shipped to Perth from London, contained 'sixty-six pounds of tea ... [and] four hundred weight of sugar'.[30]

The more prosperous shops promoted themselves in obvious ways; through the signs, motifs and decorations above their doors, on bill-boards swinging from their upper floors, and in the packing and wrapping material, printed specially for their goods. In fact as the century advanced, shopkeepers came to rely on the literacy of their customers. Newspapers, which increased in number and frequency in London and the provinces, provided shopkeepers (and many others of course) with a perfect platform to display their goods and to flaunt their claims to good, competitive shop-keeping.[31]

New shops announced their opening in the papers. In 1756 this advertisement appeared in the *Whitehall Evening Post*:

> Thomas Fletcher, upwards of Twenty six years shopman to the late and present Mr Twining, begs leave to acquaint his Friends and the Public, that he has open'd his shop... [which] sells all sorts of fine Teas, Coffee, Chocolate, etc,

He also promised,

> to oblige those who are pleased to favour him with their commands for Teas, [that he] will sell all sorts of refined Sugars at Prime Cost.[32]

Newspapers offered traders, shopkeepers and manufacturers of all descriptions the chance of promoting themselves before the reading public, but the advertisements often served specific functions. They described the locations of shops and market stalls – even of travelling salesmen. They often listed the terms on which goods could be purchased. As newspaper advertisements became more commonplace (filling page after page of the papers, to the point where the reader had to search for any hint of news), claims became bolder and the salesmanship more aggressive. Ever more shopkeepers (and producers) had learned the lessons of advertising and were following the lead of the more successful and aggressive of entrepreneurs in marketing their goods to the reading public.

Time and again local merchants claimed that they could sell tropical staples on equal terms (for quality and price) with London dealers. Indeed the reader of provincial newspapers could not escape the references to London; London merchants, London sales, London prices, fashions, goods fresh into London or via London. (Even topical news was simply cut from the London papers and reprinted in the local editions.) The most distant of provincial readers, their consuming appetite whetted by this parade of advertisements, could feel abreast of metropolitan commercial and fashionable life. If the advertisements were to be believed, the provincial consumer paid no more for his goods (despite the distance and the carriage), was abreast of the latest fashion and had access to the freshest of produce which tumbled from the holds of ships from China, South East Asia and the Americas. The purpose of this advertising blizzard was of course to sell, but at the same time it persuaded provincial Britons that they enjoyed the material benefits of London without having to endure the cost and hardship of living there.

It was inevitably a highly competitive world, sharpened still further by the entry into provincial newspapers of advertisements from London traders. Under the direct threat of losing their business to London, local shops sought to undercut their metropolitan competitors. By late eighteenth century the retail trade had taken on a recognizably modern form; aggressive marketing and pricing, discounts for cash, extensive credit facilities, mail-order, goods tailored to customers' requirements; all and more had become prominent features of late-century shops and shopping.[33]

Of all the changes in the shopping habits of the British people none was more striking than their growing reliance on tropical foodstuffs. William Stout, a shopkeeper in Lancaster from 1688, provides a host of clues. He made an annual (five-day) journey to London, returning via Sheffield, to buy and order goods for his premises. However, he bought most of his sugar and tobacco (the latter, in 1709, declared to be 'the most profitable') locally, or from Liverpool and Bristol. As a young shop apprentice, Stout had learned the routines of packaging these goods for sale over the counter, spending hours breaking down the sugar, tobacco and other goods into small packets of one and two pounds. At some point in his long shopkeeping career, those staples 'took off'. Looking back from the 1740s he noted of 1709 that there was 'not above one-quarter part of the sugar consumed here as has been since'.[34]

The working experiences of Stout and similar provincial shopkeepers dovetail perfectly, at the local level, with the national figures. In the years 1709–11 some 40.9 million pounds of sugar were imported. But by the end of the century, that figure had increased to 322 million pounds. Tea imports registered a similar quantum leap; from 122 600 to 16 million pounds. The increase in tobacco imports was less spectacular, from 10.6 to 15.3 million pounds.[35] (Tobacco had, as we have seen, reached saturation point late in the seventeenth century.) Of course these figures need be set against the background of a growing population, a rising proportion of which, from mid-century, was living in urban areas. In 1700 there were 68 towns in England and Wales with populations over 2500; a century later there were 188.[36] It was precisely in these areas that thousands of shops sprang into being, to cater for the daily needs of that growing population. By then, those needs included imported goods cultivated by British colonial settlers, African slaves and Chinese labourers.

Specialist shops which sold only a particular line of staples (tea, coffee, tobacco, chocolate) developed in the bigger towns. And it was to those specialized emporia, with their exotic range of leaves, beans and mixes, that smaller provincial shopkeepers often turned for their own supplies. The great majority of people – the lower income groups – had no direct need of such specialist shops, turning instead for tea, sugar and tobacco to their local general shop, to the small shopkeeper or even the landlord of the local alehouse. But of all the specialist shops, it is the tea shop which remains the most striking. There were for a start, vast numbers of them: 32 754 in England and Wales in 1783 and 1034 in Scotland.[37]

The massive expansion in shops selling tea was fuelled by profitability. Tea provided grocers with their most profitable items of trade. Time and again, individual shopkeepers admitted – and subsequent research has confirmed – that the British passion for tea was the most certain, the most steady and the most lucrative form of trade for shopkeepers of all stations, despite excessively high levels of taxation on tea until

1784. It seems clear enough that most tea dealers were, consciously or not, dealing in illegal tea. Since the East India Company's imports formed only a small part of the nation's consumption, the rest was finding its way into the nation's shops via 'illegal' routes.[38] Students of the trade are in no doubt that it was the enterprise and drive of the illicit tea-traders that proved intrumental in driving the tea habit deep into all corners of the British market. One enterprising illicit Scottish trader boasted that his acitivites had created shops as far south as Durham and Leeds.[39]

Within the legal trade – those men who bought the chests of tea at the East India Company auctions – a familiar pattern had developed. They transferred the tea chests to their own facilities, broke open the tea, mixed and tested it, sifting the final produce into the blends and mixes their customers liked. They knew the tastes required by the British consumer, and their in-house experts acquired those skills of sampling and blending the leaves in ways which would please the increasingly choosy customers. Tea tasting and blending thus became that delicate skill which survives to this day. The major tea companies forwarded their repackaged tea to their bigger (or important) customers throughout the country and to individual customers abroad. Twinings for example dispatched orders to the West Indies (to governors, traders and planters), to British officials in Europe, to officers serving overseas. They traded with people on the very edges of British expansion and colonial warfare; men fighting in North America in the 1760s turned for refreshment to tea ordered direct from Twining's in London. So all-consuming was the British passion for sweet tea, and so comprehensive the services offered by the major houses, that demand could be satisfied whatever the location, from the precariousness of the unsettled colonial frontier to the misery of Eton College. William Dutton wrote to his father from the Lower School;

> I wish you would be so kind as to let me have Tea and Sugar here to drink in the afternoon, without which there is no such thing as keeping company with other boys of my standing.[40]

By the mid-eighteenth century tea-drinking was a universal British phenomenon, from the highest to the lowest. It had spawned and was satisfied by a quite remarkable system of distribution centred on London's trading companies and shops, which delivered tea (and other goods) to the furthest recesses of British and colonial settlement or travel. Wherever the British found themselves, they could always find comfort in a cup of tea.

The tea industry was given an extra boost by the debate which swirled around the question of reducing the tea duties in 1784. It was a major political issue which generated enormous coverage and public attention, providing legal tea-dealers with a perfect opportunity to launch a major sales campaign when the duties were reduced. It was at this point that the major London tea-traders became seriously interested in public advertising. Previously, they had largely accumulated clients by slow, informal, trusting word-of-mouth (and of course by the reliability and quality of their service). The debate about the duties on tea served to promote its sale still further. In newspapers, in handbills, inside and outside Parliament, the British people were urged to drink more tea. They were also encouraged to shop around and to look for lower prices; the very purpose of the 1784 Act was to reduce the cost of tea to the consumer. Cheaper teas, reduced prices, bargain deals, 'the cheapest shop in town' – all such claims and more were dangled before the reader in order to lure the tea-drinking public to the shopkeeper's counter. One dealer proclaimed (perhaps not without justice) that

> should any person offer teas for less than here stated, the public may be assured they are mixed with those musty, moldy, and decayed sorts.

Another offered his tea 'for the benefit of the poor'.[41] Throughout the promotion of tea in the 1780s dealers stressed two features; their competitive prices and the unadulterated nature of their offerings (itself a sure sign that adulterated tea was commonplace).

The major London houses did not have things all their own way, for there was competition from other sources. The tables were turned when dealers in other towns placed advertisements in London newspapers offering their competitively priced teas. From Bristol and Bath, Ripon and Leeds, Newcastle and York, tea-dealers competed directly with the London companies, always claiming that their tea was no dearer (and certainly no worse) than their metropolitan rivals. There was also commercial rivalry between shopkeepers in their same town. Their rival claims were sometimes bizarre. One Edinburgh shopkeeper proclaimed that his teas were 'cheaper than those on South Bridge as his shop rent is not one-third of theirs'. Some of the bigger tea-traders sought to remain aloof from this splurge of aggressive commercial salesmanship, notably the simple, plain-dealing Quaker merchants whose trading honesty had already become a byword and helps to explain, to a marked degree, their brilliant successes in this and other businesses.[42] Most however felt unable to go down that unsullied commercial route, instead joining in the flurry of advertising which engulfed the British public in the 1780s.

The buoyancy and profitability of the tea-trade came to a halt in the years of global warfare after 1793. The war, first against the Revolution and then Napoleon, was a convulsion which consumed the nation's energies and manpower. It also, of course, severely disrupted international trade.[43] Indeed Napoleon hoped to bring Britain to its knees by economic dislocation rather than by military defeat. To help pay for the war tea duties were raised again and higher prices brought an end to the giddy excesses which had followed 1784. The trade did not pick up until the return of peace in 1815.

There could be no stopping the British attachment to sweet tea: tea-drinking was in effect a way of defining Britishness.[44] It was just as well that Britannia ruled the waves (though in the 1790s it was a close-run thing) because the supplies of tea and sugar needed to fuel the energies of the people and to lubricate their routines of sociability came courtesy of long-distance maritime trade and naval power. It was the beginning of a pattern which was to dominate commercial and strategic thinking in the nineteenth century and especially in the twentieth. Yet it was clearly in place by the late 1700s. By then, the British had become a nation of consumers, devouring goods and produce as no other nation on earth at that time. And they were addicted to foodstuffs which were brought to the doorstep by the remarkable global trading system which the British had perfected (if not invented) since the seventeenth century. Those goods, from the recesses of China, from the slave fields of the Caribbean and the Chesapeake, were delivered to British people, of all sorts and conditions, by tens of thousands of shopkeepers. It was hard to see the connection, at the point of sale, across a grubby, corner shop in poorer urban areas, but the link was clear enough; the shopkeeper was the last link between the colonial producer and the British consumer.

The British were able to consume their tropical staples thanks to that aggressive colonial power and commercial ascendancy which had come to characterize their dealings with the wider world. Their colonial outposts – trading companies, plantation settlements, military bases and the extraordinary long reach of the Royal Navy – kept in place a massive global empire which, whatever its invisible costs, yielded major benefits to all and sundry. Few counted the cost, but all could enjoy the benefits in the comfort (or bleak poverty) of their own homes. In time of course the goods of the wider world were to arrive in Britain, as well as other nations, courtesy of the strength of commercial companies. But in this, the first phase of Britain's imperial asendancy, the British had become addicted to the fruits of their empire thanks to a ruthless exercise of power. It may seem fanciful, but here was a power exercised around the world in different forms, which ensured that even the humblest of British people were guaranteed their few ounces of tropical pleasures from their nearest corner shop. Again, Adam Smith saw the point sooner than others.

> To found a great empire for the sole purpose of raising up a people of customers, may at first sight appear a project fit only for a nation of shop-keepers. It is however, a project altogether unfit for a nation of shop-keepers; but extremely fit for a nation governed by shop-keepers.[45]

# 11 The Passion to Consume

The phenomenon of material consumption is so integral an aspect of today's world that it is tempting to think of it as uniquely modern. The urge to buy – to consume – goods, to fill our private and public lives with artefacts of all sorts and conditions is the driving force behind much of the world's economy. Though the current scale of material consumption is recent, historians have come to accept that the phenomenon itself, far from being new, has been a feature of western life for at least two centuries; it was already deeply ingrained long before Britain became an industrial power.

The substance of this book has been about certain kinds of products and consumables which lay at the heart of that early consumer revolution. Few would now dispute that economic change in the course of the seventeenth and eighteenth centuries was, in large measure, driven forward by the rising power of consumer demand. Consumption of an increasingly diverse and expansive range of goods was the inspiration behind a host of innovations – technological, marketing, and organizational. And this was true not solely in Britain but in greatly differing societies where the British settled and traded. What few historians have recognized is the degree to which the urge to consume – to acquire the artefacts and luxuries of the modernizing world – penetrated far beyond the west and served to transform societies much earlier than previously imagined.

On the very rim of the European's world, on the dangerous and violent edges of European settlement and control, where colonists and settlers clung to insecure roots in alien territory, their presence prompted a desire for consumption among local peoples. Wherever they lived, traded or settled, Europeans infected locals with more than their diseases: they enthused them with the desire to own, to buy, to trade for consumer goods which came ashore from European ships. The local details differed from place to place but the overall pattern was similar. Right round the edges of Atlantic settlement and trade (and of course much further afield), the spores of western material consumption thrived among local peoples, infecting them with the urge to possess items obtainable only from the Europeans. Whatever resistance there may have been to contact with the whites (understandably, since such contacts were full of obvious dangers – of ill-health, violence and upheaval), local peoples simply could not resist what the white men had to offer. And what they had to offer was, thanks to their remarkable global trading systems, the dazzling produce of Europe and Asia.

Wherever we look, at contact between Europeans and distant people, there we will see the encouragement of consumption as part of European domination. Perhaps the most spectacular case was in West Africa, for there European goods formed the substance of the barter and sale of slaves. European produce poured into West Africa as the basis for the lucrative Atlantic slave trade. Most striking, and best remembered (though not, economically, the most important), was the metalware and hardware, especially from the Black Country. Metal bars became a popular means of exchange: 12 and 13-kilogram hunks of metal notched into smaller units for subdivision, used as currency along a vast stretch of the coast.[1] Some historians have been more impressed however by the volume of imported firearms. At the peak years of the Atlantic slave trade, Europeans imported between 283 000 and 394 000 firearms *each year*. In 1802 alone, the value of guns shipped into Africa stood at £145 661.[2] The military value of those guns was limited by problems of maintainence and supply. But, like so many artefacts from Europe, the importance of firearms transcended their firepower. They empowered and enboldened their owners and they became a much-prized and much sought-after form of trade.

Guns were only a small part of the European trading onslaught in West Africa. From the first, Africans were encouraged to consume a wide range of basic and luxury goods. From the British viewpoint, the most important commodity was that range of textiles which flowed into Africa from Britain and India. Irish linens, Scottish woollens, Indian silks and calicoes – all and more became part of the everyday life in a host of African societies. The rapid growth of the British textile industry from the mid-eighteenth century was closely linked to the African trade. An expanding volume of Lancashire textiles was manufactured for trade to Africa, and for clothing slaves in the Americas. In its turn, the consumer power that textile manufacture unleashed in Britain was directed towards the consumption of material goods (many of them, as we have seen, exotic). Those men most involved, the manufacturers in and around Manchester, were in no doubt of the importance of this African-based trade to the livelihood of their workers in Lancashire.[3] The figures speak for themselves.

In 1750 the value of cotton goods shipped from England to Africa stood at £7839. Ten years later it was worth £52 264. There were inevitably periodic slips in the graph – mainly caused by the interruptions of war – but the overall upward trend was unmistakable. By the end of the American War in 1783, exports to Africa stood at £162 724; on the eve of the French wars (1792) they had grown to £437 370.[4]

But these bare figures tell only part of the story, for African traders and merchants developed a taste for luxurious textiles from Asia which were transhipped via Britain. The 54 958 pieces of 1751 more than doubled in the next decade. By 1783 they stood at 154 675 pieces and in 1793 413 652. On the eve of the abolition of the slave trade, more than a third of a million textile pieces were imported into Africa.[5] Moreover a similar pattern was true for other European slave-trading nations. The Dutch for instance paid for many of their slaves with textiles, most of them manufactured in Haarlem and Leiden.[6]

There were of course other trinkets and baubles which European industries poured out for African consumption. Many were obviously useful – knives, pans, clocks, chains, locks. But many too were luxuries. French brandy and wines, West Indian rum, sugar from the New World and tobacco from the Chesapeake. Here was yet another of those remarkable ironies which dot the history of material consumption, for these were goods, grown and manufactured by slaves in the Americas (many of them Africans) being used for the purchase of still more slaves. Those same goods were also for the use of African slaves on board the slave ships. It was as if the cycle of exploitation came full circle. When the *Hope* set sail for Africa from Lancaster in 1792 it carried, among a varied cargo of foodstuffs and manufactured goods, rice (almost certainly grown by slaves in South Carolina) and pipes destined for use with slave-grown tobacco. It was a common practice on the slave ships to allow slaves a tobacco ration. James Penny told Parliament in 1789 that slaves on board British ships 'are then supplied with Pipes and Tobacco; both Sexes sometimes will smoak.'[7] It was important to keep slaves in good humour, especially when they had made landfall and were being prepared for sale to the planters. When the ship the *James* reached Barbados in 1626 the Captain recorded in his log: '... gave my slaves tobacco and pipes.' Later, as they were being prepared for sale, he again gave them 'fresh water to wash and Palm Oyle and Tobacco and pipes'.[8]

Other slave-grown produce found its way back to Africa and into the slave ships. In the first 41 years of its trading life, the Royal African Company imported more than 30 000 tons of sugar in part return for 100 000 African slaves.[9] It is an irony of extraordinary proportions that Africans – and even slaves in the holds of the ships – had been taught to desire the very objects which the Atlantic slave system had been devised to conjure forth from the fertile lands of the Americas.

When European slave traders set down on the coast to negotiate the price of slaves with Africans, they laid before them the most attractive of material goods; rolls of costly Indian silks, the best French brandies, the most potent of firearms, wads of tobacco and the best of European metalware. When Europeans offered shoddy or unpopular goods – cheap metals goods and baubles – Africans angrily rejected their overtures. Experience taught the Europeans that good trade could only be had via decent barter, prefaced by elaborate and profuse gift-making. 'Those who make the most acceptable presents has the most friendship from them...'[10]

Not surprisingly, pipe-smoking was common among slaves in the Americas; even in regions where tobacco production was unusual. When William Beckford described the island of Jamaica in 1790, he remarked on the fact that, throughout the island, slaves could be seen walking around smoking pipes.[11] Among the various items recovered by archaeologists from slave graves in Barbados, white clay pipes are especially numerous. Vast numbers of European pipes were exported to all the American colonies, and it is clear enough that people of all classes, from the highest to the humblest slave, smoked. And they smoked from pipes manufactured in Europe – from London, Bristol, Reading and possibly Holland.[12] Ships heading for Africa and the Americas would ordinarily have pipes in their cargoes, for sale, barter, or simply for use among the slaves on board the second leg of the voyage.

It is a curious fact that slaves in the Americas almost certainly acquired the habit of pipe-smoking not from the region where the tobacco grew, but while on board the slave ships. In time, of course, smoking and tobacco cultivation were transplanted to the the other side of the Atlantic and took root in a host of African societies. Africans smoked because they were encouraged to do so by Europeans. And for the habit to continue, the slaves required pipes – manufactured in Europe.

Those who studied British colonies in the Americas were in little doubt, by the mid-eighteenth century, that they were gazing at a remarkable source of wealth and material well-being for the British nation. Bryan Edwards dedicated his classic history of the West Indies in 1793 to his king, George III, with the ringing assertion that the islands 'are become the principal source of the national opulence and maritime power'.[13] Though it is relatively easy to tabulate the rising volume of tropical goods shipped across the Atlantic to Britain, it is less commonly acknowledged that those islands were kept at work, and were developed by, vast consumption of imported goods. Plantations – and their enslaved labouring force – could not survive without the import of British and other goods. Each year plantation accounts recorded barrels and boxes of goods unloaded from British vessels. Worthy Park received, among a varied cargo in 1789, the following items: mosquito nets, thread, copper boilers, strainers and a host of metal goods, saddles and furniture, glass, hats for the slaves, porter (for the whites), coal, lime, blankets for the slaves, linseed oil, paint, mustard, gunpowder, corks, flour, peas, cooking oil, lead, stationery, nails, shingles, chains, tools for the fields, carpenters' equipment, seeds for the gardens, cheese (from Cheshire), medicines, rope and tarpaulins. In that same year, the plantation unloaded food supplies and candles from Ireland. Moreover, many of the goods bought from other parts of the island had been imported into the island initially.[14] The plantations – direct source of so much wealth – stimulated a prodigious amount of British industry, production and supply simply to remain operational.

Planters, like slaves, could not survive without imports from Britain. Not suprisingly, many artefacts of plantocratic life – which was itself modelled on life in the metropolis – mirrored the domestic consumption of their British peers. By the mid-eighteenth century, planters throughout the islands shaped their domestic environment much as they would in Bath or Bristol. Inventories of plantations reveal the pattern. Rooksby Park in Jamaica had among its rooms a 'Tea room' complete with a mahogany tea table and a display of china. An inventory of the same place for 1809 listed '1 Old Tea Urn'.[15]

More surprising perhaps was the fact that many items had spread down from the planters to the slaves. But was it really surprising? After all, this is precisely what happened in Britain, where the propertied classes handed on their material possessions and their cult of luxury consumption to their servants. Slaves began to acquire a range of personal effects in a host of ways. They loved, for example, to adorn themselves with jewellery. Sir William Young was struck by slave jewellery in Bridgetown:

> ... there was such a swagger of importance in the gait of those (and many there were) who had gold earings and necklaces ...[16]

In Martinque he thought that 'The jeweller and silversmith's shop (Goutier's) is as brilliant as any in London or Paris'.[17]

On all sides, visitors to the islands were in agreement that, by the late eighteenth century, there was a marked material improvement taking place among the slaves. And they measured that improvement not simply in the obvious indices of daily life on the plantations, but by the sense of rising material well-being visible in most islands. Young himself thought that the material improvement among the slaves was simply a function of money: the spread of money through their ranks had an improving, 'civilizing' effect. We know for example that in Jamaica, about 20 per cent of the island's cash was in slave hands.[18] Bryan Edwards however disagreed. The reason, he claimed, was not money but a related issue:

> It is not therefore the possession of money alone; it is the new desires springing up in his [the slave's] mind, from the

> prospects and examples before him that have awakened his powers, and called the energies of his mind into action.[19]

The 'examples' were all around; in the Great House, in the towns (to which ever more slaves had access – and in which many now lived) and spilling forth from the armada of ships which plied back and forth between the islands and the ports of Europe. Slaves, quite simply, followed the route of those around them, and learned the habit (and picked up the desire) of acquiring objects: necessities, refinements and luxuries.

When Bryan Edwards reported on the improving fortunes of the upper reaches of slave society, especially the 'tradesmen and domesticks' he told of their domestic fittings:

> Many of these have larger houses with boarded floors, and are accomodated (*at their own expence* it is true) with very decent furniture:– a few have even good beds, linen sheets, and mosquito nets, and display *a shelf or two of plates and dishes of queen's or Staffordsshire ware.*[20]

Solid furniture, imported textiles, costly pottery – and all bought at the slaves' expense. Here surely was remarkable testimony to the seductive power of material consumption. Moreover the only people from whom the slaves could have acquired this habit – the only people they met who were likely to possess such artefacts – were local whites.

We need of course to be cautious about such evidence. After all, Edwards was a planter, keen to broadcast the paternal benefits of slavery (not least to the slaves), at a time of mounting abolitionist pressure. What better way of discounting abolitionists' horror stories than by pointing to the improvement in the material conditions of the slaves?[21]

Fortunately there is an abundance of parallel evidence which confirms the general point that slaves were indeed acquiring ever more material artefacts. One French planter, writing after the disasters of the Haitian revolt, bemoaned the 'foolish fancy of enriching negroes [which] was but too common and extravagent among us'.[22] Though we need to be careful about the *degree* of slaves' material well-being, it would be wrong to ignore it. But, for our purpose, if historians of the consumer revolution need evidence for the contagious acquisitiveness of material consumption, they need look, not to the plebeian cultures of the western world, but to subject peoples on the fringes of colonial settlement.

Slaves bought, bartered or were given objects which in the first instance graced the homes of their local betters. To a degree this was both obvious and inevitable. Since white society controlled the flow of all goods coming into the slave islands, they inevitably shaped the supply of material goods into the slave quarters. But it seems clear enough that slaves, like their plebeian counterparts in Europe, also developed their own craving for material items. And so many of those items were luxuries – the personal jewellery, the clock reported stolen from a slave's cabin in St Ann, Jamaica, in 1788,[23] the shelves of fashionable English pottery – these were surely luxuries. And whence came the urge to consume such items? To a degree they were encouraged in such tastes by the occasional generosity of local whites. Masters and mistresses, lovers and fathers, passed on to their favourite slaves a range of material objects – much as the British well-to-do gave goods to their own domestics. Thomas Thistlewood in Jamaica gave gifts to his favourite paramours and payment in cash for sexual favours. But more interesting still is the fact that in return one slave gave him valuable items. Phibbah, Thistlewood's mistress, was an astute trader and dealer in those goods and foodstuffs valued by other slaves. She accumulated goods and money, sold on credit and generally built up possessions left and right. She sold one of her horses for £4.10s. and on another occasion 'sold her mare Patience to the Negro man of Col. Barclay named Crossley for seven pounds. He paid her £5.10s down, and is to pay the remaining 30s in three months.'[24] On various occasions she gave Thistlewood substantial items; foodstuff and 'a piece of soap', animals for cooking, tasty morsels and on one special occasion (when they were about to part) 'gave me a gold ring, to keep for her sake'.[25]

Many of these material acquisitions stemmed directly from the slaves' work in their gardens and provisions grounds. The produce they cultivated, the animals they tended, were bartered and sold, to individuals or at markets, and the goods and money thus accumulated spent on improving their material lives or enhancing their pleasures. From an early date it was this growing material accumuluation which enabled slaves to invest such time and lavish materials in preparation for major slave 'festivals', especially at Christmas and 'crop-over'. Visitors to the islands were stunned by the ability of slaves – people, they assumed, with little but the basics of human existence – to conjure forth the most elaborate and costly costumes and decorations. The simple truth was that the slaves had became consumers. They bought, borrowed, swapped and were given a remarkable range of items produced on both sides of the Atlantic. They did not need the persuasion of early advertisers because, on the fringes of empire, they saw with their own eyes the benefits and pleasures to be had from such things. They picked up the habit of consumption from their betters. And similar stories were reported from other, hugely different parts of the British empire.

This pattern was repeated wherever we look in the Americas. Nor was it restricted to the obviously prosperous. The humble and the poor – people who seemed immune to the rise of material well-being so striking on both sides of the Atlantic – began to enjoy and use items designed for others. It seemed natural to those Americans who bridled at the encroaching power of the British over North American affairs, to attack British power where it hurt, by boycotting imported luxuries – those unnecessary 'Baubles of Britain'.[26] Americans of all sorts and conditions had, like slaves in the Caribbean, become accustomed to the unquestioned acquisition of a range of imported British goods. Indeed it is symptomatic that of all the events leading to American independence, it was the outburst against imported tea that sticks in the popular mind. But if we wish to assess the real impact of imported British goods, the most revealing evidence is to be found among the Indian peoples. There, among the native peoples of northeastern America, we find irrefutable evidence of the contagious power of material consumption, evidence which – like consumption among the slaves – throws fresh light on the whole debate about the nature of the consumer revolution in the seventeenth and eighteenth centuries.

From the earliest contacts between Europeans and Indians, the invading whites realized that Indians had access to many desirable objects. The pelts and skins so basic to Indian life were the very luxuries of European consumption, and traders paid good prices for them in a range of European currencies. Beaver for hats, otter and fox skins to trim gowns and dresses, deerskins for leather goods – these and other pelts were demanded in vast and increasing profusion. Indians throughout the regions of contact hurried to oblige. Tens of thousands of pelts passed along the complex Indian trading routes to the outposts of European settlement; convoys of Indian canoes ferried the goods to European traders. The figures involved were astonishing. Between 1739 and 1759 the Cherokee for instance 'reduced the southeastern deer population by 1.25 million.'[27] In return, the Indians acquired new habits, developing a voracious taste for imported goods. The process was summed up in an observation of 1679. The Indians had discovered that:

> many Things which they wanted not before because they never had them are by ... means [of the trade] become necessary both for their use and ornament.

They had been afflicted 'by a desire of new-fangled novelties'.

The Indians were not to be fobbed off with worthless trinkets. They quickly learned the value of the animal skins they delivered to the Europeans, in return accumulating a host of artefacts from European industries – many of which were clearly more advanced than their own crudely made items. In the words on one Indian, 'The Beaver does everything perfectly well, it makes kettles, hatchets, swords, knives, bread, in short it makes everything'.[28] Indians learned the nature of the market, and developed skills required to thrive in the competitive market place. They would take their pelts to distant traders if they thought they could get a better deal. They were choosy about the goods on offer. In short, they became discriminating and effective customers and consumers.

Historians have been able to reconstruct what the Indians acquired, thanks to two distinct but related sources; European trading ledgers and the recent archaeological work on Indian sites. Curiously enough Indians had in fact acquired European goods long before they made face-to-face contact, picking up items from abandoned settlements and shipwrecks. It was even reported that the first Indians confronting Gaspar Corte-Real in Canada in 1501 held a piece of an Italian sword; another wore Venetian silver earings.[29] As trade evolved, Indians quickly appreciated the benefits of superior European tools and pots, which were quickly adapted to the range of domestic and workaday Indian needs. But the most common acquisition was textiles. European woollens and duffels became part of Indian attire across great tracts of North America, their durability and qualities replacing many of the indigenous skins and furs used since time out of mind. They were however cloths which the Indians made up into their own garments; they rarely liked or wore European clothing, though prominent Indians might adopt contemporary colourful and buttoned regalia to enhance their own status and rank.

Imported luxuries quickly insinuated themselves into Indian life. Dyes from China, Venetian glass beads, German silverware were favourite items. But Indians were adaptable, taking other artefacts (thimbles, scraps of shiny metals) to incorporate them into their own displays and jewellery. These were however mere baubles. More significant – very much like the pattern unfolding at much the same time on the African coast – were alcohol and firearms. Indians and Africans faced similar problems in servicing and using European firearms. But those difficulties did little to deter them. The Indians wanted guns as the agent and threat of terror over their enemies; guns bestowed power and status far beyond their firepower. They were, like so many modern weapons, as powerful in their threat as in their use. It is generally recognized that this rapid and ubiquitous spread of European guns among the Indians had a deeply disruptive influence on tactics and fighting.[30]

For all the power of the firearms, there is little doubt that alcohol was much more destructive. Indians demanded and got French brandy and wines, and rum from the West Indian slave islands. It had devastating effects. Mass drunkenness, associated violence, the rise of related illnesses and the general corrosion of the stable fabric of Indian life, all and more flowed directly from the Indians' widespread and greedy demand for western alcohol. Less damaging, but no less ubiquitous, was the impact of the mirror. Now Indian men could set about their own facial paint and decorations; arrange their own coiffure, indulging in their narcissistic self-obsession that amused so many Europeans. But the mirror might also bring bad news, notably the irrefutable evidence of the deformity and ugliness inflicted by illness and disease – especially by smallpox. Men who saw their disfigured faces reflected in their British mirrors were driven to despair and even suicide.[31]

In this welter of detail a distinct pattern unfolded among the Indians. At first they were dazzled and tempted; later, they were in awe of and finally became dependent on, the artefacts of the western world. From the initial days of contact through to the more regular and ritualized dealings beween Europeans and Indians by the mid-eighteenth century, the flow of European goods increased dramatically, a fact amply confirmed by archaeological discoveries. Indeed so pervasive were European artefacts among Indians in the north-east that investigators despaired of ever finding objects unalloyed by European influences. Contemporaries were apt to describe these changes among the Indians as 'degeneration'.[32]

The impact of European goods on the peoples of North America was extraordinary. The consequences for North American animal life was even more dramatic. In places, the wildlife that bore the fur and skin sought by the Europeans was virtually exterminated by Indian hunters. When their natural supply of wealth disappeared, the Indians had little to trade with the Europeans save 'their land, their labor, or their military services, which the proliferating colonists were only too glad to buy at bargain rates'. So addicted had Indians become to these 'artificial wants' that many realized they could not live without the Europeans. There were, it is true, periodic Indian outbursts of resistance – collective efforts to purge themselves of this dependence; to get back to their natural, native ways. But the most difficult task of all was to 'learn to live without any trade or connections with the white people, clothing and supporting themselves as their forefathers did'.[33]

Despite fierce Indian reaction, despite violent efforts to turn back the clock and to live without the European and his possessions, ultimately the white man's economic power proved too strong. Indian peoples were as beholden to western material consumption as the most prosperous ranks in Britain. Indeed it is surely a sign of the remarkable power of the western economy that it had, on the eve of the American War, drawn into its orbital pull huge and distant swathes of empire, dispatching goods to peoples who were beyond the ken of Europeans. To a remarkable degree, the expansive economies of Europe – but especially of Britain – needed the peoples of the colonial peripheries to nurture their export industries.

At all the major points on the edges of the Atlantic empire – in the African slave trading outposts, on board the slave ships, in the Caribbean islands and among the Indian peoples of north-eastern America – the consumer revolution was at work. People of the most diverse kinds – people unknown to the Europeans not long before – were greedily consuming objects brought to their door by Europeans. It is clear that some European artefacts even went ahead of the first European arrivals; the flotsam and jetsam of overland and oceanic trade which found its way into the hands of people who scarcely knew what to make of it. More important still however was the fact that the people on the edges of empire were clearly in the forefront of a new wave of material acquisition. It was their consumer demands which prompted economic expansion in the British heartlands, in those key areas of economic growth (textiles, metals, foodstuffs) which had such important long-term consequences for the future growth of the British economy.

The patterns of consumption were striking from the mid-seventeenth century onwards. The flow of goods to the Indian peoples of North America, in return for valuable pelts, was remarkable. In the 40 years to 1700, woollens and metalware imports doubled; other items (tableware, sewing items) tripled. It was a curious formula for, as the native peoples were in great decline, the survivors nonetheless managed to consume an expanding volume of imported goods from Britain; fewer and fewer Indians consumed ever more goods. Moreover there is a convergence of evidence to confirm precisely when this pattern of Indian consumption took place. Archaeologists have shown that while only perhaps 15 per cent of excavated items from the period 1600–20 were of European origin, the years between 1650 and 1655 yielded artefacts which were 75 per cent European.[34]

Africans too learned to value and to desire European goods at much the same period. By the end of the seventeenth century, Africans along a vast expanse of the coast had learned to discriminate about the goods offered to them by trading Europeans. The first significant English player in the complex trading game on the African coast was the Royal African Company. By the end of the 1600s, one commentator reckoned that 150 commodities were traded on the coast. The

Royal African Company, which controlled the English trade throughout the second half of the seventeenth century, exported 27 major items to Africa. When ships unloaded the wrong items (i.e. when the English shippers got it wrong), howls of complaint issued from the traders on the coast and Africans simply refused to buy. But, in general, the main complaint by the late seventeenth century was of insufficient goods for sale. Though the broad pattern of trade was clearly imposed by the Europeans, the specific fluctuation in demand was dictated by the African consumer.

During the dominance of the Royal African Company, trade varied greatly from one part of the coast to another. The value of a slave was calculated in one place by the iron bar, elsewhere by a certain volume of gunpowder. At another spot, slaves could be had for textiles (26 sheets). At Whydah, Indian textiles were demanded for slaves. And although nominal values were placed on the heads of particular kinds of slaves, they were bought by exchanging them for that value of goods. The price of slaves had risen dramatically by the late 1600s, increasing perhaps fivefold in the last 20 years of the century, thanks to the rapid development of the slave islands. And each rise meant that more goods had to be imported onto the coast. The flow of goods seemed endless. Iron bar and copper bars, brass and pewter-ware, a range of British woollens, various Indian textiles; carpets and sheets, gunpowder, guns and knives.[35]

Nor was this African demand for imported goods restricted solely to land-based traders. The hundreds of ships which plied the Atlantic slave routes needed to be supplied. Hundreds of ships each year criss-crossed the Atlantic, servicing the slave colonies and beyond, their routes much more complex and varied than the term 'triangular trade' suggests. And each of these ships was loaded with products from the hinterland of their British port and with goods transhipped, mainly from Asia. Quite apart from the goods needed to buy the slaves, they required provisions to keep the slaves alive on the long haul across the Atlantic.

The nourishment (such as it was) of the millions of miserable Africans shipped across the Atlantic also served to fuel European industries. When the slave ships loaded, they took on board enough provisions and goods to maintain their human cargoes across the Atlantic. That millions did not survive the crossing does not undermine the point. They loaded barrels of vinegar (to clean out the slave quarters, and to rinse out slaves' mouths on arrival), barrels of beans to feed the slaves, tobacco and pipes to pacify them. The *Norman* left London in 1714, intent on securing 300 slaves, and for whom it carried food and supplies of pipes and tobacco. Agents in Africa were told by the Royal African Company in London to put on board the westbound slave ships 'twenty gallons of rum for each hundred slaves'.[36]

The business of slave trading became ever more complex, with links deep into Africa, goods shipped to Africa from the furthest reaches of Asia, and with crucial ties to a plethora of European industries. The slave trade was in fact the hub of a remarkable global system which poured consumer goods, from all corners of the world, into the holds of the slave ships, and thence to a myriad of communities in Africa and the Americas. There are of course a number of ways of interpreting this picture. The Atlantic slave system was but one aspect – albeit so obvious and discomforting because its prime commodity was human – of a much broader global trading network. In recent years, historians have been anxious to play down the role of slave exports in the economic history of Africa, pointing out – quite properly – that the slaves were only one sort of export trade; that Africa exported a greater range of other commodities. Yet, however we define this aspect of Africa's economic history, it hinged to a marked degree on the consumption of imported goods. Put at its simplest, by the time the slave economy had become a pace-setting force within the broader Atlantic trade, African consumption played a crucial role. Europeans were able to fill their slave ships because they had persuaded Africans, from a range of greatly different societies, that they wanted or needed exotic goods; that they wished to consume European and Asian goods which were unloaded from their sailing ships.

Throughout the second half of the seventeenth century, English traders tried to secure a lucrative place for themselves on the African coast. Prevailing economic orthodoxy however decreed that slave trading should be in the hands of the monopoly Royal African Company. When that monopoly was broken in 1712, English traders to Africa soon appreciated that they were entering an area of trade where consumer tastes and customer demands had already taken on a clearly defined shape. It was immediately apparent that English traders could not seduce Africans with cheap or inferior items. In the course of the late 1600s, African traders had become sophisticated consumers of imported goods, keen on what they perceived to be the best, and dismissive of items which failed to live up their expectations. Ironically, in the short term, this worked *against* British domestic industries. Africans were alert to the fact that superior goods – especially textiles – were produced elsewhere. When for instance Bristol merchants first made a tentative beginning in the African trade, their potential African trading partners already had clear ideas about what they wanted. As a result, the Englishmen had to offer transhipped textiles. Indian cloths were so obviously superior to the British that the Africans wanted the Asian variety. In the words of David Richardson: 'Bristol merchants found it difficult to convince the discerning African consumer that British-produced goods were better than those made elsewhere.'[37] Bristol was able to adapt quickly to this consumer demand, using its existing trading links with London and Holland to acquire the goods that the Africans wanted. But the fact of African consumption and tastes is crucial. English traders had to accept that Africans had already become sophisticated customers who could dictate terms to the importers and traders from afar.

To get a sense of how deeply pervasive was the influence of the Atlantic empire within Britain, we need only look at the regions and industries which supplied the ships heading for Africa and the Americas. The British slave-trading ports were scattered around the coast and ranged from the smallest, most unlikely of candidates (Poole, Lyme Regis) to the obvious (Liverpool and Bristol). They all drew upon a broad commercial and productive hinterland for the goods they shipped, quite apart for the goods they transhipped from Asia. A few examples will illustrate the network of trading and manufacturing links which moved goods from throughout Britain to the holds of the slave ships. The *Hope* left Lancaster for Africa in 1792 carrying among her cargo the following articles: rice and knives from a merchant in Liverpool, silk and cotton goods from another Liverpool house, salt from Cheshire, beads from a Liverpool trader, brass and wire from Cheadle, cotton goods from Manchester, flagons from a Lancaster tea and spirit merchant, earthenware from a Liverpool manufacturer, sails from a Kirkham sailmaker, weapons and iron goods from a Liverpool factory, foodstuffs from a local grocer, pots from Preston, chests from a Lancaster cooper.[38] Here were small towns, provincial backwaters and smallscale operators active in, benefiting from, and becoming important agents in a much broader global undertaking.

The links were direct and the benefits substantial. Slavery reached deep into the heart of British life, galvanizing men and communities (traders, growers, dealers, shops, craftsmen and others) to work towards nurturing and encouraging the Atlantic slave system. It soon became impossible to disentangle great swathes of the British economy from the course and progress of the Atlantic slaving system. Of course slavery was only one aspect of a remarkable Atlantic system for, as we have seen here, it embraced lucrative and transformative dealings with the Indian peoples of the Americas. Those of North America, after sampling the Europeans' wares, opted for what pleased them most – what satisfied their distinctive local needs. Those needs, in West Africa and North America, may often have seemed luxurious (at least to outsiders) – items which indigenous societies had managed without since time out of mind. But they quickly became integral to local society, and consumers demanded more and more. Nor was this demand a simple shout for *anything* European. North American Indians and Africans made *precise* demands of their white trading partners. Moreover those demands were in place by the mid-seventeenth century. These, the first people to experience a consumer revolution, the first to devour European goods on a prodigious and transforming scale, were people living beyond the European pale.

They were, moreover, people who prove elusive for scholars searching for the standard data basic to European economic history. What, for example, were the *earnings* of American Indians on the eve of contact? They were, as James Axtell has reminded us, people living in penury, yet how was it that, within a few short years, these same people were able to consume remarkable and increasing volumes of western material goods?[39] Though they lacked any obvious income, they had access of course to items which Europeans wanted; to the apparently boundless supply of North American pelts. And a similar story was true on the African coast, where indigenous traders could conjure forth – by means the Europeans were not always clear about – seemingly endless supplies of Africans for the slave quarters of the Americas. For those students of the origins of the consumer revolution, here then is powerful evidence, which redirects attention *away* from Britain itself, focusing it on the very edges of European trade and settlement. There was, in effect, a periphery of Atlantic consumption which depended on Europe for the importation of manufactured, cultivated and transhipped goods. And the end result from those worlds of distant consumers – distant, that is, from the metropolitan heartlands which called this trading system into being – was a remarkable rise in the material well-being of Britain itself. Historians have long concentrated on the extraordinary upsurge in Britain's economic strength because of the Atlantic system. We can now see that the whole process was clearly marked in the 50 years between 1650 and 1700.

The purpose here however is not so much to sketch the broad outlines of British economic growth as to suggest the degree to which the development of Britain's Atlantic economy was fired and then driven forward by some remarkable patterns of material consumption among peoples on the edges of British settlement and trade. Yet it is impossible to restrict these comments simply to the issue of consumption. What lies behind this discussion is an even more significant issue; of the role played by the opening of the Atlantic economy in the transformation and advancement of Britain itself. In a long and convoluted debate, stretching back a half century, historians and economists have wrestled with the question of the origins of British economic primacy from the eighteenth century onwards. If we look at the narrower focus of consumption, we can see the degree to which the peoples on the edge of British settlement and dominion formed a critical market for the British economy. These patterns of colonial consumption were clearly important in generating economic growth and broadly-based well-being in the British heartland. More than that, the first signs of modern consumption were to be seen on the very fringes of colonial life as much as in Britain itself. It was a mutually beneficial arrangement. In return for the goods demanded by colonial peoples, the British devoured – and became addicted to – the fruits of empire produced by their client and servile peoples.

# 12 Questions of Taste, Addiction – and Empire

The British people entered those turbulent post-1815 years of industrial and urban growth collectively wedded to a diet and to social habits shaped by the exotic staples discussed in this book. There were of course many other exotica which had become basic to their lives. But few others had come to exercise such pre-eminent social importance, to the degree in fact that they even helped to define the very nature of Britishness itself. Historians curious about the emergence of national identity have looked closely at the political expression of that identity, but have virtually ignored its social and economic origins. To repeat the simple question with which I began: what could be more British that a cup of sweet tea?

This book has been at pains to stress that there was much more to these British habits than the accidental, changing fads of taste and fashion. There is however one issue which needs to be addressed. Some of these tropical staples were addictive stimulants. Could this be the key to the universal consumption of tea/coffee/tobacco? Indeed the modern-day drive against those items are often inspired by their harmful effects. Too much caffeine, too much tannin – too much addiction and stimulus – have led to the development and marketing of alternative forms (decafeinated coffee, herbal teas). Tobacco is of course in a league of its own for its addictive qualities and its harmful consequences. Yet consumers of these (and other) products continue to reassure themselves by pointing to the benefits they claim for their pleasures. Tea to revive and refresh, to start the day, to calm the agitated or injured; tea-drinking interludes to punctuate daily routines, to conclude the day – all and more are so obvious because so familiar. Coffee too played similar roles. Taken to stay awake (or not taken in order to fall asleep), coffee to complete a meal, to break up the day's routines; coffee and tea-drinkers make similar claims for their chosen beverage. These very different drinks have something in common: consumers defend their choice of drink for its pleasures, for its physical effects and for its social importance. Curiously, the patterns of argument – for and against these items – reflect, in modern form, many of the claims which greeted their arrival in Britain in the seventeenth century. They – and others – were promoted (or denounced) by varying alliances of scientific and commercial interests. But in each case, objections were soon marginalized by a rising tide of public consumption.

The fact that tea and coffee occupy greatly differing social roles from one society to another provides perhaps the most telling clue to their significance. They are obviously products of particular historical and cultural forces. Why, for example (and with obvious changes and exceptions) is Britain a nation of tea-drinkers and the USA a nation of coffee-drinkers? To a degree of course the answer lies in the distinctive commercial history of those different nations. But that commercial story is itself a result of different historical trajectories. It is at this point that we need to return to the broader history of the British people. Whatever importance we might attach to the addictive or stimulating nature of these tropical staples, they were qualities which, in the British case, were mediated by the broader interests of global trade and empire. To put the matter boldly, the British people developed their social and personal habits around these staples because of the specific course of British imperial and commercial history.

This is not to deny however that 'taste' played an important part. But 'taste' itself is so culturally specific – so hugely different from one society to another – that we need to consider the historical origins of particular tastes. After all, before the seventeenth century, the British people had virtually *no* taste for any of the items discussed in this book, for the simple reason that these exotica were effectively unknown or were rarified and costly luxuries. When the British developed a taste for these beverages for example, they did so, as we have seen, by adding sugar to them. Chocolate, coffee and tea, in Britain at least, were sweet beverages. And this evolution of sweet tastes was made possible by the slave plantations of the Caribbean.

Sugar poured from the West Indian islands on a scale and with results that few could have imagined. Islands were conquered, native people effectively destroyed, nature itself transformed, by the need to cultivate sweetness. And to make it possible, Africa was scourged, millions of its peoples transported and scattered in unprecedented numbers to the edges of the British empire. This whole vast edifice was kept in place by a huge, effective and repressive military machine: the Royal Navy which controlled the sea lanes and the islands; military bases which both repelled European rivals and overawed the legions of resistant, alien slaves. Here was sweetness which flowed from military and commercial strength.

The profits of this empire – the duties imposed on the global flow of tropical produce – enriched the British nation-state. The strength of the eighteenth century British state – advanced by the instruments of its military might (especially the Royal Navy) was itself maintained by the very process it was most crucial in defending; the conduct and flow of overseas trade and dominion.[1] Merchants and their companies, planters and their agents, colonial assemblies and their representatives – these and many more complained about the existence and levels of taxation and duties on the produce they dispatched to Britain. Duties were levied on all the imported staples discussed here, and though the British statesmen and politicians might argue about the appropriate *level* of those duties, most agreed that without them, the British state would have been greatly diminished, its fiscal strength reduced and its power correspondingly enfeebled. There were powerful reasons for the maintenance and enhancement of this global system of trade and domination. Moreover, those reasons could be seen in tangible form on the dockside of maritime Britain.

Whether in the form of the East India Company's chests of tea landed in London, the massive hogsheads of crude muscovado unloaded in Bristol or the barrels of tobacco shipped into Glasgow, here were the fruits of distant empire and trade. But here too was a major form of financial sustenance for the British state itself. Clearly, state income was derived from a much broader base than this. But the proceeds of global trade and dominion were integral to British power abroad and fiscal strength at home.[2]

The British people's acquired tastes for the fruits of empire were, then, both a function of British power and a source of national strength. They were tastes which were titillated and promoted with growing emphasis and ubiquity by that range of commercial interests, keen to sell their tropical wares. Rising literacy, the printed word (in newspaper advertisements and handbills), the influence of coffee shops and taverns, the universality of shops with their own displays (grand or meagre) of goods from distant parts of the globe – all and more served to dangle the imagery and reality of tropical goods before the British people.

There was too the contagion of social usage – call it emulation – that ripple-like effect of rising material consumption, from one person, one group, one class to another. The particular form – the specific style – which consumption took itself offers a complex story of the development of British etiquette and convention. Each of these exotic items not only entrenched itself in British life, but each evolved its own highly ritualized form of usage, and acquired its own social significance; by the end of our period, each of them seemed so well-established, so integral to British life, that few stopped to consider how new, how unusual, they were. They were, in a word, thoroughly British. But of course the British were also thoroughly imperial and global in their economic outlook.

Custom came to dictate than men alone should smoke (though ladies might take snuff, a fact which itself helped to shape key areas of contemporary masculinity and femininity). Tea-drinking cut across all boundaries of class and gender, but even so, tea-drinking rituals differed greatly across the social spectrum. Everyone, as far as we can tell, took sugar in their drinks and foodstuffs. Sugar was universal – as near as possible to being a national food. Its greatest use of course was to be mixed with tea. Indeed it seems likely that tea – like chocolate and coffee – only became acceptable to British taste by the coincidence of timing: all began to arrive in Britain when the first sugars were unloaded from the new West Indian colonies.

This was of course no mere coincidence. Produce from tropical colonies, goods via long-distance maritime trade, all were the material benefits to the British of aggressive trade and rapacious settlement. Personal acquisitiveness, commercial daring, military and technical power, all advanced or sustained by the British state, these were the formative elements in enhancing the wealth of the metropolis and of incorporating the whole nation in the course of empire and trade. This nation of shopkeepers – and shoppers – had by

1800 a vested interest in Britain's commercial and imperial role in the world at large.

Critics of the British empire (notably the Americans who broke away in 1776) were alert to these complex ramifications of Britain's aggressive tendencies. Benjamin Franklin denounced what he regarded as Britain's

> Fondness for Conquest as a Warlike Nation, her Lust of Dominion as an Ambitious one, and her Thirst for a gainful Monopoly as a Commercial one...[3]

Such vices were not simply the preserve of a small governing or intellectual elite. It seemed clear enough that the urge to global pre-eminence had entered the fibre, the soul, of the British people. At one level this was entirely understandable because so many Britons, most notably the Scots, had travelled to the very limits of commerce and settlement, to trade or live often in dangerous and hostile conditions. For example, in the seventeenth century alone, some 400 000 Britons had migrated across the Atlantic.[4] And such people were in addition to the temporary sojourners – the sailors, soldiers, traders – who (with luck) returned home from distant work and postings.

Few contemporaries were in any doubt that Britain needed its trade and dominion. Few indeed complained about it. How else can we explain the fact that as late as 1787, few had made serious objections to that most rapacious aspect of British trade – the Atlantic slave trade? The reason was simple and apparently irrefutable; here was a form of profitable trade and dominion – a source of lucrative business whose ramifications reached deep into every corner of British life.

Britain's global power thus reached not only to the most distant corners of trade and settlement but revealed itself in the results of that power, in the very heart of British society itself. The material benefits of dominance over distant places and peoples (whatever the hidden costs discovered by modern historians) were there for all to see. They were stacked on the shelves of the humblest shop, in the smallest, most inaccessible of villages. Whatever taste or communal addictions the British people had acquired by 1800, however complex the associated ritual of consumption, however subtle or crude the process of promoting and marketing those goods, the whole edifice rested securely on Britain's commercial might and empire.

This was, then, no mere exchange, no accidental transmission of crops and staples. This was no haphazard collision of peoples and plants. The story of the natural substances studied here had been utterly transmuted by economic power and military might. The British enjoyed those fruits of empire as the world's pre-eminent imperial and trading nation. Now, two centuries later, we can see the British, retreated to their island home, expelled from all but a handful of colonial outposts. That first astonishing British empire has slipped away like all other empires before it. But the former imperial masters (and mistresses) continue to take pleasure and comfort from the fruits of those long-lost empires.

# Notes

## ACKNOWLEDGEMENTS

1. Alfred W. Crosby, *The Columbian Exchange. Biological and Cultural Consequences of 1492*, Westport, Conn., 1972; Henry Hobhouse, *Seeds of Change. Five Plants that Transformed Mankind*, London, 1985; Sidney Mintz, *Sweetness and Power*, London, 1985.

## INTRODUCTION

1. John Brewer, *The Sinews of Power. War, Power and the English State, 1688–1783*, London, 1989.
2. Adam Smith, *The Wealth of Nations*, 1776, vol. II, bk IV, ch. 7, part iii.

## 1 ATTRACTIONS OF THE EAST

1. K.N. Chaudhuri, *Trade and Civilisation in the Indian Ocean*, Cambridge, 1985, p. 15; Janet L. Abu-Lughod, *Before European Hegemony. The World System, 1250–1350*, Oxford, 1991.
2. Ibid., p. 21.
3. This flow of goods was, in the American context, described as 'The Columbian Exchange' in an argument advanced by Alfred W. Crosby in two important books: *The Columbian Exchange. Biological and Cultural Consequences of 1492*, Westport, Conn., 1972, and *Ecological Imperialism*, Cambridge, 1986. Though greatly influenced by Crosby's work, this study seeks to offer an alternative view.
4. C.R. Boxer, *The Portuguese Seaborne Empire, 1415–1825*, London, 1969, p. 37.
5. Ibid., ch. 2; N. Tarling, ed., *The Cambridge History of South East Asia*, Cambridge, 1992, p. 354.
6. C.R. Boxer, ibid., p. 51.
7. Ibid., p. 59.
8. N. Tarling, ed., op. cit., p. 358.

## 2 TEA

1. John Lettsom, *Natural History of the Tea Trade*, London, 1772, p. 30.
2. Quoted in P. Griffiths, *A History of the India Tea Industry*, London, 1967, pp. 3–9.
3. Ibid., pp. 10–13.

4. P. Pomet, *A Compleat History of Druggs....* London, 1712. Pomet was chief druggist to the French monarch.
5. Ibid., pp. 10–11.
6. S. Schama, *An Embarrassment of Riches*, London, 1988 edn, pp. 171–2.
7. N.H. Woodward, *Teas of the World*, New York, 1980, p. 40.
8. Ibid., p. 41.
9. Quoted in J.W. Willis Jr, `European Consumption and Asian Production in the Seventeenth and Eighteenth Centuries', in J. Brewer and R. Porter, eds, *Consumption and the World of Goods*, London, 1993, p. 140.
10. N.H. Woodward, op. cit., p. 53.
11. R. Latham, ed., *The Shorter Pepys*, London, 1985, pp. 81, 800–1.
12 K.N. Chaudhuri, *The Trading World of Asia and the East India Company*, Cambridge, 1978, p. 386.
13. Ibid., pp. 388–9.
14. K.N. Chaudhuri, *East India,* op. cit., pp. 393–4.
15. Carole Shammas, *The Pre-Industrial Consumer in England and America*, Oxford, 1990, pp. 83–5.
16 N.H. Woodward, op. cit., p. 57.
17. J.E. Willis Jr, op. cit., p. 142.
18. N.H. Woodward, op. cit., p. 57.
19. J. Stevenson, *Popular Disturbances in England, 1700–1870*, London, 1979, p. 45.
20. N.H. Woodward, op. cit., p. 58.
21. C. Shammas, 'Changes in English and Anglo-American Consumption from 1550–1800', in J. Brewer and R. Porter, op. cit., pp. 183–5.
22. K.N. Chaudhuri, *East India,* op. cit., pp. 408–9.
23. D. Vaisy, ed., *Diaries of Thomas Turner*, Oxford, 1984, p. 159.
24. J. Lettsom, op. cit., p. 62.
25. Jonas Hanway, *Letters on the Importance of the Rising Generation of the laboring part of our fellow-subjects*, 2 vols, London, 1757, II, p. 179.
26. Quoted in A. Hope, *The Londoner's Larder*, London, 1990, pp. 88–9.
27. Quoted in S. Mintz, *Sweetness and Power*, London, 1985, pp. 114–16.
28. S.T. Anning, *A History of Medicine in Leeds*, Leeds, 1980, pp. 38; 57.
29. Sir F. Eden, *The State of the Poor*, 3 vols, London, 1797, I, 496; 535.
30. J. Burnett, *Plenty and Want*, London, 1979 edn, p. 26.
31. F. Braudel, *Capitalism and Material Life, 1400–1800*, London, 1967, p. 180.
32. K.N. Chaudhuri, *Asia Before Europe*, Cambridge, 1990, p. 335.
33. H. Hobhouse, *Seeds of Change*, London, 1985, p. 108.
34. Ibid., p. 109.
35. Quoted in N. McKendrick, 'Josiah Wedgwood and the commercialisation of the Potteries', in N. McKendrick, J. Brewer and J.H. Plumb, eds, *The Birth of a Consumer Society*, London, 1982, p. 101.
36. Ibid., pp. 133–4.
37. Ibid., p. 111.
38. A. Hope, *The Londoner's Larder*, London, 1990, p. 89.
39. N. McKendrick, op. cit., pp. 113, 131, 141.
40. C. Shammas, 'Changes', op. cit., pp. 181–5.
41. H. Hobhouse, op. cit., p. 94.

## 3 COFFEE

1. R. Bradley, *The Virtue and Use of Coffee...*, London, 1772, p. 12.
2. R. Hattox, *Coffee and Coffeehouses,* Seattle, 1985, chs 2–3.
3. Ibid., chs 3–4.
4. R. Bradley, op. cit., p. 23.
5. 'Coffee', in P. Pomet, *A Compleat History of Druggs,* London, 1712, p. 129.
6. R. Bradley, op. cit., pp. 22–26.
7. B. Mosley, *Treatise Concerning the Properties and Effects of Coffee,* London, 1792, pp. 45–58.
8. S. Pauli, *A Treatise on Tobacco, Tea, Coffee and Chocolate,* London, 1746, pp. 163–6.
9. R. Bradley, op. cit., pp. 6–7.
10. Quoted in R. Bradley, op. cit., p. 12.
11. Quoted in G. Keynes, *The Life of William Harvey,* Oxford, 1966, p. 406.
12. R. Bradley, op. cit., pp. 21–2.
13. Claudia Roden, *Coffee,* London, 1977, p. 22.
14. G. Keynes, op. cit., p. 407.
15. C. Wall, H.C. Cameron and E.A. Underwood, *A History of the Worshipful Society of Apothecaries of London,* Oxford, 1967, I, pp. 4; 125; 393.
16. W. Besant, *London in the 18th Century,* London, 1902, p. 98.
17. R. Lathem and W. Matthews, eds, *The Diary of Samuel Pepys,* London, 1983, X, p. 70–1.
18. A. Hope, *Londoners' Larder,* London, 1990, p. 61.
19. Lathem and Matthews, *Diary of Samuel Pepys,* op. cit., X, p. 71.
20. A. Hope, ibid., p. 62. This may of course have been a spoof by a man.
21. Lathem and Matthews, *Diary of Samuel Pepys,* op. cit., pp. 71–2.
22. Lathem and Matthews, eds, *Diary of Samuel Pepys,* op. cit., V, p. 37.
23. Ibid., X, 107.
24. Quoted in Hugh Phillips, *Mid-Georgian London,* London, 1964, p. 58.
25. Ibid., p. 58.
26. W. Besant, *London in the 18th Century,* op. cit., pp. 313–14.
27. Quoted in ibid., p. 311.
28. A.S. Turberville, *Johnson's England,* 2 vols, Oxford, 1933 (1952 edn.), I, p. 180.
29. C. Roden, op. cit., pp. 28–9.
30. A.S. Turberville, op. cit., II, pp. 341–2.
31. John Brewer, *Party Ideology and Popular Politics at the Accession of George III,* Cambridge, 1976, p. 150.
32. Lathem and Matthews, *Diary of Samuel Pepys,* op. cit., X, p. 107.
33. See the picture, 'The Charing Cross Evening Frolick' by P. Boitard, 1756 in Hugh Phillips, op. cit., p. 105,
34. R. Bradley, op. cit., p. 23.
35. I am indebted here to my colleague Dr Simon Smith for letting me read his paper 'Specialisation in Transatlantic Trade: The Example of Coffee', 1994.
36. John E. Wills Jr, 'European consumption and Asian production in the 17th and 18th centuries', in *Consumption and the World of Goods,* John Brewer and Roy Porter, eds, London, 1993, p. 143.

37. B. Moseley, op. cit., pp. 79–80.
38. B. W. Higman, *Slave Populations of the British Caribbean 1807–1834*, Baltimore, 1984, pp. 44, 55, 59.
39. Simon Smith, 'Specialisation', op. cit., p. 6.
40. P.J. Laborie, *The Coffee Planter of St Domingo*, London, 1798.
41. P. Deane and B.R. Mitchell, *Abstract of British Historical Statistics*, Cambridge, 1971, pp. 285–9.

## 4 WAR, DISEASE AND SETTLEMENT: THE AMERICAS

1. W.D. Phillips and C. Rahn Phillips, *The Worlds of Christopher Columbus*, Cambridge, 1992, chs. 2–4.
2. D.E. Stannard, Section I.4. in K.F. Kiple, ed. *The Cambridge World History of Human Disease*, Cambridge, 1993, pp. 35–41.
3. The Indian peoples were not, of course, indigenous in the strictest sense. See K.F. Kiple, Section VII.6. in K.F. Kiple, (ed.), op. cit., p. 497.
4. K.F. Kiple, Section VII.6 in K.F. Kiple, ed., op. cit., pp. 497–503.
5. A.W. Crosby, *The Columbian Exchange*, Westport, Conn., 1972, p. 36.
6. H.N. Simpson, *Invisible Armies*, New York, 1980.
7. A.W. Crosby, *Exchange*, op. cit., p. 37.
8. Ibid., p. 38.
9. A.W. Crosby, 'Metamorphosis of the Americas', in H.J. Viola and C. Margolis, eds, *Seeds of Change*, Washington, DC, 1991, p. 79.
10. Ibid., p. 73.
11. For the latest history of this process see Hugh Thomas, *The Conquest of Mexico*, London, 1993.
12. D.T. Reff, *Disease, Depopulation and Cultural Change in Northwestern New Spain, 1518–1764*, Salt Lake City, 1991, ch. 6. See also D. Crook and W.G. Lovell, eds, *'Secret Judgements of God.' Old World Diseases in Colonial Spanish America*, Norman and London, 1990.
13. A.W. Crosby, *Exchange*, op. cit., p. 41.
14. Ibid., p. 52.
15. R. Wright, *Stolen Continents*, New York, 1992, p. 14.
16. R. Wright, ibid., p. 47.
17. R. Wright, ibid., pp. 55, 57.
18. R. Wright, ibid., p. 75.
19. R. Wright, ibid., pp. 82–3.
20. A.W. Crosby, *Imperialism*, op. cit., p. 201. But for a different, recent view, see the articles by Francis Brooks, 'Smallpox in the conquest of Mexico', and 'Disease and Population in the Conquest of Mexico: Twenty Five Years of Scholarship'. The author was kind enough to let me read these important revisionary essays before publication.
21. Ibid., pp. 199–200. See also A. Mercer, *Disease, Mortality and Population in Transition*, Leicester, 1991, chs. 2–3.
22. A.W. Crosby, *Imperialism*, op. cit., p. 201.
23. R. Wright, op. cit., p. 45.
24. A.W.Crosby, *Imperialism*, op. cit., p. 201. When Charles Darwin brought four indigenous people to Britain from Tierra del Fuego in

1831, they were vaccinated against smallpox. A. Desmond and J. Moore, *Darwin*, London, 1992, p. 106.
25. J. Axtell, *The European and the Indians*, New York, 1981, p. 248.
26. A.W. Crosby, *Imperialism*, op. cit., p. 202.
27. J. Axtell, *The Invasion Within*, New York, 1985, p. 219.
28. J.A. Merrel, 'The Customs of Our Country', in B. Bailyn and P.D. Morgan, eds, *Strangers in the Realm*, Chapel Hill, 1991, pp. 124–5.
29. J. Axtell, *Invasion*, op. cit., p. 250.
30. J. Axtell, *Europeans*, op. cit., pp. 249–50.
31. J. Axtell, *Europeans*, op. cit., p. 251.
32. A.W. Crosby, *Imperialism*, op. cit., p. 203.
33. R. Sheridan, *Doctors and Slaves*, Cambridge, 1985, ch. 9.
34. J.A. Merrell, in B. Bailyn and P.D. Morgan, eds, op. cit., pp. 123–4.
35. Ibid., pp. 124–5.
36. N. Sanches-Albornoz, 'The First Transatlantic Transfer: Spanish Migration to the New World, 1493–1810', in Nicholas Canny, ed., *Europeans on the Move*, Oxford, 1994, ch. 3.

## 5 THE INDIAN WEED: TOBACCO

1. James Axtell, *Beyond 1492*, New York, 1992 , pp. 192–3; 55.
2. Ibid., pp. 147; 313.
3. V.G. Kiernan, *Tobacco. A History*, London, 1991, p. 9.
4. Ibid. For the most recent study of tobacco, see Jordan Goodman, *Tobacco in History. The Culture of Dependence*, London, 1993.
5. F. Braudel, *Capitalism and Material Life, 1400–1800*, London, 1967, pp. 189–190. See also K.N. Chaudhuri, *Trade and Civilization in the Indian Ocean*, Cambridge, 1985, p. 31.
6. J. Israel, *Dutch Primacy in World Trade*, Oxford, 1990, pp. 264–5.
7. Simon Schama, *An Embarrassment of Riches*, London, 1987, pp. 205–8.
8. V.G. Kiernan, op. cit, p. 17.
9. Keith Thomas, *Religion and the Decline of Magic*, London, 1973, p. 23.
10. Peter Clark, *The English Alehouse. A Social History, 1200–1830*, London, 1983, p. 135.
11. S. Pauli, *Treatise on Tobacco*, London, 1746, pp. 3–4.
12. Ibid., pp. 35–8.
13. V.G. Kiernan, op. cit., p. 22.
14. P. Clark, *Alehouse*, op. cit., p. 125.
15. Ibid., p. 134.
16. Ibid., pp. 134–5.
17. B.W.E. Alford, *W.D. and H.O. Wills and the Development of the U.K. Tobacco Industry, 1786–1965*, London, 1973, p. 5.
18. *The Shorter Pepys*, Robert Latham, ed., London, 1985, p. 494.
19. Ibid., p. 820.
20. See Alan Kulikoff, *Tobacco and Slaves*, Chapel Hill, 1986.
21. Ian K. Steele, *The English Atlantic, 1695–1740*, Oxford, 1986.
22. Carole Shamas, *The Pre-Industrial Consumer in England and America*, Oxford, 1990, p. 79.

23. Ibid., p. 80.
24. Ibid., p. 81.
25. Ibid., ch. 8.
26. Simon Schama, *Embarrassment*, op. cit., p. 198.
27. V.G. Kiernan, op. cit., p. 32.
28. Ibid., p. 29.
29. Ibid., p. 34.
30. *Free Thoughts on Snuff-Taking, by a Friend to Female Beauty*, London, 1782.
31. B.W.E. Alford, op. cit., pp. 26–7.
32. Cissie Fairchild, 'The Production and marketing of populuxe goods…', in *Consumption and the World of Goods*, John Brewer and Roy Porter, eds, London, 1993, pp. 228–30.
33. V.G. Kiernan, op. cit., pp. 33–4.
34. Penny Corfield, *The Impact of English Towns, 1700–1800*, London, 1982, ch. 3.
35. Ibid., p. 35.
36. Ibid., p. 38.
37. T.M. Devine, *The Tobacco Lords*, Edinburgh, 1990.
38. John K. Walton, *Lancashire.* A Social History, 1558–1939, Manchester, 1987, p. 70.
39. T.M. Devine, op. cit., pp. v–vi.
40. S. Pauli, op. cit., p. 35.
41. Alexander Johnston, *Notebook*, 1787(?), in *Powel Papers*, Historical Society of Pennsylvania, Philadelphia.
42. V.G. Kiernan, op. cit., p. 79.
43. Ibid., p. 80.
44. Simon Schama, *Embarrassment*, op. cit., p. 206.
45. J. Aiken, *A Description of the Country from Thirty to Forty Miles Round Manchester* (1795), 1968 edn, New York, p. 187.
46. V.G. Kiernan, op. cit., pp. 81–2.
47. Ibid., pp. 87–8.
48. M. Girouard, *Life in The English Country House*, London, 1980, p. 294.
49. M. Girouard, ibid., pp. 296–7.
50. V.G. Kiernan, op. cit., p. 50.
51. Hugh Thomas, *Cuba*, London, 1971, pp. 133–5.
52. V.G. Kiernan, op. cit., p. 51.
53. Asa Briggs, *Victorian Things*, London, 1988, p. 241.
54. Brian Harrison, *Drink and the Victorians*, Oxford, 1971, pp. 158–9.
55. Piers Brendan, *Thomas Cook*, London, 1991, pp. 23, 26, 101.

## 6 THE AZTEC DRINK: CHOCOLATE

1. Ronald Wright, *Stolen Continents. The New World Through Indian Eyes*, Toronto, 1993 edn, chs 1 and 3.
2. Technically, cacao bean; common usage now decrees cocoa.
3. Henceforth the term chocolate refers to drinking chocolate. It was however quite unlike modern drinking chocolate, as this chapter will

show. The word chocolate comes from the Aztec word *xocolati*; Carlos Fuentes, *The Buried Mirror. Reflections on Spain and the New World*, London, 1992, p. 205.

4. Elizabeth Rozin, *Blue Corn and Chocolate*, London, 1992, p. 195.
5. W.H. Prescott, *The Conquest of Mexico*, London, 1909, 2 vols, I, p. 30, n1.
6. Elizabeth Rozin, *Blue Corn*, op. cit., p. 196.
7. W.H. Prescott, op. cit., I, p. 102, n1.
8. Ibid., p. 369.
9. A.W. Knapp, *Cacao and Chocolate. The History*, London, 1920, p. 8.
10. Elizabeth Rozin, op. cit., p. 196.
11. A.W. Knapp, ibid., p. 8.
12. *Cambridge History of Latin America*, Cambridge, 1984, L. Bethell, ed., Vol. I, pp. 373–4.
13. A.L. Butler,'The Indian Nectar': The Introduction of Chocolate into 17th Century Europe', Paper given to the Social History Conference, January 1993.
14. A.W. Knapp, op. cit., p. 10.
15. A.W. Knapp, op. cit., p. 18; D.H. Urquhart, *Cocoa*, London, 1955, pp. 2–3.
16. Carlos Fuentes, op. cit., p. 279.
17. D.H. Urquhart, ibid., p. 1.
18. Quoted in A.L. Butler, op. cit.
19. This issue is dealt with by Sidney Mintz in *Sweetness and Power*, London, 1985, ch. 3.
20. Quoted in A.L. Butler, op. cit.
21. A.L. Butler, op. cit.
22. M. Toussaint-Samat, *A History of Food*, Oxford, 1992, p. 574.
23. W. Knapp, op. cit., p. 12.
24. 'Historicus', *Cocoa. All About It*, London, 1896, p. 46.
25. R.S. Dunn, *Sugar and Slaves*, London, 1973, p. 168.
26. M. Craton and J. Walvin, *A Jamaican Plantation. Worthy Park, 1670–1970*, London, 1970, p. 31.
27. 'Historicus', *Cocoa. All About It*, London, 1896, pp. 49–51, for a list of the various Acts. See also D.H. Urquhart, op. cit., pp. 13–14.
28. Elizabeth Raffold, *The Experienced English Housekeeper*, London, 1801 edn, p. 316.
29. For a display of the more costly tea-sets used by the propertied orders, see the collection on permanent display in the Manchester City Art Gallery, Portland St, Manchester. For a good range of teapots, see *The Story of Tea. An Exhibition of Tea and Coffee Ware, 1700–1900*, Catalogue, South African Cultural History Museum, Cape Town, 1993.
30. Letter of John Royton, 5 April 1723, in *The Trade of Bristol in the Eighteenth Century*, W.E. Minchinton, ed., Bristol Record Society, 1957, p. 89.
31. D.H. Urquhart, op. cit., pp. 15–16.
32. G. Wagner, *The Chocolate Conscience*, London, 1987, p. 13.
33. Quoted in John Latimer, *The Annals of Bristol in the Eighteenth Century*, (1893), Bath, 1970 edn, p. 177.
34. J. Othick, 'The Cocoa and Chocolate Industry in the Nineteenth Century', in Derek Oddy and Derek Miller, eds, *The Making of the Modern British Diet*, London, 1976, p. 79.

35. W.E. Minchinton, *Trade of Bristol*, op. cit., pp. 19, 64.
36. H-C. Hui and L.H. Hui, *Shops and Shopping in the Eighteenth Century*, London, 1989, pp. 260–2.

## 7 FEEDING THE PEOPLE: THE POTATO

1. The best account of the hunger of those years is to be found in Roger Wells, *Wretched Faces. Famine in Wartime England, 1793–1801*, Gloucester, 1988.
2. J.H. Parry, *The Age of Reconnaissance*, London, 1963, p. 286.
3. R. Salaman, *The History and Social Influence of the Potato*, Cambridge, 1988 edn, pp. 101–3.
4. C. Hamshere, *The British in the Caribbean*, London, 1972, pp. 3–4.
5. R. Salaman, op. cit., pp. 142–7.
6. R. Blome, *A Description of the Island of Barbados*, London, 1678, p. 8.
7. C. Hamshere, op. cit., pp. 69, 101, 103. In B.W. Higman, *Slave Populations of the British Caribbean, 1807–1834*, Cambridge, 1984, pp. 204–18.
8. 2 July 1772, Alexander Johnston, *Memoranda Book, 1775*, Powel Papers, Historical Society of Pennsylvania, Philadelphia.
9. B.W. Higman, *Slave Population*, op. cit. pp. 205–6.
10. William H. McNeil, 'American Food Crops in the Old World', in Herman J. Viola and Carolyn Margolis, eds, *Seeds of Change*, Washington DC, 1991, p. 47. See also R. Salaman, op. cit., ch. IX.
11. R. Salaman, op. cit, p. 450.
12. R.F. Foster, *Modern Ireland, 1690–1972*, London, 1989 edn, p. 220.
13. R.F. Foster, ibid., ch. 9. For English tithes see Eric Evans, *The Contentious Tithe*, London, 1976.
14. R. Salaman, op. cit., p. 251.
15. R.F. Foster, op. cit., p. 197.
16. R. Salaman, op. cit., pp. 254–5.
17. R.F. Foster, op. cit., pp. 217–20.
18. R. Salaman, op. cit., pp. 437–9.
19. Ibid., p. 433.
20. Ibid., pp. 114–15.
21. Ibid., pp. 105–7.
22. Ibid., pp. 445–8.
23. Ibid.
24. J.K. Walton, *A Social History of Lancashire*, Manchester, 1987, p. 75.
25. R. Salaman, op. cit., pp. 454–5.
26. H.C. Darby, ed., *A New Historical Geography of England after 1600*, Cambridge, 1976 edn, p. 112.
27. P.J. Corfield, *The Impact of English Towns, 1700–1800*, Oxford, 1982, ch. 2.
28. Roger Wells, *Wretched Faces*, op. cit., p. 21.
29. R. Salaman, op. cit., pp. 479–84.
30. Pamela Horn, *The Rural World, 1780–1850*, London, 1980, p. 34.
31. Quoted in R. Salaman, op. cit., p. 488.
32. The phrase is from Roger Well's evocative book dealing with this subject, op. cit.

33. Roger Wells, ibid., ch. 17.
34. G.E. Mingay, ed., *The Agrarian History of England and Wales, 1750–1850*, vol. VI, Cambridge, 1989, pp. 303–4.
35. R. Salaman, op. cit., pp. 507–8.

## 8 THE AFRICAN GIFT: SUGAR

1. Sidney Mintz, *Sweetness and Power*, London, 1985, pp. 80–91. This early section owes much to Mintz's provocative study.
2. Carole Shammas, *The Pre-industrial Consumer in England and America*, Oxford, 1990, p. 81.
3. Quoted in Sidney Mintz, op. cit., pp. 103, 105.
4. Ibid., p. 108.
5. Carole Shammas, op. cit., p. 82.
6. A. Hugill, *Sugar and All That... A History of Tate and Lyle*, London, 1978, p. 27.
7. Ibid., pp. 27–9.
8. Sir Frederick Eden, *The State of the Poor*, London, 1797, 3 vols, III, 770.
9. Sidney Mintz, op. cit., p. 120.
10. For a good illustration of the use of sugar in eighteenth century manuals, see E. Raffold, *The Experienced English Housekeeper*, London, 1801 edn.
11. James Walvin, *Black Ivory. A History of British Slavery*, London, 1992, p. 6.
12. R.S. Dunn, *Sugar and Slaves*, London, 1977, p. 207.
13. Ian K. Steele, *The English Atlantic 1675–1740*, Oxford, 1986, p. 286.
14. James Rawley, *The Trans-Atlantic Slave Trade*, New York, 1981, p. 180. See also David Richardson, ed., *Bristol, Africa and the Eighteenth Century Slave Trade to America*, 3 vols, Bristol Records Society's Publications, XXXVIII, XXXIX, XLII, 1986, 1987, 1991.
15. R.S. Dunn, op. cit., p. 203; Sidney Mintz, op. cit., p. 73.
16. Sidney Mintz, op. cit., p. 73.
17. Quoted in Dorothy Marshall, *English People in the 18th century*, London, 1956, p. 172.
18. Michael Craton and James Walvin, *A Jamaican Plantation. Worthy Park, 1670–1970*, London, 1970, p. 52.
19. Quoted in Mark Girouard, *Life in the English Country House*, London, 1978, p. 204.
20. R. Roth, *Tea-Drinking in 18th Century America*, Washington DC, 1961, pp. 63–91.

## 9 THE CAUSE OF ALL DISTRESS: PLANTATIONS

1. R.F. Foster, *Modern Ireland*, London, 1989 edn, p. 61.
2. Philip D. Curtin, *The Rise and Fall of the Plantation Complex*, Cambridge, 1990, p. 77.

3. H.S. Fink, trans., *A History of the Expedition to Jerusalem*, Knoxville, 1969, p. 130.
4. P.D. Curtin, *Plantation Complex*, op. cit., ch. 2.
5. Richard Blome,*A Description of the Island of Jamaica*, London, 1678, p. 36.
6. Ibid., p. 37.
7. J. Walvin, *Black Ivory*, London, 1992, p. 70.
8. R. Blome, op. cit., pp. 8, 19.
9. See Bruce Roberts, *Plantation Homes of the James River*, Chapel Hill, 1990.
10. Bryan Edwards, *The History, Civil and Commercial, of the West Indies*, 2 vols, London, 1793, II, p. 10.
11. An even more revealing cameo bore the legend; 'Am I not a woman and a sister?' See back cover of the journal *Slavery and Abolition*, Cass, London.
12. Hugh Tinker, *A New System of Slavery*, London, 1974; K.O. Lawrence, *A Question of Labour: Identured Immigration into Trinidad and British Guiana, 1875–1917*, London, 1994.
13. P.D. Curtin, *The Rise and Fall of the Plantation Complex*, Cambridge, 1990, p. 176.
14. James Walvin, *Black Ivory*, op. cit., p. 309.
15. P.D. Curtin, *Plantation Complex*, op. cit., p. 178.
16. D.B. Crigg, *The Agricultural System of the World*, Cambridge, 1974, table 42, p. 224.
17. *Plantation Workers. Resistance and Accomodation*, Brij V. Lal, Doug Munro and Edward D. Beechert, eds, Honolulu, 1993.
18. For a list of these plantation crops, see George L. Beckford, *Persistent Poverty*, Oxford, 1971, appendix I.
19. See D.B. Crigg, op. cit., ch. 11.
20. S.H. Twining, *The House of Twining*, London, 1956, pp. 67–8.
21. D.M. Forrest, *A Hundred Years of Ceylon Tea*, London, 1967, p. 19.
22. S.H. Twining, op. cit., p. 71.
23. Serena Hardy, *The Tea Book*, Weybridge, 1979, p. 91.
24. George L. Beckford, op. cit., pp. 97–9.
25. P.D. Curtin, *Plantation Complex*, op. cit., pp. 196–203.
26. Ibid., p. 203.
27. *The Cambridge History of Africa*, vol. VI, R. Oliver and G.N. Sanderson eds, Cambridge, 1985, pp. 15, 78, 517–18, 534–6, 547, 550, 752–3.
28. For a severe critic, see George L. Beckford, op. cit.
29. E. Graham & I. Floering, *The Modern Plantation in the Third World*, London, 1984, p. xiv.
30. The ill-fated efforts to make Jamaican estates into co-operatives in the 1970s was a case in point.
31. See D.K. Fieldhouse, *Colonialism, 1870–1945*, London, 1981, p. 74.
32. See the list in D.K. Fieldhouse, *Colonialism*, op. cit., p. 79.
33. The phrase comes from V.G. Kiernan's title, *The Lords of Human Kind*, London, 1972.
34. See, for example, 'Foreword' by D.K. Fieldhouse, in E. Graham and I. Floering, op. cit., pp. xiv–xvii.

35. See the classic essay by E.P. Thompson, 'Time, Work Discipline and Industrial Capitalism', *Past and Present*, 1967.

## 10 SHOPS AND SHOPPING

1. G.J. Barker-Benfield, *The Culture of Sensibility. Sex and Society in Eighteenth Century Britain*, Chicago, 1992, 189.
2. Plate 30 in M. Dorothy George, *Hogarth to Cruikshank, London*, 1967, pp. 47, 49.
3. A.S. Turberville, *Johnson's England*, Oxford, 1933, 2 vols, I, p. 176.
4. Quoted in Neil McKendrick, 'Josiah Wedgwood and the commercialization of the Potteries', in Neil McKendrick, John Brewer and J.H. Plumb, eds, *The Birth of a Consumer Society*, London, 1983, p. 119.
5. Quoted in A.S. Turberville, *Johnson's England*, op. cit., I, pp. 175.
6. Quoted in N. McKendrick, op. cit., p. 78.
7. Mass-Observation, H.D. Willcock, ed., *Browns and Chester. Portrait of a Shop, 1780–1946*, London, 1947, p. 14.
8. Quoted in N. McKendrick, op. cit., p. 78.
9. *Browns and Chester*, op. cit., p. 17.
10. P.J. Corfield, *The Impact of English Towns, 1700–1800*, Oxford, 1982, p. 19.
11. Quoted in N. McKendrick, op. cit., p. 79.
12. P. Corfield, op. cit., p. 19.
13. Carole Shammas, *The Pre-Industrial Consumer in England and America*, Oxford, 1990, pp. 197–8.
14. See Ian Mitchell, 'The development of urban retailing, 1700–1815', in Peter Clark, ed., *The Transformation of English Provincial Towns, 1600–1800*, London, 1984, pp. 259–83.
15. Ibid., p. 267.
16. Ibid., pp 276–7.
17. See especially Roger Scola, *Feeding the Victorian City. The Food Supply of Manchester*, Manchester, 1992, pp. 256–7.
18. The most detailed account of shops in the 18th century is to be found in Hoh-Cheung Mui and Lorna H. Mui, *Shops and Shopping in Eighteenth Century England*, London, 1989.
19. Mui and Mui, op. cit., pp. 204–5.
20. John Burnett, *Plenty and Want*, London, 1979 edn, pp. 106–7.
21. Mui and Mui, op. cit., pp. 212–13.
22. Ibid., pp. 216–17.
23. *The Journal of William Schellink's Travels in England, 1661–1663*, M. Exwood and H.L. Lehmann, eds, Camden Fifth Series, I, London, 1993, pp. 121, 127. There is the possibility that tobacco was so universal in Cornwall because of smuggling.
24. Mui and Mui, op. cit., ch. 5.
25. Carole Shammas, op. cit., ch. 8.
26. Ibid., pp. 258–9.
27. Ibid., pp. 260–1.

28. Quoted in Mui and Mui, op. cit., p. 6.
29. Stephen H. Twining, *The House of Twining, 1706–1956,* London, 1956.
30. Mui and Mui, op. cit., pp. 223–5.
31. On the general question of literacy see David Vincent, *Literacy and Popular Culture, England, 1750–1914,* Cambridge, 1993 edn. For eighteenth-century newspaper advertisements see N. McKendrick et al., eds, op. cit., ch. 4.
32. S.H. Twining, op. cit., p. 34.
33. On the broader issues of selling and consumption, see the essays in *Consumption and the World of Goods,* John Brewer and Roy Porter, eds, London, 1993.
34. Mui and Mui, op. cit., pp. 8–9, 48.
35. Ibid., pp. 13–14. See also John E. Willis Jr, 'European consumption and Asian production in the seventeenth and eighteenth centuries', In Brewer and Porter, op. cit., ch. 6.
36. P.J. Corfield, *Towns,* op. cit., pp. 8–9.
37. Mui and Mui, op. cit., p. 251 and tables nos. 6, 7 and 22.
38. Carole Shammas, op. cit., pp. 83–6.
39. Mui and Mui, op. cit., p. 251.
40. Stephen H. Twining, op. cit., p. 44, and ch. VI.
41. Mui and Mui, op. cit., p. 257.
42. Arthur Raistrick, *Quakers in Science and Industry,* New York, 1968 edn; Mui and Mui, op. cit., pp. 265–7.
43. For a broad discussion of the impact of the wars see Clive Emsley, *British Society and the French Wars 1793–1815,* London, 1979.
44. This aspect of British identity is not explored in Linda Colley, *Britons. Forging the Nation, 1707–1837,* London, 1992.
45. Adam Smith, *The Wealth of Nations,* vol. II, bk iv, ch. 7, pt iii.

## 11 THE PASSION TO CONSUME

1. P. Curtin, et al., eds, *African History,* London 1978, p. 226.
2. J.E. Inikori, 'The import of firearms into West Africa', in *Forced Migration,* J.E. Inikori, ed., London, 1982.
3. J.E. Inikori, 'Slavery and the revolution in cotton textile production in England', in *The Atlantic Slave Trade,* J.E. Inikori and S. Engerman, eds, London, 1992, pp. 171–2.
4. Ibid., Appendix I, pp. 173–4.
5. Ibid., Appendix 2, pp. 176–7.
6. J.M. Postma, *The Dutch in the Atlantic Slave Trade, 1600–1815,* Cambridge, 1990, pp. 103–4.
7. James Penny, (1789), quoted in M. Craton, J. Walvin and D. Wright, eds, *Slavery, Abolition and Emancipation,* London, 1976, p. 36.
8. Elizabeth Donnan, *Documents Illustrative of the Slave Trade to America,* Washington, 1930, 1935, 4 vols., I, pp. 204–5.
9. K.G. Davies, *The Royal African Company,* London, 1970 edn, pp. 345–6.
10. Quoted in Colin Palmer, *Human Cargoes,* Urbana, 1981, p. 32.

11. W. Beckford, *A Descriptive Account of the Island of Jamaica*, London, 2 vols, 1790, I, p. 236.
12. J.S. Handler and F.W. Lange, *Plantation Slavery in Barbados*, Cambridge, Mass., 1978, Appendix B, pp. 251–73.
13. Bryan Edwards, *The History of the British Colonies in the West Indies*, 3 vols, 3rd edn, London, 1801, I, 'Dedication'.
14. M. Craton and J. Walvin, *A Jamaican Plantation. Worthy Park 1670–1970*, London, 1970, Appendix 1, pp. 320–3.
15. *Tweedie Estate Records*, 4/45, No. 13, Archives of Jamaica.
16. Bryan Edwards, op. cit, vol. III, p. 244.
17. Ibid., p. 270
18. R.M. McDonald, *The Economy and Material Culture of Slaves*, Baton Rouge, 1993, pp. 30–1.
19. Bryan Edwards, III, p. 283.
20. Ibid., III, p. 165. The italics are mine.
21. See his remarks in 'Preface', ibid., pp. xv–xviii
22. P.J. Laborie, *The Coffee Planter of St Domingo*, London, 1798, p. 180.
23. *Slave Trials*, St Ann, Jamaica, 19 August 1788, National Library of Jamaica.
24. D. Hall, *In Miserable Slavery, Thomas Thistlewood in Jamaica, 1750–1786*, London, 1989, p. 94.
25. Ibid., pp. 94, 79.
26. T.H. Breen, '"Baubles of Britain", The American and consumer revolutions of the eighteenth century', *Past and Present*, No. 119, 1988.
27. James Axtell, 'The First Consumer Revolution', in James Axtell, *Beyond 1492*, New York, 1992, p. 131.
28. Ibid., p. 132.
29. Even if mythological, the myth took hold. Ibid., p. 135.
30. Ibid., pp. 141–2.
31. Ibid., pp. 143–5.
32. Ibid., p. 146. But note the wise words of James Axtell about the use of this concept.
33. Ibid., pp. 149–51.
34. Ibid., pp. 145–6.
35. K.G. Davies, *The Royal African Company*, London, 1970 edn, Appendix 1.
36. Colin Palmer, *Human Cargoes*, op. cit., p. 50.
37. David Richardson, ed., *Bristol, Africa and the Eighteenth-Century Slave Trade to America*, Bristol Record Society Publications, 3 vols., I, Bristol, 1986, p. xx.
38. Melinda Elder, *The Slave Trade and the Economic Development of 18th Century Lancaster*, Halifax, 1992, Appendix B, pp. 211–12.
39. J. Axtell, op. cit., p. 129.

## 12 QUESTIONS OF TASTE, ADDICTION – AND EMPIRE

1. There has been a lively debate on the question of the profitability of the eighteenth century empire. For a recent summary see John Brewer, *Sinews of Empire*, op. cit.

2. For the most recent discussion see P.J. Cain and A.G. Hopkins, *British Imperialism. Innovation and Expansion, 1688–1914*, London, 1993, ch. 2.
3. Franklin to Lord Howe, 2 July 1776, in *The Papers of Benjamin Franklin*, W.B. Willcox, ed., New Haven and London, 1982, vol. 22, p. 520.
4. A.N. Porter, ed., *Atlas of British Overseas Expansion*, London, 1991, p. 34.

# Index